HIGHWAYS AND BYWAYS

IN

DORSET

MACMILLAN AND CO., Limited
LONDON . BOMBAY . CALCUTTA
MELBOURNE

THE MACMILLAN COMPANY
NEW YORK . BOSTON . CHICAGO
DALLAS . SAN FRANCISCO

THE MACMILLAN CO. OF CANADA, Ltd.
TORONTO

Corfe Castle : The Bridge and Gateway.

Highways and Byways

IN

Dorset

BY

Sir FREDERICK TREVES, Bart.

G.C.V.O., C.B., LL.D.

SERGEANT SURGEON TO H.M. THE KING; LORD RECTOR OF THE
UNIVERSITY OF ABERDEEN; AUTHOR OF "THE OTHER SIDE OF
THE LANTERN"; "THE TALE OF A FIELD HOSPITAL"

WITH · ILLUSTRATIONS · BY

JOSEPH PENNELL

MACMILLAN AND CO., LIMITED
ST. MARTIN'S STREET, LONDON
1914

COPYRIGHT

First Edition, June 1906
Reprinted, October 1906, 1914

Dorset Woods and Downs.

PREFACE

THE county of Dorset is small, but is yet so varied in its configuration as to present an epitome of the scenery of Southern England. It is a land of moods and changes that knows no monotony, and is indeed so full of hills and dales that there is scarcely a level road within its confines, save by the banks of streams.

It is crossed by a range of chalk downs whose lonely heights are worn smooth by the wind and are traversed only by shepherds and their sheep. To the East is the Great Heath, a wild, sandy fragment of unchanged Britain, which is still just as it was when the Celts first wandered over the island. To the North lie the glorious woods of Cranborne Chase and the enchanting Vale of Blackmore—that valley of the Blue Mist in whose soft shadows will be found the very heart of England. This valley is in the delectable hinterland, so that any who travel northwards from the sea will come in time to the hills, and when they have climbed to their summits will be able to look down upon a country beyond of rare and romantic beauty.

If they descend into these lowlands they will find that time has moved back a hundred years or so, and that they have stepped into a corner of Old England—into the England of the coaching days. In this Sleepy Hollow they will find the untroubled life of the past, will come upon such farmer's men as Gabriel Oak, will meet the tranter on the leisurely road, and will pass through many ancient villages of thatched roofs and rose-covered walls. Here too they will learn something of the picturesque bustle of the market day and of the business of the carrier's cart, or will see a little into such industries as that of sheep-washing by a trout stream and of cyder-making in a Tudor barn. Upon their ears, too, will fall, like an echo from ancient England, the quaint speech of the dialect of Dorset.

South of the hills Dorset can boast of a coast line which few parts of England can surpass for charm and variableness. There are cliffs of white and cliffs of black, sea walls of orange-yellow, and of grey and gold, bays such as Worbarrow, coves such as Chapman's Pool and Lulworth, and that steep bank of pebbles, eighteen miles in length, known as the Chesil Beach.

In the county are the ruined castles of Corfe and Sherborne, such great churches as those of Wimborne and Milton, such an old-world church as that of Puddletown and such ancient strongholds as Maiden Castle and Badbury Rings. Possibly more admirable than these are the old manor houses of Dorset—Cranborne, Athelhampton, Bingham's Melcombe, Mapperton, or Puncknowle—and the long-forgotten villages, with their homely gardens, their little drab churches, their wells, and their ponds for ducks.

The itinerary followed in the book is by these ways : The county is entered at Shaftesbury, and the road thence is taken to Poole, by way of Blandford and Wimborne, with a diversion to Cranborne. The coast is next followed from Poole to Lyme

Regis, where the road turns inland, along the western border of the county, to Sherborne. From this ancient capital of Newer Wessex the traveller moves southwards, by way of Cerne Abbas, to Dorchester. At Dorchester the journey ends.

Much use has been made of Hutchins's monumental History of the county and of the Proceedings of the Dorset Natural History and Antiquarian Field Club.

FREDERICK TREVES.

6, WIMPOLE STREET, LONDON,
    May, 1906.

CONTENTS

CHAPTER VIII

CHAPTER IX

CHAPTER X

CHAPTER XI

CHAPTER XII

CHAPTER XIII

CHAPTER XIV

CHAPTER XV

CHAPTER XVI

CONTENTS

LIST OF ILLUSTRATIONS

HIGHWAYS AND BYWAYS

IN

DORSET

HIGHWAYS AND BYWAYS

IN

DORSET

CHAPTER I

SHAFTESBURY

THERE lies to the north of Dorset—so an old writer says—
" a deep country full of pasture, yielding plenty of well-fed
beaves, muttons and milch kyne." This deep country is shut
in towards the South by a long rampart of chalk hills which
crosses the land diagonally, like the " bend " on a heraldic
shield.

It is a spur of the same great chalk plateau which farther
inland has formed the Chiltern Hills and the Plain of Salisbury,
and which carries on its smooth back the boulders of Stonehenge. On its way over the county it softens into gorse-
covered downs, dotted with sheep, or rises into hills on which
still stand the earthworks of British strongholds and the
mounds of beacons. It ends at last by a pebbly beach, as
a sheer white cliff about whose front the seagulls are ever
hovering. This deep country is very green and very homely
There is no spot like it beyond the confines of Britain. It

is so typical of the island which shelters it that it might claim
to be symbolical of the Heart of England.

The first chalk hill that steps out into the county halts
suddenly as if the wide plain had fascinated it. It forms
a steep-sided solitary ridge, on the very point of which
stands the town of Shaftesbury. Thus it comes about that
the town looks from a height seawards, seeming to be perched
upon a jutting cape or a far-venturing headland. If the sea
fretted its feet, then would there be a lighthouse on its summit
in place of a town. So steep are the flanks of this green ridge
that there is but one easy road to its crest, and that is by
the East. On all other sides such road or path as essays to
escape from the town drops down headlong into the plain.

That Shaftesbury is a very ancient place the records testify.
Those who dabble with the past suppose it was old when
the Romans climbed up to it, and that the present town was
founded by King Alfred in A.D. 880. All this is likely enough,
because in Saxon times the deep country round about was a
tangle of forest and swamp, while this bold, crisp headland
stood forth as a place where there was wholesome footing and
a clear look out. It was on the high road also from London
to Exeter. Moreover, the body of King Eadward the Martyr,
who was basely murdered at Corfe, was brought here in A.D.
980 and buried on the hill, whereby the town became sanctified
as a place of pilgrimage.

The city has had many names. It was, in the beginning, Caer
Pallador. By the time of the Domesday Book it was Sceptes-
berie. It then, with all the affectation of a lady in an eighteenth
century lyric, called itself Sophonia. Lastly it became Shaston,
and so the people call it to this day, while all the milestones
around concern themselves only with recording the distances
to "Shaston."

The chief trouble of the town in olden days was the lack of
water. Every drop had to be carried up by precipitous paths
from the lowland beneath. Dripping water-carriers must ever

have been seen mounting the slope in the summer time. They received twopence for a horse load and a farthing for a pail " if fetched upon the head."

The great glory of this hill town was its Abbey, while among the exalted ladies of bygone England must ever stand, with uplifted head, the Abbess of Shaftesbury. She had much wealth in both money and lands, gorgeous plate for the church, as well as the gift of four rectories.

It was in this Abbey that King Eadward was buried. His body was brought hither from Wareham with great pomp and solemnity, for with the dead King came the Earl of Mercia, the Bishop of Sherborne, together with the Abbess of Wilton and all her nuns. In the slow-moving procession too were the nobles of Wessex, with their retinues and their armed men. When the cavalcade came in sight the gaping folk of the plain would leave their fields, drop silently into the shuffling crowd, and tramp with the rest to the Abbey on the hill as if they walked in their sleep. As the long line of cowls and gowns, of skin jackets and sloped spears, crept up the path to the summit the droning chant of the singers would have been heard far across the valley.

Such miraculous cures were wrought at the martyr's tomb, and such grace was with it, that the sick, the sad, and the penitent came from all parts of the land to the sanctuary to seek peace. In the Abbey was also buried the Queen of Eadmund Ironside, " the last hero of the old Royal line," and, lest the record should end there, the historian is at pains to tell that it was " the place of sepulture of many persons of quality."

The nunnery was founded by King Alfred, who gave to the church of Shaftesbury 100 hides of land, " to the honour of God and the Holy Virgin and for the health of his own soul." His " medemesta dehter," or midmost daughter, Ethelgede, he made the first abbess.

The convent flourished exceedingly until 1539, when the end came. In that year of the Reformation the nunnery was dissolved, and the last abbess, Elizabeth Zouch, marched out of its gates with her nuns to the number of fifty-five. It was on March 23rd that they left the Abbey for ever ; and if it was a windy day—as it is apt to be in March—there would have been much fluttering of white frocks and hoods as the trembling and weeping women passed down out of the town. I expect that the abbess led the way, that she walked alone, with head erect and unflinching lips, while the timid nuns followed with small attempt at dignity, clinging to one another and chattering not a little.

With the procession of strong men up the hill, behind the body of the dead king, the glory of the Abbey began ; with the palpitating little cavalcade of nuns who huddled hysterically down the slope its glory ended.

There is evidence to show that life in the convent was not one of crooning monotony. Strange visitors came to the place. At one time, in the year 1313, the wife of Robert Bruce and his daughter, the Princess Marjory, were confined in the nunnery. On which occasion the King allowed the generous sum of 20/- a week for their maintenance. These two ladies had come upon troublous times. After a reverse in the North Bruce had sent his Queen, his daughter, and their ladies to Kildrummie Castle under the charge of Nigel Bruce and the Earl of Athole. King Robert then departed on his mysterious wanderings in the West Highlands, hiding and scheming.

In his absence the English came to Kildrummie, took the castle, hanged Nigel Bruce and others without ceremony, and bore away the Queen and the Princess to the abhorred country across the border. They were carried finally to Shaftesbury, where, with little doubt, the mother and daughter paced often the paths of the convent garden, looking northwards to the chalk downs of Mere, beyond which lay the road to their wild home. It is possible that in that very garden the news came to them of the great victory at Bannockburn which made Robert Bruce more than ever a king.

There were, moreover, little domestic events which must have tempered any weariness of life in the Abbey. Such an episode, for example, as the following cannot fail to have given the nuns a fluttering interest in worldly affairs as well as pungent material for conversation.

It is told that the Archbishop of Canterbury, on his visit to Shaftesbury in 1285, "excommunicated Sir Osbert Gifford for stealing two nuns out of his nunnery at Wilton, and absolved him on these conditions: that he should never after come into

Shaftesbury.

a nunnery or into the company of nuns; that he should, for three Sundays together, be stripped and whipped in his parish church of Wilton and as many times in the market and parish church of Shaftesbury, and fast a certain number of months, and not wear a shirt for three years, and not take upon him the habit or title of a knight, nor wear any apparel but of a russet colour, with lamb or sheep skins, and that he should restore the nuns to their convent to undergo like punishment. All which he bound himself by oath to do."

It would appear from the concluding part of this record that the two nuns who were stolen were not stolen unwillingly, but that they were accessories—probably with much unseemly giggling—both before and after the act. It may be surmised also that they were the two prettiest nuns at Wilton, and the coarse restrictions in the matter of apparel must have made their punishment very hard to bear. It is a base thing that a loutish sheep hide should brush a cheek which knew only the tender touch of a wimple of white linen.

Of the great church and its convent, of the Abbey buildings and of the many chantries, chapels, and shrines, no signs now exist, nor can any tell where lie the bones of King Eadward or of the Queen of the Ironside. Traces of the foundations of the Abbey were, some years ago, laid bare, and one part of the garden wall is yet to be seen, but that is all. With the Abbey have vanished three mints where coin was made, at least two hospitals, and some eight churches. They have faded away, spire by spire, gable by gable, like the turrets in the city of a dream. Gone too are both the old and the new Guildhalls, the Fish Cross, the Butter Cross, and the Cross on the summit of Gold Hill.

The records of the town show an unbroken succession of Mayors of Shaftesbury from some time before 1352. They also show that these magnates lacked not the graces of hospitality when the occasion was worthy. In the reign of Edward IV., for example, they expended tenpence "for two pitchers of wine given to the King's Justices of Assize," and on the same day is noted the liberal outlay of fourteenpence "for a breakfast of the burgesses."

Liberality was a feature of the townsfolk which extended even to the arts of bribery and corruption. In the account of the trial of one controverted election the evidence showed that "a person concealed under a fantastical disguise and called by the name of Punch was placed in a small apartment, and through a hole in the door delivered out to the voters parcels containing twenty guineas; upon which they were conducted to another apartment in the same house, where they found a person called Punch's secretary, and signed notes for the value, but which was made payable to an imaginary character to whom they had given the name of Glenbucket."

Punch, it further appears, was no less a person than one Matthews, an Alderman. He would have been long and fondly remembered by the voters of Shaftesbury, for the vision of parcels containing twenty gold coins dropping through a hole in a door into eager palms is pleasant to dwell upon.

After the destruction of the Abbey this cheery hill town fell

Old Houses, Shaftesbury.

upon evil days. No longer a burial place for Kings and Queens, no longer the goal of eager pilgrimage nor the rendezvous of nobles, it took in despair to the making of shirt buttons. At this it fared somewhat indifferently, for in one petition the burgesses plead "that the Towne has growne about 200 li. in debte: there are above 300 begging people to be releved and there are not above 30 householders in all the towne able to give releiffe."

The Shaftesbury of to-day is a bright, pleasant, and healthy town, perched on the bluff end of a ridge. Viewed from afar off it is not imposing. From the North there is little to be seen of the place except the belfry of Trinity Church and the chimney of the gas works. The writer who compares the distant town to "towered Camelot" has too modest a conception of the latter city. The best sight of Shaftesbury is from Melbury Hill on the South. From this height it appears as a steep green ridge capped on the sky line by red-roofed houses and church towers and by comfortable clumps of trees.

The town has some 2,000 inhabitants, and its disposition is of the simplest. A hot and tired-looking road hurries in from Salisbury, climbs over the hill, and, dropping down upon the other side, pushes on towards Sherborne. In its unsteady passage across the top of the ridge it makes the wavering High Street of the settlement. A few side lanes on either side complete the plan of the place.

Most of the houses, of stone and red brick, cling to that austere simplicity of design which marks the habitation a child draws on a slate—a thing of four symmetrical windows, a central door, and two chimneys giving forth a curling smoke. There are, moreover, modern villas which would not disgrace the suburbs of Stratford-by-Bow.

There will be found, on the other hand, dignified old houses with stone-mullioned windows, moss-covered walls crowned by apple blossom, lanes with brown-thatched cottages where a path of cobble stones leads through a garden to a porch of honeysuckle. Here and there are houses so low that any who will can look in at the bedroom windows, and houses which are so askew with age and so twisted and deformed that they might have been shaken by an earthquake.

The names of the streets recall the history of the old city. There are "Commons" and "Parson's Pool, Angel Lane," where was a tavern of that name for pilgrims, and Bell Street, which owned a like inn, "The Bell"; Magdalen's Almshouse or Dolhouse, of unknown antiquity; and Bymport, which was the Bind Port of the time of Edward IV.

This Bymport is a very agreeable street, which skirts the

north crest of the hill. Readers of *Jude the Obscure* will find here Phillotson's school and the little low drab house in which the wayward Sue wrought the wrecking of her life. The light of the setting sun streams in through the back windows as it did in the novel when Phillotson was lying ill. "The sunsets are mostly beautiful from here," the writer of *Jude* explains, " owing to the rays crossing the mist of the vale."

At many a point in the streets of this wind-swept town will be a bright gap among the houses whence is a sudden view of the limitless valley. It is just such a view as one might glean through a slit in the ramparts of a castle on a hill. Moreover, in any street you may come unexpectedly upon a steep, green-walled lane which drops down over the cliff to the plain as a rope ladder would drop from a tower.

Not the least headlong of these lanes is Gold Hill. It is a cobbled way, slow to climb, at the summit of which are the not unpicturesque Town Hall, the crumbling Church of St. Peter's, and the "Sun and Moon" Inn. On the right of the lane are thatched and tiled cottages, placed on steps so as to obtain a sure foothold. On the left is a very ancient wall of grey-green stone. It is an embankment wall that centuries ago kept level the Abbey garden. It is supported by enormous straining buttresses. The foot of each is planted aslant on the paved slope ; the shoulders of each lean back with fearful effort towards the line of houses on the ridge. These giants of stone seem to be holding up the town with might and main, to be cracking under the desperate burden, and to be almost swept down hill by the terrific weight. They are worthy to be symbols of Atlas holding up the world.

The ancient church of St. Peter's is the most conspicuous object in the High Street. Faded and pitiably senile, its stone is corroded by centuries of keen wind and biting rain, while its tottering doorway and porch stand by the church as emblems of venerable poverty. The deserted sanctuary seems to be shrinking into the earth ; so close are its windows to the very pavement that the curious child can peep in at the empty nave. Yet it has a noble tower, carrying six bells, on one of which still run the lines placed there in 1672 :—

> " When you hear me for to tole
> Then pray to God to save the soul."

Gold Hill, Shaftesbury.

It has a rich embattled parapet, glorious with carvings in stone of the portcullises, pomegranates, and roses of the time of Henry VIII. The roses are woefully faded, but on the mouldy sill of one of the tower windows is a sympathetic wall-flower in generous bloom.

From one brink of the hill the houses seem to shrink timidly away so that there is left a level green to crown the scarp. This is called Castle Hill. Of trace of a castle there is none, but it is recorded that those poor confused yokels, the "Club Men," fortified this place—probably with ridiculous gabions and alehouse valour—at the time of the Civil War.

On the southern edge of the ridge is a delightful wooded walk, called Park Walk, from which extends a view unsurpassed by few in England. This meditative avenue is on the very edge of the height, and it is said to have been a walk in the Abbey Park. At the foot of the hill, below the terrace, lie the thatched roofs of the suburb of St. James, with its ample gardens and its quite impressive church. The little settlement suggests a village on a beach as seen from the brink of an over-towering cliff.

The view from the Abbey terrace is across a vast, verdant, undulating valley of the richest pasture land—a plain without a level stretch in it. It ever rolls away into shallow valley and low hill, with now and then a wooded height or the glittering track of a stream. The land is broken up into a thousand fields, fringed by luxuriant hedges. In every hedge are many trees; trees follow every buff-coloured road, and gather around every hamlet or cluster of farm buildings. It is a country of dairies. Everywhere are there cows, for the smell of cows is the incense of North Dorset.

Away to the South the valley of meadows is shut in by the bank of the chalk downs. The nearest height is that of Melbury Hill, three miles distant, and to the West are Hambledon, the Shillingstone and Okeford Downs, Bell Hill, and Bulbarrow. On the East are the bare wind-driven heights, on the southern slope of which lies Cranborne Chase. As the foot of the hills is approached the pasture land ends in ploughed fields and patches of corn. The trees become fewer; the oak is changed for the fir, the dell of ferns for the clump of gorse, until at last, as the side of the slope is reached, there is nothing left but the close-cropped grass.

The great plain is intensely green, but this brilliant tint belongs only to the stretch of country about the foot of the hill, for the atmosphere which floods the valley is blue ; any mist that hangs in its hollows would seem to belong to the

The Downs, near Shaftesbury.

moonlight, while the far-off heights, on many a summer's day, are as blue as the iris.

Under the north side of Shaftesbury Hill is the suburb of Enmore Green, once famous for its wells. This very uninteresting village possesses a green no longer, but boasts still of a public well and a pump under a shed.

There was a time when Shaftesbury was very largely dependent upon Enmore for its water supply. It is evident from the following record—written in the reign of Henry VIII.— that the people of the hill town were in danger of having their water "cut off" under conditions which were not concerned with the mere payment of "water rates."

"6th March, 18. Henry VIII. Mem. That hit is the custome in the
tethinge of Motcombe, *usu longo,* time out of remembrance and mynde,
that the Soundhey nexte after Holy Roode day in May, every yeare,
every parish within the borough of Shaston shall come down that same day
into Enmore Greene, at one of the clocke at afternoon, with their
mynstralls and myrth of game ; and, in the same greene of Enmore, from
one of the clocke till too of the clocke, by the space of one hole hower,
theire they shall daunce : and the meyer of Shaston shall see the quene's
bayliffe have a penny loffe, a gallon of ale, and a calves' head, with a payer
of gloves, to see the order of the daunce that day : and if the daunce fayle
that day and that the quene's bayliffe have not his duty, then the said
bayliffe and his men shall stop the water of the wells of Enmore from the
borough of Shaston."

At Shaftesbury, as at many another Dorset town, the dweller
in cities can see something of the charm of the life of little
towns.   There is a curious absence of traffic in the streets,
and a sense that the place is deserted.   The newcomer
wonders if this is the "little town" that

"is emptied of its folk, this pious morn."

Everyone walks in the road, and from the tramp of their
feet on the crisp way it would seem that shoes here are of
heavier make than in cities.   In London the passing crowd
is dumb, for all are strangers.   Here each knows the other, so
that scarcely a soul goes by without a word of greeting.   The
boys in the streets are whistling a tune which was popular two
years ago : many people stand at street corners, as if waiting for
someone who never comes : most of the men carry sticks, and
most of the women baskets.

There is a personality about the place which is lacking in
those great cities which never slumber nor sleep.   In the
morning the town wakes up.   The householder opens his front
door and stands out in the road in his shirt-sleeves to appraise
the weather.   The idle apprentice takes down the shop shutters,
and—between intervals of gossip—places buckets, spades, tubs,
horse-collars, and other goods, according to their kinds, upon
the edge of the pavement.   The sexton strolls by to toll the

morning bell. A leisurely man drags a drowsy horse to the blacksmith's to be shod, and in a while there is the sound of a hammer on an anvil. A passing gig, that started from some farmhouse at sunrise, interests the waking town. It may carry a dairymaid on her way to a new situation, a couple of milk cans, or a confused heifer under a net.

A man proceeds to sweep the road with a besom made of a bundle of twigs according to the pattern of centuries ago. He shows a willingness to converse with everyone—man, woman, or child—who will stop to "pass the time of day with him." As something of an event a miller's cart, with a team of four fine horses, climbs up the High Street. They may have come so far that they appear to be foreign. There is always a vain, boastful dog with the waggon, who clamours that the town should stir to see his horses, his wain, his waggoner, and his sacks, all of which he regards as of unequalled magnificence.

In the evening the town goes lazily to sleep. The yawning shops close reluctantly, the long shadows of the setting sun fall across the drowsy street. The children have vanished. The lovers have come back from the lanes arm in arm. A tired dog is asleep in the centre of the road. Lights go out in the windows one by one, until the place is silent and dark. The visitor from the city falls asleep, lulled by the unwonted odour of a blown out candle and of a pillow that has been embalmed in lavender. Possibly about midnight a single horseman trots into the sleeping town, and in a while two horsemen clatter out again along the same road. From which it may be known that an anxious man has come in from the country to fetch the doctor, and is taking him back as if by the bidding of some Habeas Corpus.

CHAPTER II

A PILGRIMAGE TO MERE

MERE, although in Wiltshire, is so close to Shaftesbury that it is well to make a journey thither, if for no other reason than for its association with William Barnes. William Barnes, "the Dorset poet," and one of the most remarkable of men, lived for some twelve years at Mere, keeping a school in the town. Barnes's father was a farmer who held Rushay Farm near Pentridge, and here in 1801 the boy William was born. The family soon moving to Bagber, by Sturminster Newton, it was at the National School in the latter place that young Barnes was educated. On leaving school he became a clerk to a solicitor, and finally in 1823 he started a school at Mere. In 1827 he married Julia Miles, the daughter of an excise officer, the subject of endless admiration in his poems and the delight of his life. It is probable that at Mere his most pleasant years were spent, for there were times of great difficulty ahead. He worked incessantly at educating himself. He was familar with all European languages. His diary was written in Italian, in which his wife ever figures as " Giulia." He could read Hindustani, Persian, Arabic, and other unwonted tongues. He was a very accomplished musician, playing himself the flute, the violin, and the piano. He wrote innumerable books besides his well-known poems, and was learned in geology and archaeology. More curious still, he was a competent engraver

on both wood and copper, so that he illustrated not only his
own works by such engravings, but also the books and mono-
graphs of his friends.

The way to Mere from Shaftesbury is by Motcombe, a hamlet
of gardens at the foot of the hill.   In the spring the little place
is as full of white blossoms as is a temple cloister in Japan.

Most of the cottages are of faded stone, while against each
drab house-end some affectionate tree in blossom will be climbing.   The houses are facing all ways, as if they were shy of the
road or were undecided which way to turn.

The ancient church is appropriate to the quiet settlement.
A tablet upon its north wall calls abruptly upon the stranger to
" Behold the end of all flesh in Elizabeth."   This same
Elizabeth proves to have been wife to Sir William Webbe, and
the tablet further states that "this most obsequious wife,
indulgent mother, hospitall neighboure, discrete and religiouse
matrone, changed this mortal for immortalitie, Jan. 7,
A.D. 1627."

The country between Motcombe and Mere is flat and
inclined to be bare.   Straight ahead, on the horizon, towers a
range of jade-green downs, smooth, rounded, and steep.   They
rise up like a long masterful comber gathering to break on a
helpless beach, so that it seems as if the pent up mass of
the downs was about to burst forth thundering on to the
plain.

On these bare heights were the homes of our forefathers of
the stone and bronze ages.   Indeed, on these very hills was
once a British metropolis, as can be seen by the many
entrenchments and earthworks which still stand, by the crowd
of tumuli, and by the old trackway which even now can be
followed across the heights, and which was the great West-going
road before the Romans came.   It is very evident why the town
stood where it did.   The flat land to the south of Mere was all
forest and swamp, trackless and treacherous.   It was a wilderness of pitfalls, a Slough of Despond, a jungle haunted by

wild beasts and outcast men, a place shuddering with perils and alarms.

It is easy to picture a Briton of the humbler kind trudging with his wife along this way. They would be moving perhaps from Hod Hill in the South to the White Sheet Hill just beyond Mere. In this passage they would best follow first the River Stour and then the Shreen water, and so come to this very flat between Motcombe and the downs. The Briton who belonged to the " smart set " of the time—to the set who carried a bronze sword—would go by the trackway along the open heights. The simpler folk no doubt would hold to the valley, and, when they had pushed beyond Motcombe, would see ahead the solid down which was their goal. Plunging along through the swamp, sinking now and then waist deep into mire, struggling through gloomy thickets and clambering over fallen trees, the two travellers must have looked upon the bright, firm, shadowless hill ahead as a crest in a Celtic Paradise.

The man who tramps northwards is strong and agile, with a broad head, a fine brow, prominent cheek-bones, and a determined chin. He is clad in skins which have been well scraped and neatly sewn together with a bone needle and a tendon thread. He carries a bow and stone-tipped arrows, a handful of stone-headed spears, and in his belt a stone axe. He is as lithe as a panther and as swift as a reindeer. His wife, who follows in his steps, is a creature of beautifully moulded limbs, with the grace of the most splendid of all animals. Her eyes are blue and unfaltering. Her fair hair is arranged with bone pins according to the latest style, as learnt when she attended the great gathering at Stonehenge.

Like the modern woman, she has many anxieties. Over her shoulder hangs a blue-eyed baby in a skin bag. She is worried about her jewellery, which consists of a necklace of boar's teeth, sea shells, and jet. She has a cooking pot to carry which is very fragile, and in which she has packed her bone needles, her best hair-pins, and the horn-handled stone knife

given her by her husband on their engagement. There is a
danger of the pot being broken or of the contents falling out
as she stumbles through the knotted swamp. Moreover, she is
carrying a pouch full of stone arrow-heads and bone fish-hooks,
which her husband has placed in her charge with emphatic
admonitions. Were not his last words to her, as they walked
down Hod Hill, " Now, do take care of these arrow-heads; and
are you quite certain you have packed up our best stone skin-
scraper ? "

She must once in a way trip and fall over a trailing bramble,
and after she has clapped her hands to her neck to make sure
that her jewellery is safe, and jerked the baby straight, she will
search for such of the precious arrow-heads as have dropped
afield. Her husband keeps on his way, and if she be long in
the search, he mimics the barking of a wolf to make her
hasten. It is probable that when she catches him up she
pants out her terror of wolves (smiling to herself at his clumsy
imitation), and whispers that she has no fear so long as his
strong arm is nigh. When the simple man's vanity is
sufficiently flattered she confesses with sighs she has lost an
arrow-head, but he is very magnanimous, for she (knowing how
proud he is of his talent of mimicry) has just added that she
is sure the wolf she heard was a very large wolf.

Mere stands on the outermost edge of the plain, at the foot
of the downs—a little grey town with a bare hill for a background. Before reaching the place, the road passes a cluster
of picturesque cottages and a mill. Here is the river called
the Shreen water. Most of the Dorset streams have pretty
names, for besides the Shreen water there are the Bride River,
the Simene, and the Bibbern Brook.

The hill over against Mere is called the Castle Hill. On its
summit can still be seen traces of the ramparts of that fortress
which Richard, Earl of Cornwall, built here in 1253.

The " George Inn," on the other hand, has been rebuilt and
so modernised that it attracts no particular notice. Its claims

to distinction depend upon the events of a single day—a certain 5th of October in 1651. It was a Sunday afternoon when four persons rode up to the inn—a Colonel Robert Phelips and his man Peters, followed by a lady riding pillion with a man-servant. The lady was Miss Juliana Coningsby, and the man-servant—an untidy-looking yokel—was his Majesty Charles II. escaping from England.

On this particular occasion the King was hurrying from his hiding place at Trent to the shelter of Heale House. The Battle of Worcester was fought on September 3rd, so the Merry Monarch had been long playing the part of a hunted fox. In ten days' time, however, he was safe in a boat off Shoreham and was making for France.

At the inn at Mere on this notable Sunday afternoon Colonel Phelips took a drink with the landlord in the cellar. The landlord, seeing Charles standing aloof from the rest, said to the shy countryman, "Thou lookest like an honest fellow : Here's a health to the King." Charles failed to respond very readily to this toast, whereupon the loyal Boniface, turning to Colonel Phelips, remonstrated with him for having such a loutish fellow in his service.

It is probably of its church that Mere is most proud, since it can boast of a noble tower, of fine wood carving, and of a monument to the pious founder, John Bettesthorne, who died over 500 years ago.

Hidden behind the church is the old chantry house, where William Barnes kept school. Here he dreamed and studied, worked in his garden, or took walks with his ever-beloved Julia. In his biography the house is described as "a roomy old Tudor building, with large oak-wainscotted rooms, whose wide stone-mullioned windows were entwined with greenery. It had a large garden and lawn, at the bottom of which ran a flowing stream, here widened into a pond overshadowed with trees."

As it was then so is it now. The back gate of the little

house opens into the churchyard, the front garden looks over the open country, for the quondam school is on the very outskirts of the town. The house is low and of dull stone. Around the garden is a ruinous, lamentable old wall covered with briars and brambles. It seems as if the wild country had grown up to the place and had crept over it, while upon the forgotten house had fallen the hebetude of extreme old age. The garden the schoolmaster loved is in a state of some decay. There is still the clear water pond at its foot, and still to be seen "near this pond a favourite nook where William Barnes often came with his Petrarch in his pocket to pass a few happy leisure moments." [1]

In his Italian diary is many times the word "zappando" (digging), to show how his time was spent, and once is the entry "Giulia malata—giorno triste" (Julia is ill—the day is sad).

A pleasant way back from Mere is by way of the lanes to Silton, where is the lonely church. This church is on a green knoll in the midst of a solitude. The village of Silton, although it had a place in the Domesday Book, has vanished off the earth, save for two or three cottages, from a sight of which the church is shielded by a belt of rook-haunted trees.

There is a mumbling graveyard, covered with long grass, which fades into the hay fields around it. The narrow path to the church might be for the ghosts of the ancient village, were it not that a single oil lamp stands by the wicket gate to light the footsteps of the living. The church is very old. On its squat ivy-covered tower a venerable sun-dial lazily notes the hours, but there is no one to look up at the record. There is within a beautiful fan-traceried roof, and without are grinning gargoyles, very marvellous to see, but there are none to be pleased by a sight of them.

In this church of the village-that-was is at least one strange

[1] *Life of William Barnes.* By Leader Scott. London, 1887. Page 27.

thing. It is a florid and boastful monument to a Justice of the Court of Common Pleas—a certain Sir Hugh Wyndham, who died in the summer of 1684. From the turmoil of a London law court there could be no more perfect refuge than this church on the knoll at Silton.

Farther on the road to Shaftesbury lies Gillingham. It is a sprawling, uninteresting town, with a drab church too large for it, and many new red brick houses which are elemental in their ugliness. Gillingham is making haste to become an up-to-date town, but in its advance there are things it finds hard to put away. Fields full of buttercups will creep up innocently among its breweries, its sacking stores, and its bacon-curing establishments. A garden steps in here and there between its business abiding shops. A pear tree in full blossom clings to the wall of the " Cash Grocery, " while the town water cart, of the latest pattern, is filled at a little stream that runs chuckling through the town.

At one time there was a forest about Gillingham. Queen Elizabeth called at " Her Majesty's Park and Forest of Gillingham." It was well cared for too in those days, since a record, still surviving, tells how John Allen and Richard Whitehead, "regarders of the Park, " charged certain keepers of the same of stealing " many loads of oaken boughs praysed at 20d. the load." It was " deafforested " by Charles I., but the deer were not totally destroyed until the end of the seventeenth century.

In this forest was a palace built by some Saxon or Norman king. It stood half a mile from the town, by the banks of the River Lodden. It became the Sandringham of the time, for both Henry I. and John came hither, while Edward I. spent a Christmas in the palace, as records show. Traces of the great rampart and moat are still to be seen. They stand in a green close, called the " King's Court," and there are those who declare that they can trace the outline of the building itself, which they say was shaped like the letter L.

CHAPTER III

HERE lie the towns of Stalbridge and Sturminster Newton. The road to Stalbridge is across a very comely country, wherein are many picturesque villages. East and West Stour are, however, not of this type.

At East Stour was the farmhouse in which Henry Fielding the novelist lived with his first wife, and where he indulged in those extravagances which brought him to speedy poverty and which he never had the opportunity of repeating. His wife was a Salisbury beauty, Miss Charlotte Cradock by name—the " Sophia Western " of his most famous novel. Her fortune of £1,500 enabled the young couple to live at East Stour for a year or so as " county people." When the money was exhausted he changed into a poor playwright in a back street in London. The beautiful Charlotte survived this misfortune some seven years, whereupon Fielding consoled himself by marrying her maid.

The house at East Stour was rebuilt in 1835, but the back part of the present building is so evidently old that it may have belonged to the original structure. The famous locust tree, which was 10 feet 6 inches in circumference and had an elder bush growing " in the middle of its body," is no more. There is, however, by the farmhouse an old garden wall which must have been standing in Fielding's time, and which would be familiar to him if he revisited this region of the earth.

Among the notables of West Stour was a certain physician named William Watson. He was a native of the village, and, having obtained an M.D. degree at Oxford in 1683, he returned to this quiet spot to practise. He seems to have been an eccentric quack, of a type that appealed eagerly to the rustic mind. There is a portrait extant of him in boots and spurs, with a hanger and cane. He has so truculent a carriage that he would pass rather for a buccaneer than for a healer of the sick. On Sundays the people flocked to him from every part of the country, as he saw all comers for the modest fee of one shilling.

Near the Stours is Stour Hill, a lofty and narrow ridge running northwards. From this windy height is a superb view of the country in an unbroken circle. To the West is Somerset, across the green Vale of Blackmore, which vale can here be seen to the greatest advantage. On the East are the hill town of Shaftesbury and the great chalk downs, while to the North rise the heights beyond Mere.

A little way down on the west side of this steep slope is the hamlet of Kington Magna. The name of Kington Magna— the great town of the King—would rather befit London than this tiny, sequestered place, upon which ever fall the very last rays of the setting sun from across the Blackmore valley.

Kington Magna was an ancient demesne of kings before the Conquest, and figures conspicuously in the Domesday Book. The fact that it commands one of the most beautiful views of the famous vale in some part accounts for the esteem in which it was held. In the reign of King John it is recorded that "John de Ingham—the then owner of the Manor—being dead, William de Boterelles gave two coursers and a Norway goshawk for licence to marry Aubrey, his widow, besides a fine of 300 marks which she paid for licence to marry."

A marriage licence was evidently costly in those days, but it is not at once manifest why Aubrey had to pay so much more than William. It is to be hoped that William, as years passed by, had no reason to regret the two coursers and the goshawk.

The present village straggles down hill like a small mountain stream. In the approach to it one meets with an ancient church, which stands upon a platform or bastion as if it watched over the hamlet below. Its fine ivy-clad tower is sheltered by yew trees which seem as old as it is itself. Such is the situation of the churchyard on the precipitous incline that if the recumbent dead could but lift their heads a little they could look down the whole fair sweep of the valley. Near the church is the venerable Manor House, with a rookery behind it. The hamlet—Aubrey's hamlet—lies below, buried in green, a zigzag line of red and brown roofs, with a fringe of apple blossom along the unseen road, a glimpse of a swinging gate, of a yellow rick, and of white clothes drying in an orchard.

Those who are curious in ancient things may descend to the floor of the valley, to the church of Buckhorn Weston. They will find on the tower a sun-dial with the date 1577 upon it, while in the church are some of those remarkable paintings on wood which were common in Dorset churches in bygone days.

The panels preserved at Buckhorn Weston are six in number, serving to represent Christ, the Virgin Mary, David, St. Cecilia, and in two examples an angel descending from heaven over some inhabited place. These pictures were originally on the front of the singers' gallery, but as that structure is now pulled down, the ancient panels are preserved in the tower.

There is also in the church a monument on which is the recumbent figure of a mysterious man. The features of the unknown have been worn away, his tomb is nameless and dateless, while so unfamiliar is his costume that none can declare his status or his occupation. I may say that this unknown of Buckhorn Weston is clad in a " taberda " which reaches half-way down the thighs; over his shoulders falls a " scapular," while about his waist is a belt, studded with lozenges, from which is suspended a pouch.

On the way hence to Stalbridge are the two very charming villages of Stour Provost and Fifehead Magdalen. Stour Provost is a typical Dorset village, which has probably remained unchanged for the last hundred years. There are the quiet street of thatched cottages, the ancient rectory, a still more ancient farmhouse, and a little old church with a low tower and some lancet windows. Fifehead Magdalen—the place of five hides dedicated to the Magdalen—is a hamlet rather

Stour Provost.

than a village. It is shrouded in green, and some of the cottages with dormer windows in the thatch are evidently very old. Hutchins speaks of this little place—which belonged once to the nephew of William the Conqueror—as "as pleasant a spot as any in the county of Dorset."

Those who are in search of picturesque villages in this part of the country will find the two just named to their liking, and they may complete the list by adding the villages of Witchampton, Tarrant Monkton, Winterborne Zelstone, and Ibberton.

In the Dorset village the cottage may be of grey stone or of white plaster. It will in any case be covered with creepers of some kind or another, possibly with ivy, but more often with roses, jasmine, or honeysuckle. Lavender bushes will reach to the window sill, and hollyhocks or sunflowers to the window top. The love of flowers, the delight in bright blossoms, and the petting of gardens are features in every Dorset village. Against the end wall of the cottage there will generally be a pear tree trained, or the wall may be hidden by a clump of elder bushes or by a pink may tree. Bare it will not be. The cottage is apt to be low, so low that it would be simpler to alight from the bedroom window on to the path than to descend the ladder-like stairs. The casements of the windows open outwards, and are made of small square or diamond-shaped panes. Sometimes the upper windows are so small and so close under the overhanging thatch that, when only two in number, they gleam like a Skye terrier's eyes from under its shaggy hair. The ground floor windows of the cottage have a white curtain drawn across their lower half on a string. This muslin generally blows outwards when the window is open, revealing geraniums in pots on the broad sill.

The thatched roof may be of any tint of grey, yellow, or brown. It may be covered by creepers, or green or golden with moss. Occasionally stalks of immature wheat grow out of it. Birds find a retreat in its motherly bosom, and the house martins are fond of building their nests under its eaves. However little the space by the cottage, there will be a trim garden in front of it full of old-fashioned flowers such as stocks, pansies, pinks, fuchsias, and wallflowers. There is often a porch over the door, which will be covered with something green, while by the side of the entrance will as likely as not be a blackbird in a wicker cage, or possibly a magpie. In the garden is a well, or a row of bee-hives behind a clump of red poppies, while not far off will be an orchard and a pig-sty, or a picturesque stack of wood for the winter.

To the garden will be a gate which closes with a simple iron latch.   Of all village sounds, the one of most human interest is the click of this latch as the gate falls to.   It marks the neighbour's gossiping visit, the lover's shy call, the home-coming of the tired husband, the slinking back of the prodigal, the first venturing forth of the baby, and the last home-leaving of the lad who is away to the wars.   Thus it comes about that the little history of the village is to be recorded in the click of its garden gates.   The last poem written by William Barnes, or

Fifehead Magdalen.

rather dictated by him when he was dying, was "The Geäte a-vallèn to," from which these verses are taken :—

> " Drough day sheen for how many years
>   The geäte ha' now a-swung,
> Behind the veet o' vull-grown men
>   And vootsteps of the young.
> Drough years o' days it swung to us
>   Behind each little shoe,
> As we tripped lightly on avore
>   The geäte a-vallèn to.
>
> And oft do come a saddened hour
>   When there must goo away

> One well-beloved to our heart's core
>   Vor long, perhaps vor aye.
> And oh ! it is a touchèn thing
>   The lovèn heart must rue,
> To hear behind his last farewell
>   The geäte a-vallèn to."

The dialect of Dorset in which these lines are written has by no means died out. If it has vanished from the towns, it is still the speech beloved in the village, and dear to the hearts of those who gossip over garden hedges or grow eloquent around the much-stained table of the inn.

Speaking of this very poem, Barnes said to the daughter who records his life : "Observe that word ' geäte.' That is how King Alfred would have pronounced it. If the Court had not been moved to London, then the speech of King Alfred—of which our Dorset is the remnant—would have been the Court language of to-day."

A characteristic feature of the village is the manor house, which, when it survives, is usually found to be converted into a farmhouse. The old homestead will be of grey stone or faded red brick, with stone-mullioned windows divided into three vertical sections or lights. The casements are filled with small square leaded panes, while the middle one of the three opens outwards. Over the wide window is a drip-stone, which gives it a semi-ecclesiastic appearance. Often some of the old casements are blocked up with stone, or an odd window, oval or round, has been interpolated in the wall, as in the beautiful house of Thane's Farm, near Motcombe. The roof will be of chocolate tiles, of drab stone slabs, or of thatch. It is apt to rise into gables and to be broken in upon by dormer windows. Imposing chimneys of weathered stone or of delicate red brick crown the manor house.

There is usually a fine stone porch which would shelter a dozen folk, and which has seen, no doubt, the welcoming of many a bride and the agonised embrace of many a farewell.

Over the porch is a quaint little chamber, about the interior of
which no passer by can fail to be curious.   Possibly an old

A Dorset Farmhouse.

grandmother sits within, watching the road through the low
curtains, or a housewife bending over needlework.

Certain of these manor houses have bay windows carried
up to the second floor, or an oriel window which would befit
an ancient college.   The wall between the windows may be

covered with ivy, or more often with roses. There will be an old garden about the manor house, upon which has been expended centuries of affectionate care, a moss-covered garden wall with stone gate-posts, or a box hedge with a couple of clipped yew trees. Round about are great farm buildings and the picturesque litter and prowling life of a farm.

As examples of the more beautiful of the many manor houses in this part of the county may be mentioned Anderson Manor, near Winterborne Tomson, and the house at Hamoon. The former, of red brick, has a tiled roof with fine gables, and a bay window above the porch, which is carried up two stories; the latter is the most charming thatched manor house that could, I think, be found anywhere in this part of England.

Continuing on the road to Stalbridge, one comes by pleasant by-ways to Marnhull, the "Marlott" of Hardy's novels, and the home of "Tess of the D'Urbervilles." It is a disappointing village, prim and stiff, with houses mostly of slate and stone, together with many villas of the Brixton and Camberwell type. It is as little rustic as a place on the edge of the Blackmore Vale could be. Its long listless street crowns a modest height above the River Stour. Leland calls it "a good uplandishe towne," and there is no doubt that it held a place of greater importance in the past than it does now. Once there was a cell here belonging to Glastonbury. It enjoyed the right to pasture six cows and one bull at Marnhull from May 3rd to November 22nd, so that the Abbot might be supplied with milk and beef during his summer visit.

The mention of bulls calls to mind that there was an annual bull-baiting held here, in the Valley Meadow, on the third day of May. It was a very popular meeting, but it led unhappily to violence and riot, and finally to actual bloodshed. The spectators were wont to express their opinions as to the merits of the bulls by fighting among themselves and by beating any who differed from the views they held. The fights thus begun

in the Valley Meadow extended beyond Marnhull, and im-
plicated those peaceful villages of which the bulls under dis-
cussion were the pride. So it happened that in 1763 bull-
baiting in Marnhull was "put down."

The town, however, was not bereft of all sources of excite-
ment when the exhausted bulls were led for the last time back
to their respective hamlets by heated men with bleeding scalps
and black eyes. In 1795 the English Benedictine nuns of
Paris sought refuge here. Their black frocks and veils gave
little grounds at first for more than curiosity. That the people
of the place "said things" about the nuns and their doings is
very probable. In the course of time, however, a nun unfortunately died, and the sisters buried her in the back garden
of the house. Whereupon the *ci-devant* bull-baiters of Marnhull rose as one. They were not disposed to discuss any
rumoured "goings on" in the convent nor raise a question
as to the burying of people in back gardens, but what they
would not and could not stand was the fact the corpse had
been buried "without the coroner." These quiet ladies from
Paris had yet to learn that enshrined in the English heart
is a jealous esteem of inquests and a reverence for the secret-
probing coroner which cannot be tampered with. By reason
of this ignoring of the coroner the nuns "became obnoxious,"
and to such a degree were they made to feel their own
offensiveness that they shook the dust of Marnhull from their
feet for ever.

According to a statement of a rector of the place, who wrote
about it in 1778, "Marnhull was always remarkable for tall
people, both men and women." This same rector also serves
to show that the modern lament over the depopulation of the
country and the cry "Back to the land!" were acute no less than
125 years ago. In his comment upon affairs he deplores that
all the able-bodied men are migrating to the large towns in such
extent that "few are left for agricultural purposes but infirm old
men and boys."

There is at Marnhull a singularly handsome church, the fine tower of which is a landmark for many miles around.

On one of the tombs it contains is the recumbent figure of a knight in armour, reputed to be Thomas Howard, Viscount Bindon, who died in 1582. His two wives lie on either side of him. The effigies are in alabaster, and their mutilated condition is explained by the statement that much of the alabaster " has been stole to make dies for coining." The Viscount is a huge and powerful man, but the wives are singularly small and delicate. They are not only exactly alike in height and in such features as have escaped the ravages of the coiner, but they are clad in precisely the same costumes : the same pretty headdress of linen, the same simple bodice, the same clasped cloak. As they wear necklaces which are identical in pattern, it is evident that the jewellery of the first wife descended to the second, and that the latter either inherited her predecessor's very clothing or copied it with a devout and complimentary exactness which may possibly be unusual.

This little town seems to have made somewhat of a speciality of epitaph writing, as is made evident by many choice inscriptions in the church and by the following by a rector of Marnhull upon his clerk, John Warren, who died in 1752 at the age of ninety-four :—

> " Here under this stone
> Lie Ruth and old John,
> Who smoked all his life
> And so did his wife :
> And now there's no doubt
> But their pipes are both out.
> Be it said without joke
> That life is but smoke ;
> Though you live to fourscore,
> 'Tis a whiff and no more."

A pleasant road across the luxuriant Vale of Blackmore over the River Stour and the Bibbern Brook leads to Stalbridge.

This is the Staplebridge of old days, described by Leland as "a praty uplandishe toune of one streate meately well buildyd, which was privilegyd withe a market and a faire. The market is decayed : the faire remaynithe." The townlet is placed upon an isolated hill rising out of the valley. From the summit of this height there is a haze-encompassed view of the Vale of Blackmore, which in June, after a week of rain, is dazzling by reason of its greenness. The district is given up to fields for

Stalbridge.

pasture and to dairies, so that he who is not well versed in the characteristics of cows, their lives and times, is regarded as a foreigner.

The town, with its radiating streets, sprawls over the hill like a starfish. It is not a "praty" town now. It possesses a neat row of semi-detached villas worthy of the suburbs of Hull, a place where "petrol" is sold, and shows a general leaning to slate, iron railings, corrugated iron, and much bill-posting. There are, on the other hand, a few thatched cottages, some fine old roofs of stone outlined by moss, quaint alleys and ancient

D

gardens, with here and there a white bow window filled with geranium blossoms.

In one street is a venerable stone cross raised on four steps, tall and of much grace,and tanned by the sun a rich yellow brown. Carved upon it, they say, are figures of the Saviour, the Virgin, and St. John, with sundry shields and coats of arms, but the lower sculptures have been well-nigh obliterated by centuries of babies' hands and the upper carvings by the rain.

In the much-restored church are pillars with capitals of angels' heads and texts, and for a font a smooth bowl of stone like a kettledrum. On one altar tomb—so old that all knowledge of its date is lost—is the recumbent figure of a corpse in a shroud. It is a gruesome object, for the body of the unknown is so profoundly emaciated that the ribs appear as entrenchments through the skin. His head reclines on a pillow with roses. What is most noticeable about him is the very determined expression of his mouth, as if on the set lips was the resolve to get no thinner under any possibilities.

People with names which would have pleased the eighteenth century playwright are buried in this place. Among them are Ismond Plainewit, 1658, Matthew Foole, 1659, and Temperance Collins, 1666.

Of the great house which stood in Stalbridge Park, where King Charles I. dined with the Earl of Cork, no trace remains beyond the stone pillars of the main gate, which are surmounted by the heads of needlessly ferocious heraldic beasts. Robert Boyle, the natural philosopher, once resided at Stalbridge House, where indeed he carried out his early chemical experiments. He must often have passed this gate, and smiled at the unnatural animals who snarl from its summit.

The road from Stalbridge to Sturminster Newton passes by Bagber, where William Barnes spent his early days. He was educated at the day school at Sturminster, so that the road between the farm and the school must have been very familiar

to him, as he trudged it every day. Somewhere along this
road was a haunted house, about the locality of which the
poet provided no information, beyond that "a dark and gloomy
lane led to it." He seems—in one of his visits to the old
home—to have pointed out the spot to his grandchildren.
"That was the lane," he told them, "your grandfather was
riding down when all at once he saw the ghost in the form of
a fleece of wool, which rolled along mysteriously by itself till it

The Cross, Stalbridge.

got under the legs of his horse ; and the horse went lame from
that hour and for ever after." [1]

Sturminster Newton—the new minster town on the Stour—
was, according to Leland, "no greate thing," while he further
adds that "the buylding of it is mene." Of the manor
house, however, he is so indulgent as to say, "It is a
thauncyent buylding, portly and strong, able and mete for a
knight to lye in." The manor house, the minster, and the
new town have long since vanished, although in the Domesday

[1] *Life of William Barnes.* London, 1887. Page 305.

D 2

Book, among sundry owners of land in the place, was no less
a person than Gosceline, the King's cook, who held four hides
here.

The town is "meately" placed, for a gracious river winds
round about it, its water-meadows are ever green, while behind
it rise the bare heights of the Dorset hills from Hambledon
to Bulbarrow. The view of the minster town from the near
village of Hinton St. Mary is excellent indeed. In that
uninteresting hamlet, by the way, lived one William Freke,
who published *A Dictionary of Dreams*, and died in 1744.
Hutchins, speaking of this author, states that "His under-
standing was deranged," and adds, as if in mitigation of his
lunacy, "but he acted as a Justice of the Peace many years"

Sturminster is a pleasant town enough, a quaint admixture
of the would-be-very-new and the needs-be-very-old. It is
approached from the South by an old stone bridge with
pointed arches, which opens on an avenue of trees and a
causeway edged with white posts and rails to mark the road in
times of flood. At the end of the vista of trees there comes
into view a comfortable medley of thatched roofs, buff walls,
outjutting gardens, and moss-covered sheds. No two houses on
the way from the bridge are alike, nor are they in line. Some
are on the level of the road, while others mount up behind a
raised path, bounded by a railing from which a child is
commonly hanging head downwards like a bat.

In the centre of the town is the semblance of a square, to
which all roads lead. Here are an officious gas standard carrying aloft the latest pattern of lamp, the stump of an ancient stone
cross, and the town pump. The latter is of wood, is small,
black, and vixenish. On it is a notice spitefully warning the
passer-by that he will be prosecuted if he does it hurt, and
adding further that no children must use the exclusive structure. There is a sourness in this, for all children delight to play
with pumps.

There are two picturesque old taverns in the town. The more

imposing of the two has walls of faded red and grey brick, while the other is a low building, covered by a thatched roof with dormer windows in it. A gateway leads under this house to the stable yard, and over the passage is a little chamber where those who lie within can hear the occasional rumbling of a cart under the floor and the ceaseless twittering of birds above the eaves. The upper windows of the inn have the sleepy look of half-closed eyes, but the lower windows are modern, glaring, and alert.

Near the church is the Boys' National School, where William Barnes was educated. As the schoolhouse was in his day so is it now—a small drab building with a stone-mullioned window

Sturminster Newton.

and prominent buttresses, which, with the red brick chimney, save it from being mistaken for a barn.

The castle which defended Sturminster Newton stood on a steep mound by the bridge. The mound is still there, scored by scrambling paths made by boys, but the castle is not. In the place of the stronghold is an orchard, in whose centre is a pale ruin almost hidden by ivy, brambles, and elder bushes. There are stone walls within this thicket, and many perfect Gothic arches. The ruin forms, however, no part of the old castle, but is all that remains of a rectorial house which was probably occupied by a monk from Glastonbury who lived here to look after the lands of that Abbey.

The way back to Shaftesbury may be by Hammoon. Hammoon—the "ham" or dwelling of the Mohuns, its ancient lords—is a little oasis of orchard and cottage in an expanse of water-meadows about the Stour. In one old house in this delightful hamlet it is possible to see to what an exquisite tint of pale rose common red brick may change after a century or two of sun and rain, and how well that colour blends with the

Hammoon Manor House.

velvety brown of an ancient thatch and the green of a lusty creeper.

Here also is a manor house which is, I think, the most picturesque of its kind. It is a long, low building of ash grey stone, with a thatched roof and fine bay windows with stone mullions. In the centre is a graceful stone porch, with a small chamber over the pillared doorway. The beauty of this dignified old homestead is enhanced by contrast, for close to it is a modern villa of the usual suburban type.

CHAPTER IV

CRANBORNE CHASE

THE glory of Cranborne Chase has well-nigh departed. Cut into on all sides by the woodman's axe and the plough, nibbled at on all opportunity by the land-grabber, it has dwindled at last to a little oasis of wild country on the borders of Wiltshire and Dorset. Here it remains—as Mr. Hardy says —" a truly venerable tract of forest land, one of the few remaining woodlands in England of undoubted primeval date, wherein Druidical mistletoe is still found on aged oaks, and where enormous yew trees, not planted by the hand of man, grow as they had grown when they were pollarded for bows." Here is a secluded piece of England which has changed but little since the days of King John, when probably the " walks " and the halter tracks were first made through the great forest.

The Chase came to King John through his wife—an heiress of the house of Gloucester. He gave up the lady—by the process of divorce—shortly after he was raised to the throne, but he did not at the same time surrender her possessions at Cranborne. It remained on and off a royal forest until James I. granted it to the Earl of Salisbury, by whose family a portion of it is held to this day. There was a time when the Chase extended on the North to Shaftesbury and Salisbury, and was encircled on its other sides by the Stour and the Avon. It had then a perimeter of over eighty miles, while through the centre of it ran the great Roman road from Old Sarum to Exeter.

There were certain lodges in the ancient Chase, as well as certain " walks " and trackways through it, each of which was under the charge of a ranger. It was alive with deer and game of all kinds. As late as 1828 there are said to have been 12,000 head of deer within its confines.

The Chase became a happy hunting ground for adventurers of many kinds. There were, first of all, certain gentlemen of the district, who formed themselves into a body of " deer hunters." These aristocratic poachers had unlimited " sport " in the Chase, for besides mere deer hunting there were frequent and bloody combats with the authorised keepers of the Chase, as well as with poachers who were not of the hunters' " set." Hutchins gives the portrait of a noted deer hunter, painted in 1720, in his cap and jack. The cap looks like a straw beehive, while the jack is a long quilted and ornamented coat that could have withstood much buffeting.

Later on the Chase proved a famous resort for smugglers, who found its many shady hollows convenient for the hiding of such goods as they landed at Poole or Swanage. It was a ready retreat also for thieves, murderers, and criminals of every grade, because shelter was safe and agreeable, and food was always at hand. If to these frequenters of the glens be added common deer stealers, poachers of small game, blackmailers, tramps, and vagabonds, with others who followed the humbler paths of vice, it is no surprise that in time the Chase became an unholy haunt which had to be " put down " as a mere covert for wickedness.

In 1830, therefore, it was disafforested, and silence fell upon the place for ever. No longer was the stillness of the night broken in upon by the crackling rush of startled deer, by the yells of throttled poachers, or the wrangling of thieves over bags of booty, nor were men to be come upon digging pits by lantern

light in which to hide spirit kegs or an occasional excise officer
with a hole in his skull.

" The place, however, still possesses great charm, and an old keeper, who
had lived all his life there, testified to the same when he said, speaking of
a sermon he had heard in which the beauties of Paradise were descanted
on, ' It seems by the account to be a desperate pleasant place, but I do
now believe, notwithstanding what the parson said, that if there was but a
good trout stream running down Chicken-Grove Bottom, Ferndich Wake
would beat it out and out.' " [1]

Those who visit the Chase from Shaftesbury—the most convenient centre—and who go thither on foot or by bicycle or on
horseback will find the way by Berwick St. John agreeable.
This village lies at the foot of Winklebury Hill, on the summit
of which is a British fort encompassed by a rampart and a
ditch. A little beyond the village is a grass lane sunk deeply
between high banks, which in the spring time are covered with
blue-bells, violets, and primroses. The flowers clothe not only
the banks, but also the green roadway itself. This secluded
lane leads by a track across the hill to Cranborne Chase.

I cannot help thinking that it was by this muffled road that
the Duke of Monmouth fled after the battle of Sedgemoor.
The record says that in his breathless journey he left Shaftesbury
on the West and crossed the high-road by Berwick St. John.
As he was making his way to that harbour of refuge, Cranborne
Chase, he would have found this hidden path a most ready
route. In July too it would have been full of shade, so that he
and his few companions might well have rested for a while in
its untroubled shelter.

When the lane reaches the hill side it enters a primitive turf
road of a curious kind. The track is entrenched ; it winds up
and round the hill in spiral fashion, to open finally upon
the bare down. It is so deeply cut into the side of the slope

[1] *Dorset.* By Frank Heath. London. Page 131.

that those who walk the road are hidden from sight.   Indeed, it would hide a troop of horse.   There is little doubt that this ancient way was dug out by the same Britons who reared the camp on the summit.   It made a safe and secret entry to the stronghold from the North, from the quarter towards which the hostile country lay.   One may suppose that many a herd of oxen and many a company of women and children have been hurried up this cutting on occasions of alarm.

The road is steep, and as the wayfarer plods up it he may fancy that at the next bend, clear against the sky line, he will meet one of those who made the road—a rugged man with red hair and blue eyes, clad in skins, as shown in Boehm's statue of him in the garden by the Larmer Tree.   He may possibly be tearing down in one of those cars drawn by rough ponies which Caesar has described, and of which that soldier had such reasonable fear.   It was of the "strepitus," or rattle, made by these cars that Caesar mostly complained, which noise would seem to have exceeded even the "strepitus" created by the motor-car of to-day.

The green gully at last opens upon the south slope of the hill, upon a wide solitude where runs that old Celtic road called the "Ox Drove" or "Ridgeway."   This venerable track, which long preceded any Roman road, runs for many a breezy mile across the county.   It was no doubt mainly a route for cattle in their passage from one settlement to another, for it kept to the hill top, to the bare ridge, as being the only way safe from ambush, wild beasts, and opportunity for straying, since the lowland was at the time a mere tangle of forest and swamp.

Just below the Ox Drove lies Cranborne Chase, which, although it forms at this point a part of Rushmore Park, is yet so little disturbed that it is still the primitive forest of two centuries ago.

A wilder stretch of the Chase (crossed on the way back to Shaftesbury) between Ashmore and the upper Blandford road may be selected as more characteristic of the spot.   From

Ashmore, or from the high downs near by, it is possible to look down upon the wandering wood and upon that rough, mysterious country which runs northward to the gap in the hills in the wake of the Roman road.

At one's feet is a rolling woodland, backed by white clouds in an azure sky.   Over the Chase is a blue mist, which hangs in the winding glens like the smoke of incense.   On the outskirts of the forest, in the springtime, are patches of ploughed land which are almost rust red, together with light green stretches of springing corn and clumps of dark pines, while at the very edge of the wild is a fringe of white may blossom and yellow gorse.

There is a green way through the wood, a track made of gilt-bronze moss and miniature grass nibbled short by rabbits, with ever on either side banks splashed by primroses.   Far away beneath the undergrowth is, here and there, a patch of blue-bells, so closely clustered that they look in the shade like a deep, blue pool.   Between the primroses and the bluebells are white anemones and violets beyond number.   The place is rustling with birds ; every tree is budding, and everything that grows is bursting with life.   A holly bush or a tree trunk looks almost black against the pale new leaves.

Here is an avenue centuries old cut through the wood, straight as a street, but so paved with moss and primroses that it looks like a lane of gold.   Here is a clearing full of felled trees and piles of faggots, with white chips from the axe lying among bluebells.   Last of all is a deep wooded glen, creeping mysteriously through the forest, its floor of grass, its wall of bushes and spring flowers—a place shut away from the world, where the sky is narrowed to a bright gap between the tree-tops.   This is just such a glen as belongs to the country of the " Idylls of the King."   Here is that level stretch of turf in the heart of a lonely wood, where it was seemly that two knights should meet in mortal combat while the banks re-echoed the thunders of their horses' hoofs, and any lull of silence would

be broken by the whimperings of the distressful maid. This
glen, which might be known as Lancelot's Glen, is designated
by the modern map-maker as " Stubhampton Bottom."

To return once more to Rushmore, it is well when in that
quarter of the Chase to visit Woodcuts, where are to be seen
the most perfect remains existing in England of a British-Roman
village. This settlement has been scientifically explored and
described by General Pitt-Rivers, whose exhaustive investiga-
tions into the works of the early inhabitants of this country are
quite unrivalled.

The village is situated in a far corner of a gorse-covered
common, amidst a country like that of the New Forest. It
is a village of pit-dwellings, the situation of the various pits
being still distinct in the form of little green hollows and
dimples. Some of the deepest holes are lined with stone, and
were evidently cellars or store places beneath the dwelling.
It is needless to remind the reader that the basin-like pits
were roofed over, and that the dome-shaped covering was
supported by a pole planted in the centre of the hollow.
Around the village are ramparts and ditches. Many of the
trenches are evidently for drainage rather than for defence, for
the country was wetter in pre-Roman days than it is now.
The little townlet is divided into definite quarters, and is
provided with at least three well-marked entrances. The
evidence collected by General Pitt-Rivers goes to show that
this village was occupied from the commencement of the
present era to about A.D. 360. It can therefore claim that
its ruins are as ancient as those of Pompeii, which was
overwhelmed in A.D. 79.

In the unique and magnificent museum which General Pitt-
Rivers has established at Farnham can be seen a model of the
ancient town and a collection of the curious things which were
found therein. It must have been a somewhat crowded village.
Numerous hearths which served as public kitchens have been
uncovered, together with certain hypocausts lined with stones

and provided with a rough flue, in which bodies were cremated at one period of the village's history. The ramparts were completed by a wall of daub and wattle work, for fragments of such a wall are to be seen in the museum.

The many objects discovered within the ramparts furnish an insight into the life of the little place. These include flint implements of the late stone age, which no doubt belonged to the still half-savage men among the conquered people, who hunted for the community, who killed wolves and boars, and brought their spoils in through the gate with no little exultation. Then there are many Roman coins, both in silver and copper. These must have come from Italy, or at least from Gaul, and have been carried hither in the pouches of men who knew the Eternal City, and who fretted at a life in a damp island, peopled with boors and oppressed by a dismal sky. They had, no doubt, many tales to tell of Southern cities, of Italian summers, and of the wonders of the great world of Rome.

Rude pottery was found in the settlement, as well as spoons and pins made of bone, with uncouth ornaments of teeth and shells. These would have belonged to the dwellers in the poor quarters of the village, in the Whitechapel of Woodcuts. In the course of the digging, too, were revealed fine bracelets of bronze, with fibulæ and brooches of exquisite workmanship. There were dainty ladies, therefore, at one time in the west end of the village; and they too, one may suppose, found the coarse life by Cranborne Chase very irksome to bear, for both the men and the manners of the island of their exile must have been but little to their liking. Between the rough hunter with the flint spear-head and the little lady of the bronze brooch there was a great gulf fixed.

In these, as well as in other excavations, one is impressed with the carelessness of ancient people, with the way they left their money and their jewellery (as the Americans would say) "around." Roman coins indeed seem to have been scattered over the earth of Britain like seed.   When the ruins of London come to be dug up by some new man—he will need to be later than Macaulay's New Zealander—it is to be wondered if the spade will disclose endless sovereigns and gold rings, or come upon a stratum of watches, snuff-boxes, and spoons.

General Pitt-Rivers found many skeletons at Woodcuts. Some of these were in the outer ditch, and he suggests that they were " probably thrown in alive and stoned to death."   About one burial pit at least, which he opened up, there is an element of tragedy.   It contained two adult skeletons, one sitting, the other standing erect.   Between them a child had been cast in head downwards, killed by a sword cut which had pierced the back of its skull.   Here, blurred in the reading, there comes to the light again the fragment of a story which has lain buried for nearly 2,000 years.

Besides the wonderful museum at Farnham, the traveller in this part of the shire should visit the Larmer Tree.   The Larmer Tree stands on the boundary line between Wilts and Dorset. It is traditionally the spot where King John was wont to meet his huntsmen when staying at his hunting box at Tollard Royal.

Upon the old tree has fallen an eternal winter, for it is long since dead.   Its roots are still in the ground and its leafless branches still rise skywards, but its trunk is ignominiously held up by a post and a chain.   It is a wych elm, and it leans helplessly against the new Larmer Tree, a young and sprightly oak. Under the wych elm the Chase Courts, they say, were held for the settlement of all matters relating to the Chase.   By the generosity of General Pitt-Rivers the beautiful grounds about the Larmer Tree are open to the public.   They contain Boehm's vigorous statue of "The Hunter of Early Days"— a Celt mounted on a shaggy pony—as well as quarters for picnic parties, a band-stand, and an open-air theatre—luxuries hardly to be looked for in a secluded wood some ten miles from any railway station.

The small village of Tollard Royal will be found in a hollow among the downs on the return journey. The little place derives its name of Royal from the fact that King John, in the right of Isabella his wife, held a knight's fee there. The venerable church, with its ivy-covered tower, is very picturesque. It contains, in the form of a recumbent figure, whose face has been rubbed absolutely smooth by centuries of village hands, a monument to Sir William Payne, who died in 1388. A black urn, set in a comely white marble niche, holds the ashes of the illustrious General Pitt-Rivers. Affixed to one wall of the church is a plain cross crudely constructed from two pieces of common wood. Underneath is this pathetic legend :—

> " This cross of wood first marked the
> Spot were
> The Hon. Alice Arbuthnot
> Was killed by lightning, 21 June, 1865.
> As it once stood on the Schildhorn Alp,
> so it is now placed unaltered
> In this church where she was married
> Eight weeks before her death."

Opposite the church is the famous building known as King John's House. It is overgrown with ivy, and its chocolate-coloured tiles are partly hidden by moss. It is a building of the thirteenth century, of which period two characteristic windows with stone seats still exist in the walls. The rest of the lodge belongs to Tudor times, and the beautiful oak-panelled rooms are of that date. The house, with its colossal beams, its wonderfully carved mantelpiece, its cavernous hearth, and its collection of ancient furniture, is of the greatest interest.

Hence to Shaftesbury the road may be taken to Ashmore and the Chase, as already mentioned. Or the descent from the heights may be made by the " Zigzag "—a steep and sharply bending road that creeps cautiously down the hill side. From the summit of the Zigzag there is a view over a wide stretch of country, the highlands of which are little altered since the days of the Britons, and are covered still by their tumuli and entrenchments, and crossed by their breezy highway, the Ox Drove.   The smooth downs roll away on either side of the road like great seas, while at their foot, on the North-east, are the " level meads " of the Vale of Chalk.

CHAPTER V

THE ROAD TO BLANDFORD

ALONG this road, about a mile beyond the hill on which stood Melbury Beacon, is the little settlement of Compton Abbas. The modern village, that all can see, is by the roadside, and is bald and bold enough. There is, however, a shy lane which leads to a glen at the very foot of the downs, where, hidden among orchards and trees, the shrunken old hamlet will be found. It is one of the many buried villages of the county. By the side of its thatched cottages is the ancient graveyard, where, in a wilderness of rank grass and tombs, fowls have made a pleasaunce of their own. Under a yew tree is the stump of the village cross, which even yet compares favourably with the Jubilee obelisk in the new churchyard. The church is gone, but its square tower, covered with ivy, still stands. It has for its only background the smooth, immense rampart of the downs. On the very summit of this tower a pear tree is growing, and the genial farmer who lives near by states that, although the tree blossoms every spring, it has not increased in size these twenty years. In picturesqueness the dwellers in Compton Abbas have gained little by the exchange of " old lamps for new."

Following the main road, one soon comes to the beautiful village of Fontmell Magna, which still boasts of a maypole. It lies in a hollow by the side of the Fontmell Brook, and is as

E

pretty a spot as old cottages, old gardens, and old orchards can make it. In the centre of the village is a very ancient tree with seats around it, where the gossips of the place congregate to mumble over flocks and herds, and the affairs of pigs.

The church is one of the handsomest in Dorsetshire. Its line of rectors goes back to one Stephen Prewett, who

Compton Abbas.

ministered here in 1303, at which time the living was owned by the Abbess of Shaftesbury. The church has many interesting features. Under the battlement over the north aisle there is carved, amidst various figures and coats of arms, the following writing, which bears the date of 1530 :—

> O ᛗᚫᚾ
> ᚴᛃᚱ ᛒᚫᚱᛖ
> ᛏᚺᛟ ᛁ'ᛗᚫᚾ

("Oh, mankind, bear thou in mind") The rest of the message is lost, and none can tell what it was mankind should keep so earnestly in his thoughts. Besides this, there are pillars crowned by angels, a Norman font, and an old carved screen with upon it the heads of "Water King and Esbell his wif."

In the churchyard is a pale stone cross to Philip Salkeld. " In respect to his Memory," the inscription says, and then follows :—

> " Born Oct. 13, 1833, at Fontmell.
> Died Oct. 11, 1857, at Delhi.
> Wounded mortally in blowing open
> The Cashmere Gate."

Fontmell Magna: The Maypole.

None will forget how this lad of 24 and his five comrades crept up to the Cashmere Gate in the dawn of the morning of September 14th, and by the glorious heroism which cost most of them their lives made the capture of Delhi possible.

When the powder bags had been placed Salkeld stood by with a slow match in his hand to fire the charge. Before he could apply the spark he was struck down by two bullets. As he fell he contrived to hand the fuse to a sapper named Burgess, telling him to fire the bags. The light, however, went out, and before Burgess could rekindle it he fell over into the ditch mortally wounded. Finally the match was applied by

E 2

Smith, another sapper, who miraculously escaped, and lived to wear the Victoria Cross he had so gallantly won. He and Bugler Hawthorne were the only two of the company who survived. Lieutenant Salkeld had had his thigh broken by one bullet and his arm shattered by another. The arm was amputated, but his case unfortunately proved no exception to

The Gossips' Tree : Fontmell Magna.

the rule that in this period of the campaign few men survived the removal of a limb.

Poor Salkeld died on the Ridge, the dismal, stony, sun-scorched Ridge, that waterless, fever-stricken boulder heap the British held for 104 days of a tropical summer. Fontmell to Delhi! The cross looks over the thatched cottages of the village, over the gardens by the brook, over the clusters of apple trees, to the great quiet downs beyond, dotted with sheep. It is the very picture—green and cool—which must have fluttered many a time through the brain of the wounded man as he lay dying on the dusty, burnt-up Ridge.

I may mention in connection with this memorial that on the high-road between Haselbury Bryan and Sturminster Newton is a plain brick bridge over the River Divelish, on each wall of which is inscribed on a stone, " Salkeld. 1857. Delhi." In the neighbouring church of Fifehead Neville are monuments to the Salkeld family.

Farther on the Blandford road is Iwerne Minster, a village of some size, beautifully situated, and possessed of many charming old cottages. It must at one time have been very picturesque, but it is in process of being metamorphosed into red brick. The low thatched cottages are gradually vanishing, to be replaced by bold houses of gaudy brick and tiles.

Iwerne serves to show one phase of the village of the future— the well-to-do, unblushing village of red brick, which for the bread of quiet beauty offers the stone of harsh unseemliness. It is impossible to complain of this with any show of reason. The low thatched cottage embedded in creepers is to a varying extent unhealthy ; it is probably damp, is certainly ill ventilated, and usually lacking in light and the first needs of sanitation. The red brick house can claim to be " hygienic," but by some ill fortune most things that are hygienic—whether they be clothing, food, or buildings—are unpleasant and unsightly. Even the hygienic person, with his fusty undergarments, his dismal diet, and his axioms about drains and traps, is not attractive. It is unreasonable to require that the inhabitants of villages should occupy unwholesome dwellings merely to please the æsthetic tastes of the passer by. The exquisite old thatched cottage, with its tiny windows of diamond panes, must go, for the man of drains has spoken, and with it will vanish the most characteristic feature of rural England.

That the unhealthiness of the gracious old cottage is no matter of surmise is enforced by the evidence of poor health among villagers. The men, who live in the open air, may be hearty enough, although they are not always so robust as they look. The stay-at-home women, on the other hand, are very commonly the subjects of anæmia and not infrequently of tuber- culosis. The life of a really poor woman in a remote village

must be woefully and injuriously dull, and those who spend thousands of pounds in providing holidays for city folk might remember that cottagers are not exempted from the need of change simply because they live in the country. In support of this I may quote the following paragraph from a London journal :
—" Those who view the increase of insanity in these islands with alarm are apt to attribute the deplorable growth of lunacy to the pressure of modern life, and especially the struggle for existence in great cities. They picture the simple countryman living the 'simple life' in reasonable content, and keeping a sound mind in a healthy body, while the dweller in crowded areas succumbs to nervous strain. Upon this picture the fifty-ninth report of the Commissioners in Lunacy, just issued, turns the hard light of facts. According to this summary, it is the countryman who goes mad sooner on the average, while the much-pitied towns-man, in spite of strain and competition, remains sane enough to be called upon to look after him." [1]

One remark I overheard at a small wayside station will, per-haps, impress the town-dweller with the isolation of some village lives. A woman, who had evidently walked far to take the train, having deposited her great bunch of flowers and queer parcels on the bench, exclaimed with evident fervour, " Oh ! how nice to see a railway station once more ! "

The church of Iwerne Minster is famous in the possession of a stone steeple, a distinction belonging to no other churches in Dorset, except those at Winterborne Steepleton, and Trent. It contains, too, certain Norman and Early English remains. The building has—like many other churches in the county— suffered from the ravages of restoration. At the beginning of the last century the spire was taken down and only rebuilt to half its former height—" the remainder went to repair the roads, says the tradition." [2] The curious shutters which once closed in the chancel windows are gone ; gone is " the square aisle with

[1] *Daily Telegraph.* Sept. 12th, 1905.
[2] *Proceedings of the Dorset Field Club.* Vol. XVI., page 47.

a fireplace, belonging to the Bower family "—the great folk of Iwerne; while with both has vanished the gilt dove that rested upon the top of the sounding board.

Among the tombs of many Bowers there lies buried here John Willis, one of the most eminent writing masters in the kingdom. "His copies were equal, if not superior, to copper-plates." For thirty years he kept at Iwerne a school for teaching writing, and so great was his fame that scholars flocked to him from all parts of the country. He died in April, 1760, having acquired a considerable fortune.

The village of Steepleton Iwerne near by is reduced to one house and a church. The house, a large and motherly structure, has taken the lonely little church under its wing, and has made a place for it in the garden, between the mansion and the stables. It is a very humble church, with an ancient wooden porch, a stone-tiled roof, and walls which are nearly hidden by ivy. There is an unexpected Norman arch over its altar, because the chancel was fashioned out of the base of a Norman tower. What may be termed the precincts of the church are lost among flowers. The diminutive churchyard spreads out over a shady lawn, which forms a bank for a stream as well as a promenade for a family of swans. The benevolent ladies of the house evidently tend this little sanctuary with pious care, and have made of its burial place a veritable Garden of Sleep. So secluded is the tree-encircled church that few who pass along the Blandford road have any inkling of its whereabouts.

The road has now reached the line of the Dorset heights, and passes under the shadow of two famous hills—Hod Hill and Hambledon. Both were important British strongholds some two thousand years ago, for they commanded the passage of the Stour. Hod Hill would appear to have been rather a fortified town, and Hambledon a fortress or military camp. On the summit of Hod Hill the defences, strong and well-fashioned, are left in a perfect state. There still remain the double rampart and the fosse the Celts built, together with the square

earthworks thrown up by the Romans in the north-west
corner of the enclosure. The main entrance, towards the
Blandford road, is guarded by a double line of entrenchments.
Within the inner wall are many dimples in the grass to show
where the pit dwellings of these ancient people stood.. They
had certainly chosen an " eligible site," for the view from the
ramparts is most magnificent. It embraces the whole of the
verdant hinterland, the winding Stour, and the curling wave of
the chalk downs. It looks down, too, upon the little church of
Steepleton, which from this height might be a chapel to our
Lady of the Garden.

On the site of the old encampment is a mossy grass, sprinkled
with many violets, cowslips, and daisies. These flowers, one
may suppose, are the living descendants of those that grew
here when the place was peopled, when fair-haired Celtic
children picked them, watching the while their fathers
toiling at the earthworks with horn picks and palstaves of
bronze.

Hambledon was a much larger and stronger place than Hod
Hill. Its entrenchments are still immense and formidable.
They rise tier above tier, rampart and ditch, rampart and ditch.
They are best to be seen at the north end of the camp from the
roadway leading to Child Okeford. In general character this
camp follows the model of that at Badbury Rings. On the
south-east side, where the approach is easiest, the rampart
mounts to the height, even now, of 29 feet. The whole hill
is steep, bare, bold, erect—a fine bluff down, with ever a look
of menace on its front. It was undoubtedly a stronghold of
the first importance, and even now it seems incomplete without
a battery of heavy guns.

The entrenchments of Hambledon have been defended—one
may suppose—in turn by Britons, Romans, Saxons, and Danes.
Their last defenders, however, were a party of despairing yokels
led by a vicar, and known as the " Clubmen." They received
their name either from the bludgeons with which they first armed

themselves or from the club or association they formed the better to carry out their designs.

These designs were simple enough. During the great civil war between the Royalists and the Parliament the countrymen in Dorset, Wilts, and Somerset had small comfort. Of the merits of the quarrel they knew nothing. All they did know was that heated bodies of armed men appeared from time to time on their lands, some shouting for the King and others for the Parliament. Whenever they met they fell to grievous fighting. Although the ends they had in view were evidently opposed, they displayed—so far as the countryman was concerned—one common trait. They trampled down his corn, pillaged his villages, borrowed his horses, and " commandeered" the contents of his barns.

In due course the worried, half-beggared villagers rose in their uncouth strength, not to join this faction or that, but to protect their hearths and homes, their stock-yards and their sheep-pens. It was no doubt a stirring call to arms. Every hamlet mustered its lumbering quotum of red-faced countrymen ; and a fine show they made when they gathered at the village cross, valiant with much ale, gay with ribbons and flags, wept over by wives and sweethearts, and hoarse with shouting " For England and our homes ! " Each man carried some murderous arm which was no doubt terrible in the eyes of his household—a club, an ancient halbert, an axe, a scythe-blade, a pitchfork, or possibly a pistol or a real sword. Each warrior, one may be sure, had his pockets stuffed with cheese and bread and the ruddiest apples from his orchard. They are credited with one mark of distinction, a white cockade.

They mustered at last some 5,000 strong. They petitioned the King, but he ignored them ; they " beat up the Parliament quarters at Sturminster Newton," but with no effect. Poor red-faced, clumsy patriots, they were doomed to do nothing but come to grief. They entrenched themselves on the Castle Hill at Shaftesbury in the summer of 1645, but Cromwell encompassed them, drove them away like blundering sheep, and took some fifty of them prisoners, whereupon they determined, with much bloodthirsty shouting, to release their leaders. Aglow with this worthy purpose, they found themselves—in some muddle-headed way—entrenched within the ramparts of Hambledon. They numbered now only 2,000, but were all filled with the resolve to hold Hambledon to the death. Whoever entered that stronghold would find nothing but corpses! Their general was the Rev. Mr. Bravel, the rector of Compton Abbas, the ivy-clad tower of whose church still stands within view of the hill. The worthy rector was so determined and of such iron mould that he threatened "to pistol whoever surrendered."

Cromwell sent fifty dragoons to deal with this desperate garrison of Hambledon. As the horsemen advanced they were fired upon. The surrender of the hill was demanded, but the reverend rector of Compton declined that proposal with contempt. The Clubmen were posted behind the great earthworks, the passage through which was so narrow "that three horses could scarce march abreast." On the road from Shroton to Child Okeford there can be seen on the hill top, and against the skyline, just such a passage as this. The dragoons, however, did not bother much about Celtic defences. They simply mounted the hill, attacked the "Death or glory" yokels, and overcame them "after a short dispute." As Cromwell words it, "they beat them from the work, and did some small execution upon them: I believe killed not twelve of them, but cut very many."

Not a few of the garrison escaped by sliding down the smooth side of the hill, after the manner of Bank Holiday folk. Many were taken prisoners, among the number being no fewer than four vicars and curates. They were imprisoned for the night in the church of Shroton at the foot of the hill. This church, which had been rebuilt only four years previously, is still the village church.

Cromwell's account of this episode of Hambledon Hill is contained in a letter dated from Shaftesbury, August 4th, 1645, and addressed to "The Right Honourable Sir Thomas Fairfax, Commander-in-Chief of the Parliament Forces." He concludes as follows : " We have taken about 300, many of which are poor silly creatures, whom if you please to let me send home they

Shillingstone.

promise to be very dutiful for time to come, and will be hanged before they come out again." [1]

It is probable that these well-meaning but ridiculous warriors lost no time in returning to the villages they had left with such *éclat*, hiding their white cockades in the bracken by the way, and their arms in the nearest ditch.

A little while ago, when an old cottage was being pulled down in Wootton Fitzpaine, a sword of the Stuart period was found concealed in the thatch. One might venture to suppose that it was hidden there by one of these " poor silly creatures " who defended the great fortress of Hambledon, or possibly that

[1] Carlyle's *Cromwell.*.   Vol. I.

it was bestowed in the roof by a wife who thought that her good man had had enough of soldiering.

The traveller who wishes to see more of the interior of the county might turn westwards a little beyond Hod Hill and follow the foot of the downs as far as Stoke Wake. In the language of guide books, this region " will well repay a visit." All the way the road keeps under the shadow of the hills, and for a mile or so follows the wanderings of the Stour.

The downs, as seen from the highway, are magnificent. They are rolling southwards on their way to the sea. Now and then a great round bluff lurches out towards the road, and the road turns timidly aside. Each moulded down is as smooth and glistening as the haunches of a racehorse. The surface of these hills is of slippery grass, tufted here and there by patches of gorse, or wandered over by companies of sheep, while on occasion there is a great scar in the slope, as if a Titanic spade had laid bare the white chalk beneath. This is assuredly the country of " The Lady of the Lambs," of whom it is written :—

> " She walks—the lady of my delight—
>   A shepherdess of sheep.
> Her flocks are thoughts.   She keeps them white ;
>   She guards them from the steep.
> She feeds them on the fragrant height,
>   And folds them in for sleep."

The first place of moment by the way is Shillingstone, which is by interpretation "Schellings' Town," for it belonged in Norman times to the family of the Eschellings. In the annals of the manor there comes an entry, made during the troublous reign of King John, which runs as follows : " Alice, wife of John Eschellings, owed 15 marks that her land might be in peace and in the King's protection, and that her lord might not pass over the sea with horses and arms."

Poor Alice Sit-by-the-fire probably learnt that peace is not to be purchased for 15 marks, and that it is not always well to put faith in princes—especially of the type of King John.

It is to be hoped that her lord lived all his days at Shillingstone, and that when at last he did "pass over the sea" it was
without the clatter of horses and arms. She may have had
that peace at least, but beyond it I expect that Alice Sit-by-
the-fire got little for her 15 marks.

Shillingstone is a roadside village of some charm. It still

Shillingstone Cross.

can boast a maypole, although the spirit of May dances and
the cult of the May Queen have long died out. The rural
Pan, if he will celebrate the dawning of the summer, will
neither deck himself with flowers nor tune his pipe, but will
rather take an excursion train to London, for there is a station
at Shillingstone.

The very beautiful and graceful village cross has been

restored, or indeed made new. It stands in the roadway, a delicate Gothic pinnacle, with an orchard and a thatched cottage for a background. There is a handsome church in the village, with certain Norman and Early English remains in it, together with a restored roof, the beams of which have been ridiculously painted and gilded. The pulpit was given to the

Okeford Fitzpaine.

church by one Keen—a merchant of Bread Street, London— who fled hither in 1666 to escape the plague.

Not far from the village is Hayward's Bridge, which crosses the Stour at a point where was once a very ancient ford—the Oakford, from which the name of the villages around is derived. Near this ford (as well as near the place of crossing at Stourpaine) are to be seen small earthworks, which were no doubt outposts to defend the passage of the river. They would command the approach from the South to the camps of both Hod Hill and Hambledon.

Okeford Fitzpaine, the next place along the road, is as

pretty an old-world village as will be found in this green hollow
of the shire.   It derives its name from the great family of the
Fitzpaines.   In the reign of Henry III. there is a record to the
effect that Robert Fitzpaine and William Gollis were acquitted
from the payment of certain dues upon the estate, the ground
for the special indulgence being "their good services to the
King at the battle of Lewes."   There is a fine suggestion of
devotion in this, but as a matter of fact Messieurs Fitzpaine
and Gollis were not only fighting against the King at Lewes, but
they, with others, had actually taken him prisoner.   As Hutchins
explains, "the rebellious barons had his seal, and acted what
they liked in his name."   Fitzpaine and his friend no doubt
chuckled to themselves when they added that stirring sentence
about their good services to the King at the battle of Lewes.
It was probably a family joke for generations.

The village is of some size, being made up of two rambling
streets in the form of a cross.   It is a part of the Dorset of old
days.   The church is kept locked, as are so many in this
county.   The following inscription, copied from one of the
bells before it was recast in 1820, is perhaps as curious as any
feature in the building itself :—

> " I often have been beate and bandge :
> My friends reioyce to see me handge :
> And when my friends doe chance to die
> Then I for them aloud will cry.
> 1658."

At Belchalwell, near by, is a church which has been deserted
by its village, of which but a few cottages now remain.   The
church is placed on a solitary mound commanding a near view
of the downs.   It has a little low square tower and an
elaborate Norman porch.   Roses are climbing over the
chancel windows, and when I visited the place in June a
turbulent assembly of bees had established a colony under the
ancient eaves.

The beautiful old-fashioned village of Ibberton— a jumble

of thatched cottages, gardens, and orchards—lies in a green bay made by a curve in the downs. If the sea could reach it there would be found, in the place of the village, a sheltered cove in an amphitheatre of hills. The church is so high up on the slope that the view from the churchyard extends far beyond the northern limits of the county by way of the Black-more Valley.

Some good soul, long ago, gave an acre of land here " for the ringing of the morning bell." To understand the gracious-ness of this bequest one must picture the hamlet in the dawn of a day in May, when the mist has barely melted from over the thatched roofs, when cottage windows are being thrown open to the sun, and then at such hour hear floating down from the silent hill the greeting of the morning bell.

Below the church a spring breaks out of the rock and finds a way through a thicket of fern and bramble to the village. It bears the local name of Stachys' well. This does not serve to keep green the memory of some worthy well-digger of forgotten days, but commemorates the fact that the spring was dedicated to Saint Eustachius. The holy man's name being inconveniently long, the villagers amiably changed it to Stachy.

When Stoke Wake is reached there is a sense of a coming to an end of all things, for the few houses which make up the tiny settlement are lodged in a far hollow at the foot of the hills. So very steep are the downs as they circle around the hamlet that it would seem to be enshrined like an image in a niche in a wall. This green sanctuary is so beset by trees that Stoke Wake is not easy to discover. Were this spot in Japan there would be a temple, brilliant in red lacquer and gold, far up among the woods, so that the worshipper, after a toil-some climb, would feel that he was alone with the mysteries of the world.

Towering above Stoke Wake is the bare rampart of Bul-barrow, which forms almost the highest point in the county. On this same bold down is the Celtic camp of Rawlsbury, a

formidable ring of earthworks and one of the most commanding hill stations in the South of England.   It crowns the sky
line of the hill, the northern slope of which is very steep.   The
defences are made up of double ramparts and ditches overgrown for many centuries with grass.   On the eastern side,
where the approach is readiest, the entrenchments are doubled.

It is needless to say that the view from the summit of Bulbarrow is most magnificent.   As Hutchins says, the outlook to
the North and the North-east " surpasses all imagination."   For
miles there stretches a waving valley of green fields, with trees
in lines, in knolls, in avenues, in dots ; a red roof, the glitter of
a trout stream, the trail of a white road, and at the end
blue-grey hills so far away that they seem to be made of a
sea mist.

The church of Stoke Wake is new.   In the old church there
was painted against the north pillar the figure of a beggar,
underneath which was written, " He that loveth pleasure shall
be a poor man."

Returning to the main road, we come to Blandford by
Bryanston, the seat of the popular Lord Portman.   This place
was the Town of Brian de Insula or de Lisle, a baron of note
in the reign of King John.   The estate was owned for many
generations by the Rogers family, and was finally purchased
from them by that Sir William Portman who took an active
part in the suppression of Monmouth's rebellion in 1685.   The
Portmans were already a family of note in the county of Somerset in the time of Edward I.

Blandford Forum takes its name from being a market-place
situated upon one of the chief fords of the Stour.   It is a brown,
prim, comfortable town on a slope leading to the river.   As
Mrs. Gummidge mourned over the "old 'un," so Blandford
mourns—but with a finer melancholy—over its fires.   It developed the habit of having fires in 1579, when it was nearly
destroyed.   During the Civil War, in the year 1644, it was
sacked and plundered for its loyalty.   Then came other fires

F

in 1677 and 1713, and finally that conflagration in 1731 which was to merit the title of the Great Fire.

It broke out at 2 p.m. of a June afternoon, at a tallow-chandler's house, and it never ceased until it had destroyed all but forty houses in the place. Small-pox happened to be raging at the time, and to the fire may be given the credit of stamping out the epidemic. The sick were laid out under hedges in the fields and gardens, as well as beneath the arches of the bridge. In spite of the transport but one died—"a strong argument," says Hutchins, "for the cool regimen." The church was destroyed, but the distressed inhabitants at once erected a "tabernacle of boards" for temporary worship.

The town, indeed, has had many troubles. It has not only been much burnt, but it has been pawned; in the reign of Richard I. the manor was mortgaged by Robert FitzParnel, then Earl of Leicester, to Aaron, a Jew of Lincoln. It owned, on the other hand, not a few consolations. It was once famous for bandstrings—when neck-bands and ruffs were worn—as well as for its point lace, which was said to be the finest in England, and valued at no less than £30 sterling a yard.

Near by the church—which is ugly, and only tolerable from a distance—is a classic fountain, erected " In rememberance of God's dreadful visitation by fire. 1731." The fountain sheltered by this pillared shrine appears to have been represented by a pump, for an inscription states that in 1768 John Bastard gave £100 " to keep this pump in repair and supplying the lamp with oil and a man to light the same every night from Michaelmas to Lady Day for ever." For ever ! Alas ! the pump has long since been replaced by a pipe and tap from the waterworks, while there is no oil lamp for any to light from Michaelmas to Lady Day, yet scarcely 140 years have passed since it was to have been tended for ever.

As may be supposed, there is nothing ancient left in Blandford. It is simply a bright, flourishing country town, and a good halting place for any who are exploring the shire.

The town is seen at its best when viewed from the grey
many-arched bridge which crosses the Stour. The river here
is a lazy stream, flecked with water-lilies, fringed with rushes,
and so overhung by trees that the swallows fluttering over its
surface seem to be sporting in a green cloister. Between the
river and the town is a "level mead," yellow in the spring with
buttercups, which creep up to the very garden walls. Beyond
the meadow is a medley of red gables, brown roofs, and clumps

Blandford.

of trees, out of which rises with some dignity the tower of the
church.

There are no suburbs, happily, to Blandford. Beyond
the last line of houses is the untrampled country, so that
a window on the fringe of the town will open over a corn
field, and cows will rest under the shelter of orchard walls.

Two houses at least, which escaped the great fire, serve to
show what manner of place Blandford Forum was before the
last trouble fell upon it. One is Ryves's Almshouse, a long,
comely, wrinkled building of brick in one story, bearing the

date 1682. The other is an old red brick mansion, a solid, self-assertive house, with imperious chimneys, a very high roof, and haughty windows. There is a rugged, un-English look about it, which some ascribe to the influence of a certain German doctor, Frederic Sagittary, who lived here before the fire. He graduated at Oxford in 1661, and was so gratified with Blandford that he caused his son, John Sagittary, to succeed him in his practice in the place.

Blandford can boast of many eminent men. Notably of Bishops. William Wake (1657–1737), Archbishop of Canterbury, Samuel Lisle (1683–1749), Bishop of Norwich, and Thomas Lindesay (1656–1724), Archbishop of Armagh, were all natives of this town. Of the last named it is tersely recorded that " he was of loose life but of ready wit."

By Blandford St. Mary there lived at one time " Governor " Pitt, grandfather of the first Earl of Chatham. He was an East Indian merchant, and for a while Governor of Fort St. George. He became known to fame as the possessor of the Regent diamond. The stone was found in 1701 at the Parteal mines, on the Kistna, by a slave, who fled with it to the coast, where he sold it to an English skipper, who in return murdered him. It is curious to note that the slave had secreted the rough gem in a wound in his leg. As this foreign body weighed 410 carats, the slave effected a surgical feat of some interest. Pitt was reported to have obtained possession of this diamond " by a stretch of power," but he declared solemnly that he had purchased it for 48,000 pagodas—which I understand to represent about £20,400. Anyhow, he sold it in 1717 to the Duke of Orleans, then Regent of France, for the sum of £135,000. Governor Pitt lies buried in the little rustic church of Blandford St. Mary, where a tablet discourses in Latin upon his virtues. A flying slave, a villainous sea captain, a murder on a beach, the Court of Louis XV. in Paris, and this humble ivy-clad village church make up the incongruous elements of the story of the great diamond.

CHAPTER VI

BEFORE starting upon this expedition to the border it is interesting to consider how the county came by its shape and what determined its boundaries. It is needless to refute the myth that King Alfred one day sat him at a table and divided his England into counties by the simple drawing of lines upon a map.

Dorset, like other shires, has been carved out of the rugged island by the point of the sword, by the flint arrow, by the javelin of bronze. Its borders have been fashioned by fighting men with desperate patience and with unheeded shedding of blood. Each coast county has its little history of conquest: of the beaching of boats, of the march inland, of the creeping border, of the stand made at the final frontier.

There is little doubt that, so far as Dorset is concerned, the present shape of the shire was given it by the Celts, the tall, fair-haired men who came over from Gaul, the round-heads who built the round barrows and had learned how to work in bronze. These were the men whom the Romans found in possession of the coast when they descended upon it, and whom they named the Durotriges. These Dorset Celts were people, no doubt, of one tribe, who held together in their venture, whereby they founded a new settlement beyond the seas which came at the end to be a compact kingdom.

Their first care on landing would be to drive the "natives" northwards, and then to strengthen their own frontiers against attack from other adventurers who were pouring in from over the Channel. The said natives were a non-Aryan people, called Iberians by some, Euskarians by others, men with long heads, who raised the long barrows, and whose sole weapons were of wood or stone. The ancestors of these short, dusky people had walked over on dry land from what is now the Continent, follow-ing the route of the Jersey steamer which carries the "tripper" of to-day. The round-heads would land at Poole, Studland, or Swanage, would creep into Lulworth Cove or beach their canoes on the sands of Weymouth or of Worbarrow Bay. To the West they would find good landing at Eype, at Burton Bradstock and Charmouth, or at the foot of the glen at Lyme.

Once ashore, they would climb the sea downs and build their camps on heights which were within sight of the blue tideway. There are the strongholds of Purbeck, of Flowers Barrow, of Chalbury, and of Portisham to bear witness to this. Moving inland, they would come, on the East, to the Great Heath and the delectable valley of the Frome, on the West to the Marsh-wood vale, and in the middle land to that lofty ridge along which now runs the white high-road from Dorchester to Bridport. Creeping northwards towards the far off Dorset hills, they would push across the lowland, following the streams and building forts or earthworks as they went.

Their greatest fortress was Maiden Castle, which commands the rich Frome valley. To the right stood, and still stand, Woodbury and Weatherby, and to the left the mighty fastness of Eggardon Hill. The long lines of entrenchments they made in their advance run from East to West, with always the ditch on the northern face. Miles of these earthworks yet survive, held in great peace by rabbits and overgrown with ferns. Such are the Battery Bank, which traverses the heath between Wareham and Wool, and Combs Ditch, which crosses the Blandford road by Winterborne Whitchurch.

In time the adventurers would reach the green haven of
the hills, and, climbing their summits, would look down upon
a Promised Land lying northwards, gracious and luxuriant ;
upon the Blackmore Valley and the lowlands of the Stour.
Far away they could see that the smiling country was shut in
by the circle of a sombre forest, beyond whose confines was a
country known to none. Here on wind-swept ridges they threw
up their advanced line of forts, Hambledon and Hod Hill,
Rawlsbury and Nettlecombe Tout, Cerne and Chelborough.
From the hill tops they could look back to the sea, and on
either hand could view the borders which were to circumscribe
their new principality.

On the East, as a natural frontier, were the impassable
swamps about the Avon and the Stour, and here lies the border
of the county still.   The great fortress at Badbury Rings and
the outpost at Duds Bury helped in after years to strengthen
this line.   On the West the frontier would no doubt have been
the valley of the Axe.   At the present day the boundary is
artificial by reason of certain exchanges with Devon, but it
is evident that along the river bank lay the ancient barrier.
Here was the weak side of the little kingdom, for the Celtic
Damnonii of Devon seem to have been troublesome neighbours.
Both banks of the river were strongly held.   Fort answered to
fort across the timid stream.   On the Dorset side will be
found the strongholds of Hawkesdown and Musbury (both now
in Devon), of Coney's Castle, Lambert's Castle, and Pilsdon
Pen, while on the west of the river still rise the earthworks of
Blackbury, Widworthy, Stockland, and Membury.   On the
North the sturdy principality was shut in by the vast forest
which extended from Pilsdon Pen to the watershed of the
Thames, and which has left little trace in the county except in
the primrose glades of Cranborne Chase.

There would seem to have been but one easy passage out of
this encircling forest, and that was by the downs on the North-
east.   This way of escape is represented by the high-road from

Blandford to Salisbury, which road I propose now to take.   It
may be that as the Celts advanced the Iberians retreated into
this north-east corner, for it is curious that here are to be found
the chief long barrows of the county—the long barrows,
namely, of Pimperne, Eastbury, Chettle, and Gussage.

The earthworks which have been alluded to are obviously
of varying dates, for they are the relics of the warring of
centuries.   They would have been garrisoned in succession by
whoever held the land and by whoever were the Empire-
makers of the time.   Moreover, it would appear that all were
not strictly military works, but were destined for the humbler
purpose of "laagering" cattle.

It was through the North-east passage into Dorset that the
fate of the county came.   If the "natives" of old time
escaped by that way, and if the Celts—when the Romans
landed—found safety along the same path across the forest gap,
it is certain that down the Roman road which replaced that
path the West Saxons swarmed to the final conquest of British
Dorset.   As a result of that conquest the little kingdom
became a mere shire of Wessex, but for all that, so far as its
boundaries are concerned, "Dorset has continued Dorset alone
from time immemorial."[1]

The road from Blandford to Woodyates—on the North-east
frontier—is long, rough, and bare ; a straight, determined,
uncompromising road, which, regardless of hill or dale, makes
direct for Salisbury.   It passes across a series of bare chalk
downs which are rolling seawards like barrel-shaped waves.

From the top of one crest the traveller can see to the summit
of the next, while on every height are tumuli and earthworks.
There are sheep on the downs and larks in the air ; otherwise
the way is singularly lonely, and only peopled by the dead.   It
is indeed a little-changed piece of Celtic Britain.

In the first dip along the road is Pimperne, a straggling
hamlet of small interest, with a fine but over-restored church,

[1] *County and Town in England.*   By Grant Allen.   London, 1901.

which has succeeded in retaining its handsome Norway doorway and a worthy Norman arch.   It has gained in one matter,
that there has been restored to it a carved stone cover for
its ancient font, which cover had long lain hidden in an
outhouse.   The manor of Pimperne was granted by Henry
VIII. first to Catherine Howard, and then to Katherine Parr,
and it is to be noted that the grant, in either case, was "for
life." The slumbering old parsonage is the one interesting house
in Pimperne.   It was built, they say, in 1530, but exuberant
creepers almost hide its Gothic window, together with the niche
beneath which are carved the arms of England and France.

Pimperne was famous long ago for its maze. This "remarkable piece of antiquity" was made of banks of earth about a
foot high.   It was the delight of the rustics on certain days of
the year to thread this labyrinth, which was of very complex
pattern, as is shown by Hutchins in the plan he gives of it.   It
was ploughed over in 1730, and somewhat later the pleasaunce
was turned into a burial ground.

Robert Frampton, Bishop of Gloucester, was born at
Pimperne in 1622.   His father was a farmer.   As a Royalist
he joined in the attack upon the Clubmen in their ridiculous
defence of Hambledon Hill (page 56).   His next move in
life was curious.   He was appointed chaplain to the English
factory at Aleppo, where he remained twelve years doing good
deeds and acquiring great influence.   He returned to England
in 1667 and married, but, hearing that plague had broken out
in Aleppo, he hurried back to his old charge immediately after
his wedding.   He remained away for three years.   Later in
life he was imprisoned in the Tower on suspicion of plotting
against the King, and while there visited Judge Jeffreys, "whom
he found in a very sad and melancholy state." • Pepys, having
once heard this good man preach, wrote of him as follows :
"The truth is, he preaches the most like an apostle that ever I
heard man, and it was much the best time I have ever spent in
my life at church."

On the grassy heights above Pimperne is a very perfect long barrow near to the road, while on the slope below it are the remains of a British settlement. The hamlet lies sheltered, but the sepulchre stands boldly up against the sky line. The road now drops into a dell where runs the Tarrant, a sparkling brook, bustling and rapid. The valley it follows is trivial, a mere gully winding through bare downs and set about by hamlets and orchards, by fields full of buttercups, with now and then a stone bridge and occasionally a mill. There are no fewer than seven villages in this mild glen, all dignified with the name of Tarrant.

Tarrant Gunville is a pretty village, approached by an avenue of trees. Its quaint old church is almost lost among amiable gardens. On the outside of the chancel wall there is a stone carved with this cheerful script :—

> HERE . LITHE . S.T.D. PARSON.
> ALL . FOWRE . BE . BUT . ONE.
> EARTHE . FLESCHE . WORME . AND
> BONE . MCCCCCLXVII.

Here, surrounded by a lordly park, is the once famous East-bury House. It serves to tell the story of a " person of importance in his day," with whom Robert Browning " parleys " in a poem of seven long stanzas. This " person," George Bubb, was the son of an apothecary in Weymouth. In 1720, when twenty-nine years of age, he inherited a fortune from his uncle, one George Dodington. He became thereupon George Bubb Dodington—a man with an ambition. He took to politics, and played his puny part so well that he was raised to the peerage under the sonorous title of Baron Melcombe. His uncle had commenced the building of Eastbury in 1718 ; the Baron finished it in 1738, at a cost of £140,000. The house, according to Hutchins, was " one of the grandest and most superb in the county, and indeed in the kingdom." The apothecary-peer aimed at becoming a patron of literature. He held a species of court at Eastbury, of which Thomson, Fielding, Young, and Christopher Pitt were the chief luminaries. Thomson speaks of Eastbury as placed

> " Where simple nature reigns, and every view,
>   Diffusive, spreads the pure Dorsetian downs
>   In boundless prospect,"

while for the *soi-disant* Maecenas he claims a character of cultured nobleness.

Eastbury House.

Poor George Bubb Dodington left to the world a diary, which was no doubt intended to become a classic, but which is now merely treasured as " the odd self-revelation of a flunkey." He aimed at immortality, but is only remembered by " the scoff that greets his very name." He died in 1762. In 1795 all but one wing of the house was taken down and sold piecemeal by Earl Temple, who had previously offered an annuity of £200 to any gentleman who would occupy it and keep it in repair.

The wing of the house which remains is of dull stone, square, solid, and sombre, with a pompous colonnade along its front to give it dignity. The most charming feature of the place is the gateway to the park. The great stone gate-posts stand out like ghosts in the shadow of aged trees. A round bridge leads to a white wicket, while on either side of the bridge is a stretch of grass, marked off from the road by a chain swinging from acorn-shaped posts of stone. It is just such a gateway as opens into one of Marcus Stone's leisurely gardens.

At Tarrant Hinton, lower down the stream, is a singularly

Tarrant Hinton.

picturesque church, full of architectural interest, while Tarrant Monkton, just beyond, is a village of much fascination. Half asleep in the sun and away from the world, it remains little altered and unspoiled. It is a shy hamlet of thatched cottages whose walls are heavy with creepers and are hedged around by flower gardens and many orchards. That most rudimentary centre of commerce, the village shop, as well as the thatch-roofed inn, are glorious with yellow roses. The air is full of the scent of blossoms, of the odour of burning wood, of the hum of bees. There is a low stone bridge of three arches over the chattering stream, which here forms a bathing-place for ducks and a rendez-vous for such calves as lounge vacantly about the village street,

At Tarrant Rawston the hamlet has vanished, leaving only a genial farmhouse, in the garden of which is a tiny church. It is a low, ivy-clad building of stone and flint, with a red-tiled roof, but with neither steeple nor tower. Within are stiff old pews, as well as a little wooden gallery approached by a door in the outer wall. It is as much a feature of the garden as was the rustic Greek temple of some sacred spring.

At Tarrant Rushton, again, the settlement is reduced to little

Tarrant Rushton.

more than a church and a water-mill. The church, small and comely, is one of the most interesting in Dorset. Dating from 1150, it contains a Norman arch, some Early English windows, a leper window, and three remarkable hagioscopes. Built in the eastern face of the chancel wall are two round, red pots of common earthenware. They are empty, and contained when found neither bones nor treasure. These strange vessels are "acoustic vases," of the type found in the walls or under the floors of certain churches both in England and on the Continent. They are supposed to have had for their object the enriching of the voice. The Rev. J. Penny, in his admirable account of Rushton Church,[1] gives the following quotations bearing on these hollow jars :—" In the month of August, 1432, after Brother Odo le Roy, the Prior, had returned from a general chapter, it was ordered that pots should be put into the choir of the Church of Caens, he stating that he had seen such in another church, and that he thought they made the singing better and resound more strongly " (*Chronicles of the Celestins of Metz*). Again, in the Churchwarden's Accounts of Wimborne Minster for 1541 is this entry : " Payd for 2 potts of clay for wyndfylling of the Church, 8*d*."

Over the south door is a very archaic carving accredited to the tenth century. Its interpretation has been the subject of much dispute. In the centre is a lamb bearing a cross, out of whose mouth issues " something of a serpentine form." This " something " is assumed to be a fish, and to thus represent the Christian symbol ἰχθύς, *a fish*. The other figures—a man with a book and another with a bird—are equally curious and still more hard to be understood.

On the hill above the untidy hamlet of Tarrant Keynston is Buzbury Rings, a Celtic earthwork. It consists of a circle of entrenchments, composed of a stout vallum and a ditch. It was an oppidum or fortified town, as well as a "kraal" for cattle. In the centre of the enclosure are the depressions which mark pit-dwellings. The wild people who lived here could boast of a superb view over the far-stretching downs and along the green Tarrant valley. Within these ancient and deserted fortifications there is now a curious object—the putting-green of a golf-course. The rampart that the Britons built up so laboriously with their horn picks has thus degenerated into a bunker, while into the fosse there drops, in place of the stone-headed arrow, an American golf-ball.

Of Tarrant Crawford, where a queen lies buried,[2] nothing is

---

[1] *Proceedings of the Dorset Field Club.* Vol. XVIII., page 55.

[2] Joanna, queen of Alexander II. of Scotland, and daughter to King John of England.

left but an ancient farmhouse and a still more venerable church. This is a village church of olden days which has happily escaped the hand of the restorer. Its ivy-clad tower, its Early English windows, and its humble porch are still as they were known to the villagers of centuries ago. Within are old high pews, with doors, and a general bare rusticity. It is lit by a few candles fixed to the walls, and must be a solemn place on a winter's night, when the wind is howling over the downs and the Tarrant is in flood.

To return to the high-road. Some six and a half miles from Blandford there is a green lane which—as the country around is dreary and bare—appears very inviting. It leads to a wooded hollow, to a shady oasis wherein are hidden the village of Chettle, with its great trees, its charming cottages, and its noisy rooks. The utter seclusion of this delightful place made it good to live in during troublous times.

Now, the great family who long owned Chettle was that of the Chafins. One Thomas Chafin opposed the advance of the Duke of Monmouth, and commanded a troop of Dorset horse at the battle of Sedgemoor. Certain of his letters to his wife, "Nan" still survive. Monmouth landed at Lyme on June 11th, 1685, and on June 16th, 1685, Thomas writes to his wife, who was away from home. The letter—addressed from "Mrs. Bestlands, Dorchester"—runs as follows: "My dearest creature. I am very well soe far on my journey. . . . My cos Strangways was killed as he was takeing horse. Mayjor Stiles saved himselfe in a plat of kidney beans : Mr. Churchill of Muston saved himselfe by running up into the garrett." After recounting these acts of valour, he continues: "I was forced to take Collington (a servant) knowing noe other soe fitt : therefore if you be pleased to come home you must send to Chettle either for Will Horner or Will Lambert. Horner and the colt would draw you home almost as well. I have Thomas Clements and the gardiner, well armed, with me." Other letters show that "dearest Nan" entrusted herself to

Will Horner and the colt and went home. Later on Thomas Chafin sends her an account of the battle of Sedgemoor. His last letter is from "Greenes Street, London," under date July 16th, 1685. He had seen the King and kissed his hand. He ends: "I hope to be at home on Saturday sennight. The late Duke of Monmouth's head was severed from his body yesterday morning on Tower Hill about 10 or 11 forenoon. Lord Grey will soone be there too. Blessing to the bratts. Soe farewell, my dearest deare Nan."

In the beautiful church of Chettle Thomas Chafin lies buried, as a tablet on the wall sets forth. He died in 1691, aged forty-one. By his side lies his "dearest deare," who survived him fourteen years. The gallant Nan was the daughter of Colonel Penruddock, who "was beheaded for his loyalty in the castle of Exon, May 18th, 1655." She had eleven children, and in this very church she and her family worshipped.

Chettle House stands in a fine garden which borders on the churchyard. It is a dignified building of red brick faced with stone. It cannot claim, however, to be the home to which "Nan" hurried with the help of Will Horner and the colt, for the house would appear to have been rebuilt about the time of Queen Anne.

Hutchins gives this note about Chettle. "In a wood near Mr. Chafin's house is a fine plantation of Scotch fir trees. They were bought in a small box about 60 years ago, when they were about two inches high, by Geo. Chafin at the Cocoa Tree coffee house in London. They were sent to Dorset and planted in his kitchen garden, and when of proper growth were transplanted into the wood. Their prime cost was 2s. 6d. : they are now worth more than £1,000."

Beyond Chettle the road mounts up over Gussage Hill, a bold open down, bare but for a short, tough grass. From the summit it can be seen that the county is narrowing, that the boundaries are closing in upon the high-road. To the North-east is the gap through which the road escapes, and upon it the

Pentridge Hills are advancing from the right and the highlands of Cranborne Chase from the left.

There was once a city on this hill, on the crest of the whale-backed down. Still are there to be seen long lines of entrenchments, a fortified enclosure, the outlines of a British town, and traces of ancient trackways. The place is now a vast solitude which is visited only by sheep, while everywhere over the wide ruins lies a soft coverlet of green.

Of such a spot as this Robert Browning has written in a famous lyric :—

> " Where the quiet-coloured end of evening smiles,
>   Miles and miles,
>   On the solitary pastures where the sheep
>   Half-asleep
>   Tinkle homeward thro' the twilight, stay or stop
>   As they crop—
>   Was the site once of a city great and gay,
>   (So they say)
>   Of our country's very capital, its prince
>   Ages since
>   Held his court in, gathered councils, wielding far
>   Peace or war.
>
>   And such plenty and perfection, see, of grass
>   Never was !
>   Such a carpet as, this summer-time, o'erspreads
>   And embeds
>   Every vestige of the city, guessed alone,
>   Stock or stone—
>   Where a multitude of men breathed joy and woe
>   Long ago."

The traveller may be tempted by a sign-post, two miles northwards, to turn aside to the village of Sixpenny Handley. It is well, however, to resist such attraction, since this strangely named place is, I think, the ugliest village in Dorset. Its title, it may be said, has no connection with the coinage. At one time there were two " hundreds " in the district, one the hundred of Sexpena, the other that of Hanlega. They were

G

fused together in due course, with the result that the principal settlement became distorted into Sixpenny Handley.

We now come to the border of the county and to the famous Woodyates Inn, famous as a posting house in the old coaching days and memorable by reason of its dim association with the Duke of Monmouth. The unfortunate Duke, escaping from the battlefield of Sedgemoor, passed through Berwick St. John, as has been already noted (page 41), and reached Woodyates by way of Cranborne Chase. Here he and his few companions were compelled to abandon their exhausted horses. They hid their saddles, turned the horses loose, while Monmouth for greater security adopted the dress of a shepherd. From Woodyates the forlorn party started to tramp to Poole across the New Forest and the Great Heath. How ill they fared, and how it came to pass that they were fated never to see the grey harbour of Poole, history has placed on record.

The inn is by the road side, and has hiding shyly behind it a meagre hamlet. The old hostelry is now much neglected, and seems indeed to have scarcely survived the indignity of being changed into an up-to-date tavern. The ancient portion of the house is uninteresting by reason of uncouth improvements and unheeded decay; the modern part is tawdry and deplorable. About the little inn is an air of utter loneliness and the look of the long-forgotten. The venerable innkeeper knew something of cycling clubs, but little of Monmouth. "I have heard tell," he admitted, "that they have put the old inn into the history books, as you may say," but beyond that he did not venture.

Some half mile from the inn is the border. On one side of the highway rises the range of Pentridge Hill, on the other are the heights of Cranborne Chase. Between is the gateway of Dorset. The road from the North approaches the frontier over the barren level of Martin Down. Drawn right across the road is the frowning entrenchment known as

Bokerly Dyke. It is made up of a high rampart and a deep fosse, the ditch being on the northern side. It can be traced for miles, for it is placed ever upon strong ground, and was supported, there can be little doubt, by the New Forest on one hand and by Cranborne Chase on the other. This venerable earthwork, thrown up some 1,500 years ago, makes a vivid and dramatic boundary to the shire. Here was the outpost; here the fighting line. By this route the vanquished Iberians fled northwards, and over this grim bank the victorious Saxons poured into the county in eager hordes until they held it to the sea.

How desperate must have been the fighting about Bokerly Dyke the numerous barrows in the district show. The modern high-road now cuts boldly through the deserted rampart; there are no longer parleyings at the ditch, while for centuries the outpost has been picketed only by rabbits and has heard no challenge but the song of the skylark.

At this very spot the great Roman road, the Via Iceniana, or Icknield Street, enters the county from Salisbury. It can be traced readily southwards from Woodyates to Dorchester, and thence to Bridport. It follows for a little way the Bland-ford road, then crossing the downs as the grass-covered " Ackling Dyke," it makes a highway at Witchampton, and enters then the great fortress of Badbury Rings. From Badbury it takes an arrow line to Dorchester, disregarding hedge and ditch, coppice and brook, with never a turn either to the right hand or to the left. At Stinsford it joins once again the modern motor-traversed road.

In no part of Dorset can the actual undisturbed Roman road be seen at greater advantage or for greater extent than about Woodyates. It approaches the gap in Bokerly Dyke across an open down. It is a raised road, grown over with green, and with a faint ditch on either side of it. Although time and the rain, the mole and the burrowing rabbit, have softened its harsh lines, it is still a stiff, sternly-drilled road, as

straight as a spear shaft and as stolid as a marching veteran.
Many a cavalcade has passed along this way, many a hunting
party, many a marauding band; its stones have rung to the
clatter of Roman arms, have re-echoed the tramp of Saxon and
Dane, and have moaned under the rustle of captive feet.

It is now a lonely road, deserted and forgotten, a mere ridge
across the down. Here and there its formal line is broken by
patches of gorse, or is cleft by a common cart road. From
Bokerly Dyke it can be followed northwards until it is lost
among the brambles and bracken of Vernditch Chase. From
the high-road it can be traced seawards across the uplands,
where, on a far off crest, it vanishes against the sky.

Near by to Woodyates is the village of Pentridge. Here, at
a place called Rushay Farm, William Barnes, the Dorset poet,
was born. In the churchyard of this drear hamlet is a Jubilee
monument in the form of an indifferent flagstaff supported by
three wire stays, and decked with a suitable tablet to record the
name of the donor of the pole.

On a wall in the restored church is the following vicarious
testimonial to the Bankes family :—

"To the Memory of
ROBERT BROWNING,
of Woodyates, in this parish, who died Nov. 25, 1746,
and is the first known forefather of
Robert Browning, the poet.
He was formerly footman and butler in the
Bankes family."

Those who are indifferent to rough roads may now make
their way to Cranborne by way of Boveridge, where is an ancient
almshouse with thatched roof and verandah and fine brick
chimneys. So out of the world is this dim retreat that it may
be commended to any who seek such peace and seclusion as
even the cloisters of a convent may lack.

Cranborne is a townlet filling a dip in a somewhat bare

country. A straggling, absent-minded little place, it has apparently small purpose in life. There still runs through it that " fleting bek " which Leland admired, and which he says " passid down thorrogh the streat self on the right hand." It is the River Crane. Cranborne has figured fitfully in history since the time that Aylward the Fair founded an Abbey there to

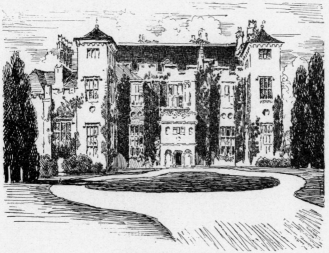

Cranborne Manor House.

which the Priory of Tewkesbury was subordinate, and since Matilda, Queen of William the Conqueror, was the lady of the manor. Its houses are now mostly modern and of red brick. There are some ancient cottages existing, among the more picturesque of which is one declared to be the birthplace of the Stillingfleets.

The most famous member of that family was Edward, Bishop of Worcester, who was born here in 1635. He was so handsome a man that he was nicknamed " the beauty of holiness." It was he who was asked by Charles II. why he always read his sermon when preaching before him, yet used no notes on other occasions. The Bishop replied that "the awe of so noble an audience and the seeing before him so great and wise a prince made him afraid to trust himself," and in return ventured to ask the King why he always read his speeches before the Commons, when he could have none of the same reasons. To this the King answered, "I have asked them so often and for so much money that I am ashamed to look them in the face."

Cranborne can still boast of two great possessions—its church and its manor house. The church is one of the largest in the county. It was built in 1252, on the site of a Norman church, one door of which still exists. The ancient font is another relic of the thirteenth century building. The heavy, solid, square tower has Perpendicular Gothic windows, while the escutcheons of Richard, Duke of York, and Cecilia his duchess are displayed on either side of the entry. In spite of the fact that the building was irretrievably mutilated by a disastrous "restoration" in 1855, it still possesses considerable charm. There are fine monuments in the church to Hoopers and Stillingfleets, as well as a marble tablet to an Eliot who is represented by a very depressed-looking lad, huddled in a chair, with one elbow resting on a human skull, while in the other hand he holds some flowers aimlessly. One of the most interesting objects in the church is a carved oak pulpit belonging to the fifteenth century, and bearing the initials of Thomas Parker, Abbot of Tewkesbury, who died in 1421.

When the chancel was rebuilt in 1875 the workmen discovered that fragments of the marble effigy of a knight had been used, with flint and rubble, in the building of the wall. It was shown that the figure was habited in armour of ring-mail, and had been once resplendent with gilt and bright colours. Dr. Smart believes this to be an effigy of that Robert le Fitz Hayme who built Tewkesbury Abbey and who died in 1107.[1] He is inclined to think, too, that it was placed here by Robert, the first Earl of Gloucester. If so, these fragments

[1] *Proceedings of the Dorset Field Club.* Vol. VIII., page 34.

of the man in ring-mail recall the story of a strange wooing and of the founding of a great peerage. Robert of Gloucester, the

The Garden Front, Cranborne Manor House.

natural son of Henry I., was enamoured of Mabel, eldest daughter of the above-named Robert le Fitz Hayme. The fervency of his wooing may have been heightened by the knowledge that she was an heiress to great wealth, a circumstance which no doubt made the King also indulgent to the match. The rest of the narrative is told by another Robert—the rhyming monk—in the following manner : " When the King made the proposal that she should marry his son, she was against it and long withstood it, and when the King often solicited her, she at last answered like a good and courteous maiden—'Sir,' said she, 'I see plainly that your heart is set on me more for the sake of my inheritance than of myself ; having such an inheritance as I have, it would be dishonourable to me to have a lord who had not two names. My father's name was Sir Robert le Fitz Hayme,[1] and that inheritance ought not to be any man's that was not of his rank ; therefore, for God's love, let me have no man for a husband who has not two names whereby he may be known.' 'Damsel,' quoth the King, 'thou sayest well in this case ; thy father's name was Sir Robert le Fitz Hayme, and I will take care that my son shall have one as fair, for his name shall be Sir Robert Fitz le Roy.' 'Sir,' said the maiden, 'that is a fair name and of great repute as long as he shall live, but what shall his son be called, or any other of his descendants ? Unless care be taken of that also, they may soon come to have no name !' The King perceived that the maiden said nothing unreasonable, and knowing that Gloucester was the chief part of her heritage, 'Damsel,' said he, 'thy lord shall have a fair unobjectionable name for himself and his heirs ; his name shall be Robert, Earl of Gloucester, and he and his heirs shall be Earls of Gloucester.' 'Sir,' quoth the maiden, 'then I like this well.' "[2]

In such wise did the courteous and astute Mabel become a countess, and it is to be hoped that she ever "liked this well."

The manor house of Cranborne is as admirable a building of its kind as any in England. The body of the mansion is

---

[1] He died two years before this wooing.

[2] Seyer's *History of Bristol.* Vol. I., page 353.

supposed to date from the time of Henry VIII., but the present charming and characteristic features of the place are due to the Cecils, who became lords of the manor during the reign of James I. The first Earl of Salisbury added the exquisite Jacobean porches, and the figures of Justice and Mercy which stand above the door to bear witness to the time when the courts of Cranborne Chase were held in the Great Hall, and when burly rangers and rugged deer hunters hung about the gateway. There was a dungeon, too, in those days for the safe keeping of poachers, weather-stained men of the bracken, who were as wild as the game they chased.

The structure has been put in order within recent times, for when Hutchins wrote of it the hall was the only good room in the house, while the bailiff was its only inhabitant. This lonely man may well have been haunted by spectres of those kings and nobles who had once idled through the empty rooms.

The house is a venerable building of grey stone, whose old tiled roof is guarded by valiant battlements and crowned by spire-like chimneys of red brick. There are long, narrow, mullioned windows in the wall, a courtyard entered through an ivy-covered arch, and a walled garden which projects a quadrangle of dainty colour into the dull and uncultured meadow. This ashen, faded manor house, this ghostly château of romance, arising on the confines of a prosaic town, is like an old English ballad whose melody breaks upon ears that have been dinned by the noise of coarse streets.

Not far from the town of Cranborne is Castle Hill, where, on the end of a ridge, rises a solemn and most remarkable earthwork. It is surrounded by trees, and consists of a steep, imperious mound, in front of which is a small arena closed about by a crescent-shaped rampart. The whole work is circular, is small, and is approached by but one entrance, which is on the side towards the sea. This, in the days of early Britain, was a meeting place where the hundred court was held, where justice was dispensed, and where the bard or druid chanted the wild gospel of the time.   On a stone on the summit of the high mound the judge would sit, while the people would gather around in the arena at its foot or on the rampart which shuts it in.   When all were assembled the judge would arise and open the session with the cry,   " Truth against the world, and in the face of the sun." [1]

Wimborne St. Giles.   The Alms House and Church.

The traveller would do well to return from Cranborne by Edmonsham and the Gussage hamlets.   At the former village is a very fine old manor house, built in 1589, and for many generations the seat of the Hussey family.   It is grey with age, and, seen through a gap in the dark trees which surround it, this relic of the reign of Elizabeth, with its wizened gables and pale walls, looks like a mist in the wood.

Near by is Wimborne St. Giles, the seat of the Earls of

[1] *Proceedings of the Dorset Field Club.*   Vol. IV., page 134 ; Vol. XI., page 147.

Shaftesbury.   The house, a square, uninteresting block, dates
from the sixteenth century, but has been the subject of many
additions, renovations, and "improvements."   It stands in a
magnificent park, through which the Allen River flows.   The
village, composed mainly of modern red-brick cottages, is
severely prim and tidy, and parades the air of being much
pampered and well endowed.   By the roadside, in a state of
extreme senility, are the village stocks, which have long out-
lived any reminiscence of roystering and beer-swilling.   About
the only contemporary of the stocks remaining is the ancient
almshouse, covered with roses and wistaria—a picture of a
beautiful and dignified old age.

The church, rebuilt in 1732, is elaborately decorated inside
with much painting, with copious gilt and overwhelming ornament.   It is crowded with monuments to the Ashley family, among
which is a very beautiful memorial to Sir Anthony Ashley (who
died in 1627) and his wife.   There are among other miscellanea
an archaic effigy of a knight in chain armour, accredited to Sir
John de Plecy, who was gathered to his fathers in 1313, as well
as a female statue carved in Naples four hundred years later,
representing "polite literature mourning the death of her most
distinguished votary" in the person of the third Earl.   This
very ornate church seems out of place.   It would rather belong
to a pompous town than to a secluded hamlet, and affords a
jarring contrast to the humble sanctuaries in the country
around.

The austere house in the park, the birthplace of that Anthony
Ashley who was the leading member of the Cabal, is associated
with many queer stories.   If any could have visited the mansion
on a certain night, in the times of the Stuarts, they would have
come upon a curious spectacle.   They would have found the
hall and the long dining-room deserted but for a few giggling
servants.   In the cellar, however, they would have discovered a
party of gorgeously dressed gentlemen sitting around certain
casks from which they were drinking.   In the centre of this

group was a King, in the person of his Majesty Charles II. He had proposed adjournment to the cellar after dinner as a

The Village Stocks, Wimborne St. Giles.

place better suited for the appreciation of wine. The company were generally hilarious, and among them was a certain Edward Hooper of Boveridge, whose jollity was so exuberant as to make him especially noticeable. So delighted was the King with his drolleries that he bade the facetious Hooper kneel before him and to rise " Sir Edward." That the wag rose with some difficulty is probable, since the historian states that "in the event the whole company were completely drunk." He further adds that "his Majesty paid his obeisance to the centre cask, to perpetuate which piece of good fellowship a crown was placed in the middle of the cellar arch, which remains to this day." This same Sir Edward Hooper, the knight of the cellar, lies buried in Cranborne Church under a fair and imposing monument. He died at the age of forty-eight, and it may be that his excessive merriment had not a little to do with his somewhat early decease. As to whether a crown still adorns the middle arch of the cellar at Wimborne St. Giles, I have no knowledge.

The Gussage villages, three in number, lie along an infant stream, which is crossed by the Roman road. Gussage All Saints, the largest of the settlements, contains some of the most ancient and most primitive thatched cottages to be found in Dorset. It has a church like a college chapel, while records say that "Imbertus Pogeys held the manor by gift of King Henry III. by service of one pair of gilt spurs." Gussage St. Michael boasts of an ancient church and of a phenomenal yew tree. Gussage St. Andrew is not easy to find. It may have been a place of note when King John gave two hides here to the Abbey of Shaftesbury, "with a certain nun named Elviva." Now the village is represented by a farm, a house or two, a pond —which on a summer's day will be full of heated cows—and a derelict church in an open field. The church may be mistaken for a long low barn. It is very old, and in the matter of styles very undecided, for it displays a lancet window, a Decorated Gothic window, as well as a square window with small panes of the type common to cottage bedrooms. So very quaint is this miniature building that it is well worth the trouble involved in searching for it.

Between the Gussages and Blandford are Moore Crichel

and Witchampton.   At Crichel there lies buried Isabel
Uvedale.   She died in 1572.   According to her monument,
she was famous—

> " For wisdome, manners, modestie, discretion, love
>   and curtesie,
>   With many a conninge propertie to grafte in her
>   gentilite."

It is incidentally noted that this gentle lady was the mother
of " thyrtene childrene," and that she " perpetuall fame shall
have."

Witchampton is one of the most beautiful villages in the
entire county.   Placed in a wooded dip by the Allen River,
it is like a garden in a dell.   Many of its thatch-roofed
cottages are almost hidden by roses, while there is hardly a
wall of faded brick that is not covered by jasmine or honeysuckle.   The village is everywhere ablaze with flowers.   There
are flowers in the churchyard, about the lych-gate, and
around the low square tower; flowers growing alike on stable
roofs and between the stones of courtyards.   There are
the ancient manor house with its crown of gables, the little
stream with its mill and its venerable stone bridge, and the
water meadow with its ivy-clad ruin of the Abbey Barn.
This garden hamlet has remained unsullied by the world, and
provides a dainty realisation of rural England in its ancient
simplicity.

CHAPTER VII

THE surprising village of Milton Abbas is best approached from the South, from the Milborne road. The way leads up a shallow valley through which a small stream dawdles. As the traveller draws nigh to Milton the valley begins to close in, its banks grow steeper, while its slopes—till now quite bare—become covered with trees from foot to summit. The road, which so far has traversed a mere dip in the downs, now sinks into a wooded glen, at the shadowy entrance of which it vanishes. Once in the wood it makes a bend, and on a sudden the hidden village bursts into view.

The first impression is one of amazement, for the place is both extraordinary and unexpected. Indeed, there is nothing like to it in any part of England.

Milton Abbas consists of one long, straight street mounting up hill through a thicket. On either side of the way are mathematically placed cottages, all exactly alike. Twenty on one side and twenty on the other. The space between any two adjacent houses is the same, and in every space is a fine chestnut tree. The cottages are square, have yellow walls, thatched roofs, and an arrangement of windows characteristic of the common doll's house. Between the rows of dwellings and the road is a lawn-like stretch of grass. On either side of the highway, with precise repetition, is the unvarying line maintained—yellow house and chestnut tree, chestnut tree and

yellow house.   Two only out of the regiment of cottages have
dared to break forth into bow windows.   In the centre of the
settlement are a prim church and an almshouse, somewhat over-
redolent of charity, while at the end of the avenue of yellow
houses is a quaint little thatch-roofed inn.

It is impossible to be rid of the idea that this is a toy town,
a make-believe village, a counterpart of the Hameau at Versailles.

Milton Abbas.

The visitor may begin by regarding the strange yellow and green
street as ridiculous ; he will end by owning that it is possessed
of a rare charm.

Milton Abbas is a model village grown old. Its story is very
simple.   When Joseph Damer, afterwards Earl of Dorchester,
became possessed of the Milton estates, he found the ancient
village squatted indecently near to the spot where he intended
to build his mansion. With the fine, quarter-deck high handed-
ness of the eighteenth-century squire, he ordered the offensive
object to be removed, and it was so. The old, untidy hamlet was

entirely demolished as soon as the new Milton Abbas had been
erected well out of sight of the great house. This was in 1786.

The quaint and all-of-one-pattern village is not the only surprising thing in this part of the county. From one end of the
toy town a road leads to a wood, into whose shades it dives
deeper and deeper, as does many a road in the children's story-
books. It comes in time to the edge of the coppice, where is
a great grass valley ringed about by hills. The woods creep
down to the foot of the slope so as to form an amphitheatre of
trees. Here, on a lawn and amid the flower-gardens of a
private mansion, is a cathedral! No other building is in sight.
It is a strange thing to meet with—a great grey house and
a great grey church standing, side by side, in a hollow in
a wood. The place is a solitude, green and still, shut off
from the world by a rustling ring of wooded hills. Such is
Milton Abbey.

The mansion house is neither beautiful nor impressive.
"It occupies the site of an abbey founded by Aethelstan
in 938 for secular priests, who were made to give place to
Benedictine monks in 964. At the dissolution it was given
by Henry VIII. (for £1,000) to Sir John Tregonwell, his
proctor in the divorce from Queen Katherine. From the
Tregonwells it passed by marriage to Sir Jacob Bancks, Secretary to the Swedish Embassy (b. 1663), and then by purchase,
in 1752, to Joseph Damer, afterwards Earl of Dorchester.
With the exception of the hall, the whole of the monastic
buildings were pulled down in 1771, when the present house
was built by the Earl of Dorchester from the designs of Sir
William Chambers. It is a large quadrangular mansion with
a central court, and is constructed of white limestone, alternating
with layers of flint. It is a curious example of its architect's
notions of the Gothic style. The only interesting part of the
house is the monks' hall or refectory . . . a stately apartment
with a roof of Irish oak." [1]

[1] Murray's *Wilts and Dorset*. London, 1899. Page 567.

H

The Abbey church is a superb Gothic building, with an elaborate tower, many beautiful windows, and many exquisite flying buttresses. It dates from the twelfth and fourteenth centuries, has been admirably restored, and is one of the most elegant of the many minsters in England.

The church inside is swept and garnished, but so empty as to give the impression of being abandoned. It needs such a crowd of worshippers as throng with restless feet the aisles of a Continental cathedral, whereas Milton Abbey is used only for the prayers of a small but devout district. The altar-screen, which dates from 1492, is a marvel of carved stone. The canopied sedilia are singularly dainty. The great oak tabernacle for reserving the Eucharist is said to be unique in England, while among many wonderful sculptures in stone is the rebus of Abbot William de Middleton, dated 1514, and composed of the letter W, with a pastoral staff by the side of a mill on a cask, or tun, and by inference therefore Mil-ton. Two archaic paintings are to be found on the rood-loft. They are said to belong to the time of Edward IV., and to represent respectively King Aethelstan and his mother. The lady—who was buried in the Abbey—holds in one hand an enormous glove, and in the other a strange bird, reputed to be a hawk.

There is one monument in the church which is, I think, the most commendable of all. It is to Caroline, Lady Milton, who died in 1775. The effigies of both Lord and Lady Milton are carved in marble upon an altar tomb. The little lady is exquisite beyond all expression. She is fully dressed in a simple costume of the time. She lies back dead. Her head drops on a pillow over which her loosened hair has tumbled. Her hands fall by her side inert and helpless. Her feet—cased in tiny shoes—are the feet of those who have trodden their last steps. The figure is tender, delicate, realistic, lamentable. By her side her husband reclines, his head resting on his hand. He is assumed to be alive, and to be gazing upon her with a look stupefied by grief. He wears a bag wig, a sword, and

pompous robes.   He is uncouth, foppish, and ridiculous.   He
is living, she is dead.   His grotesque self-importance and too
prominent concern   only serve   to intensify her simplicity,
her stillness, her dreamless sleep.

Monuments to husbands and wives are to be met with in
almost every ancient church, and present certain interesting
variations.   The two are generally shown lying stiffly side
by side like Noah's Ark figures packed· away in a box.   The

Milton Abbey.

Milton monument is a remarkable departure from this type,
and I may here mention two other memorials in the county
which are not of the conventional pattern.

In Wimborne Minster is an altar tomb, erected in 1444, to
John Beaufort, grandson of John of Gaunt, and to Margaret
Beauchamp his wife.   The effigies were prepared by the
direction of their daughter, Lady Margaret Tudor, mother of
Henry VII.   The two lie side by side, he a burly fighting man
in full armour, she a slender and pretty woman, in robes of
state.   She wears a veil under her coronet and a jewel on her
breast.   Their two right hands are firmly clasped together, and
so natural is the action that the impression remains that it was

H 2

thus they died. He has taken off his gauntlet the better to hold her hand, while the empty glove is pressed to his cuirass.

As a contrast to this tender and dignified memorial might be named a monument in Beaminster Church to George Strode (d. 1753) and his wife (d.1746). Mr. Strode is dressed as a Roman citizen in toga and sandals, and reclines, with evident effort, upon a pillow. Mrs. Strode, in semi-Roman attire, is by his side. She holds in her hand an eighteenth century book, to the open pages of which she is directing Mr. Strode's attention. Her attitude appears to be that of rebuke, his of supercilious indifference. No doubt the meaning of the artist was good, but the result is deplorable.

Those who stroll over the smooth lawns around the Abbey Church will hardly realise that they are walking over the site of the ancient town of Milton. This old town has been graphically described by the Rev. Herbert Pentin.[1] It was a place of many streets and of many taverns. It possessed a brewery of great renown, as well as a grammar school founded in 1521. At this school were from 80 to 100 boarders, while among the scholars of one time was Masterman Hardy, Nelson's captain. There were over 100 houses in the town as distinct from the parish. It almost surpasses belief that the whole of this ancient settlement, its rectory, its school, its almshouses, and its redundant inns, were all swept off the earth because one Joseph Damer decreed that the town "was too close to his residence, and proved an annoyance to him." He fell upon the little place and destroyed it, as Vesuvius overwhelmed Pompeii. As a rebuke to sentiment "he had all the headstones in the churchyard removed, broken up, or buried."[2] In the making of his gardens, too, he was annoyed by the obstinate turning up of the bones of the vulgar parishioners of Milton, and so great was his disgust that of these sturdy yeoman no remains are now to be found.

[1] *Proceedings of the Dorset Field Club.* Vol. XXV., page 1.
[2] *Ibid.*, page 5.

On the summit of a wooded hill behind Milton Abbey is the minute Norman Chapel of St. Catherine. It is approached by a long straight stair, the steps of which are of the greenest turf. Chapels on the tops of hills were often dedicated to St. Catherine of Alexandria, since the legend says that the body of that saint was buried by angels on the summit of Mount Sinai. The chapel, which is now once again used as a place of worship, has been sadly mutilated in past years. The destroyer of the old town of Milton turned it into a labourer's cottage. After this vandal's death the little shrine fell upon even more evil times.

Those who are interested in the fate of ancient churches will find at Liscombe, near by, an early Norman chapel (with a Transition Norman arch and rounded pillars), the nave of which is used as a bakehouse and the chancel as a place for storing logs.

From Milton Abbey it is well to go on to Bingham's Melcombe, because the road thither is most delightful. It mounts up to the hills through the Abbey park and through the out-of-the-world hamlet of Hilton, in whose handsome church are twelve ancient paintings on wood which are curious to see.

The church is almost as large as the hamlet, and was once famous for its ancient glass, all of which, however, was destroyed in 1730 " by some idle person."

The way climbs to the crest of the Dorset heights, between Nettlecombe Tout and Bulbarrow. From this high road the traveller can survey the whole county from Mere to the Purbeck hills. The land lying Northwards—the blue-misted hinterland —is rich, luxuriant, and fair to see, a cavalier country of flocks and herds, and of many trees. The country to the South is work-a-day, austere, and bare, seamed by the plough and scraped by the harrow, a haunt of the wind-driven sea-gull in winter ; a sober, puritan country.

Bingham's Melcombe lies in a sheltered cove on the southern side of the hills, where it would seem to have sought refuge from the turmoil of the world. It stands far away from any highway, and is ten miles distant from any town or railway station. The little place consists merely of a church, a manor house, and sundry farm buildings. The ancient church, of stone and flint, slumbers by the side of a soothing brook within a circle of trees, which from a distance wholly hide it and its squat tower. Within are many monuments to the Bingham family, as well as the manorial pew, which still retains its old oak seats.

The house is an exquisite and most picturesque example of the manor house of bygone days. It is probably the oldest house of its kind in Dorset. For more than six centuries it has belonged to one family, the Binghams. The house would appear to have been built in the reign of Edward I. It has been modified and added to, but the building that is now to be seen is practically the manor house as it was in the time of Edward VI. Bingham's Melcombe, indeed, bridges over the long gap between Edward VI. and Edward VII.

The house is small and low, and of two stories. The avenue which leads to it is guarded by stone eagles, the Bingham crest. The little mansion is of grey stone, warmed by many centuries of sun. In front of it is the gate-house, a sturdy stronghold, with walls which are nine feet thick in places, which are backed by massive buttresses and pierced by heavily-barred doors. Behind are the courtyard and the chief wing of the habitation. This little flagged square is as quiet as a convent cloister, a place of mullioned casements and quaint gables, where pigeons strut on the stone terrace or perch on the pinnacles above the great oriel window. To step into this grey quadrangle is to find oneself back in the England of the middle ages. There should be at least on the terrace a knight in a plumed hat, a lady with ringlets, and at the gate a pretty waiting-maid and horses with pillions.

The present owner of Bingham's Melcombe thus describes the manor :—

" The house rambles round three sides of the court with sweet meander-
ing irregularity. There is hardly one straight line, one right angle, or one
dead level in the whole. . . . The court is on two levels, the higher
reached by two short flights of weather-beaten stone steps opposite to each
other and meeting on a common landing, which by their colouring, their
shape, and their surroundings recall the storied flight of steps at Haddon
Hall. The retaining wall is built of the small grey bricks of the olden
time, which in their interstices give birth and sustenance to a wealth of

The Court-yard, Bingham's Melcombe.

flowers and ferns which almost hide it from view. Along the terrace,
above the steps and the wall, are large bushes of hydrangea, which, laden
as they are with bloom during three full months of the later summer, blend
their delicate pink with the greys and browns, the yellows and russets of
the surrounding masonry. There is nothing which is grand or grandiose,
staring or stately, about the whole. It is simply restful and homelike ; but
the oriel projecting from the old hall, with its lofty gable, its weathercock
with the date 1661 still visible on it, its mullioned windows, its delicate
traceries, its graceful finials, half revealed and half concealed by Virginian
creeper and topped by eagles ready for their flight, its massive and deeply
chiselled coat of the Bingham arms, all in warm Ham Hill masonry, is a
very dream in stone, an ideal of Tudor domestic architecture." [1]

---

[1] *Bird Life and Bird Lore.* By R. Bosworth Smith. London, 1905.

Within are ancient oak chairs and chests, cabinets and settles, massive chimney-pieces, blocked up doors, a powdering-room, narrow turret stairs of stone, and endless cupboards.

In the old-world garden around the house are an ancient bowling green, a great yew hedge, fourteen feet high and eighteen feet deep, dating from the time of Henry VIII.; a "lovers'

The Bowling Green, Bingham's Melcombe.

seat," a "lovers' walk," a water-wheel and fish-ponds, a "ladies' garden" for summer flowers, and a circular dovecot of stone.

At Cheselbourne, near to Bingham's Melcombe, I sought in vain for the tomb of Mrs. Urith Basket, who, "being *full* of good works and days," departed this life in 1707; yet the village is probably but little changed since Mrs. Basket wrought her good works in it.

Admirers of Thomas Hardy's novels should visit Milborne St. Andrew, the "Millpond St. Jude's" of *Far from the Madding*

Crowd, where is also the "Welland House" of *Two on a Tower.*
This house was once the residence of the Mansell Pleydells,
but since 1758 it has been turned into a farmhouse. It is a
stolid building, in a wide park, composed of a body and two
wings with high-pitched, Flemish-looking roofs. Standing quite
alone in the park are two great stone gate-posts surmounted by
trophies of arms. They look lost and foolish, like two "supers"

Winterborne Zelstone.

in a play who have forgotten their cue and still linger on the
empty stage.

The old-fashioned and picturesque village is full of reminiscences of the time when it was the chief posting place between
Blandford and Dorchester. An effigy of a white hart—once
the glory of an inn of that name—is even now no mean
feature of the small town. The church has a fine Norman
doorway and other features of interest, while in the churchyard
is a stone to William Rice, "the first man who ever hunted a
pack of roebuck hounds." William the huntsman died in
1826, aged seventy-eight.

Between Blandford and Milton Abbas runs the Winterborne,

a little stream which owes its title to the fact that it runs only in the winter time. There is a rivulet of like name and habits in the South of the county. Both brooks issue from chalk hills, flow as clear, gushing rivulets all the winter, and then, about June, suddenly dry up. This is no doubt due to the cessation of a syphon action in connection with reservoirs of

Winterborne Zelstone.

water in the downs. The local sages can foretell, almost to a day, when the rush of the burn will cease.

All the villages along these rivers take the cognomen of Winterborne, and thus it comes about that there are no fewer than fourteen Winterbornes in Dorset.

Of the Blandford Winterbornes the following are worthy of some consideration. At Winterborne Clenston and at Anderson are ancient manor houses. The house at the latter place is a remarkably fine and stately building. It is of faded red brick faced with stone, has high gables and towering chimneys, handsome stone-mullioned windows, and a general bearing of great dignity and charm. The village has vanished, so that the manor house and the church are left alone, one on either side of the faithless stream.

On the downs above Clenston is the British earthwork known as Comb's Ditch. It is composed merely of a rampart and a ditch—with the fosse ever on the northern side—which can be followed across the country for miles. Although much grown over by grass and weeds and riddled by the rabbits, it is still an impressive relic of the once great line of defence.

In the church of Winterborne Kingston is a tablet to George Strangeways, who died in 1569. This man's great-grandson, George Strangeways, a major in the King's army, shot Mr. Fussel with a carbine in his lodging near the "Palsgrave Head" tavern, Temple Bar, on February 11th, 1659. There is nothing of special note in this unhappy incident, but there is in the sequel. Strangeways was tried for the murder, but refused to plead, in order to preserve his estate and prevent a public punishment. "He was pressed to death in the press yard in Newgate, February 28th, and was buried at Christchurch, London" (Hutchins).

It is worth while to turn aside to visit the hamlet of Winterborne Zelstone, for it is as rustic and picturesque a spot as will be found anywhere in Dorset. It is composed of a few old thatched cottages, a little inn, a little shop, a little bridge, all fitfully disposed along a grey road by the side of the fickle stream. In the early summer the water of the brook is almost hidden by forget-me-nots and extravagant weeds, while the meadows around are at their greenest.

Next to it is Winterborne Tomson. The village of this place has long ago departed, leaving behind only the manor house, some farm buildings, and a lowly church. It is among the outhouses that the church is to be found, for it is merely an appendage of the farmyard. It is a wizen old building, curiously small, with no more architectural pretence than a barn. Its east end indeed so fails in distinction as to present only a blind, round wall. Were it not for certain Gothic windows of a hesitating type and a squat bell gable, there would be small excuse for claiming that the building was a church at all.

The poor little sanctuary has long been deserted ; the windows are broken, and birds roost on the pews or under the cove roof. The churchyard is knee-deep in grass and weeds, while

The Deserted Church, Winterborne Tomson.

its one surviving tomb is hidden by wild undergrowth. Inside will be seen the village church as it was one hundred years ago. The ancient oak pews are high and provided with doors. The pulpit is surmounted by a sounding-board, a needless vanity, since a whisper could be heard from the altar to the door. On the pulpit desk is a red cushion ; beneath is a cramped stall for the clerk. Opposite the pulpit is the manorial pew, still furnished with cushions and hassocks of ancient pattern. The altar is a plain oak table, covered by a red cloth, at which the rats have been tugging. At the west end is a singing gallery approached by a ladder-like stair. In the church porch hangs the rope for the bell. In each window bench weeds are growing, while everywhere is the taint of mould and the dank odour of decay.

As the little place was when the diminished congregation walked out of it for the last time so is it now. Some may have gone back for old memories' sake, or to look once more at the altar steps where they were married, but beyond this the chuch has been left as reverently alone as if it were the chamber of the recently dead.

CHAPTER VIII

THERE are two roads from Blandford to Wimborne—one by the river, and one by Badbury Rings and Kingston Lacy.

The river road brings us to Charlton Marshall, an uninteresting village with a prim, old-maidish-looking church. The place was at one time the scene of a lurid drama in which the chief part was played by one John Truelove, gent. Master Truelove had practised for many years in London as a surgeon, and having acquired a small fortune, retired to this riverside hamlet to end his days. Probably he found the change from the great city to the Dorset village too extreme, for he seems to have taken to riotous living and to have stumbled into money difficulties. Anyhow, on a certain day in October 1742 he knew that he had to anticipate a visit from the Sheriff's officer.

He prepared for the arrival of this official in the following original manner. He sent away his children, discharged his servants, and having filled his bedroom with furze, he locked himself in the house and watched for the coming of the man of the law. In due course the Sheriff's officer appeared, and after trying the doors in vain, stepped, no doubt, into the road and looked up at the retired surgeon's house. Whereupon John Truelove, gent., set fire to the furze in his bedroom, and when the house was well ablaze came to the window, glared at

the amazed officer in the road, and then shot himself with
a pistol. Having thus performed his last operation, the surgeon
fell back into the burning room, and so withdrew himself for
ever from the gaze of obnoxious men. The house—which was
to have been the refuge of his old age—was entirely destroyed.
The chronicle of this tragedy ends with the following unpleasant
anatomical inventory : "Nothing remained of this unfortunate
man but some of his bowels, part of his backbone, and one of
his feet in a shoe."

The road on its way passes under Crawford Castle, a well-
preserved British fort, whose lofty rampart hangs at one point
over the cutting of a railway. Between these two works of
man, which are here in such close company, there stretches a
gulf of centuries filled with the clamour of spade and pick,
with the clank of anvils, the glare of fires, and the bursting
breath of steam.

Beyond the castle is Crawford Bridge, the most picturesque
bridge over any Dorset stream. It has nine old arches of grey
stone to carry it over the river, to make a shelter for the trout
and an echo for the water as it tumbles over the pebbles.
There is some bravado about the ancient bridge, for on the up-
stream side it thrusts out angular buttresses of enormous
strength, to show that it could stem a torrent if the need arose.
In 1506 the bridge was in ruins, and as money was scarce, an indulgence of forty days was granted to any who contributed to
its repair. The money paid for this object was to be kept in
a box, and Edith Coker, Abbess of Tarrant, was appointed
receiver of the same. At the present day, when the bridge
needs attention, the work is undertaken by the County Council,
who grant no indulgences and need no successor to Edith
Coker.

Nearer Wimborne are Sturminster Marshall, a large straggling
village with a maypole, and Corfe Mullen, where it is well to
halt for a while. This simple place possesses a charming
old church with a low, ivy-covered tower and an Early English

chancel—a church of warm colours, such as the painter in water
colours loves. Near to the church is a little old manor house
of faded brick. It is now a farmhouse, standing derelict in
a bald waste. Tall chimneys crown a roof burnished with
yellow moss, a valiant buttress holds up the sober wall, while
a most delicate bow window looks out over a dismal pond and
a rough railing which encloses nothing. The house is like
a dainty satin shoe found on a rubbish heap.

I gather from Hutchins that this tiny mansion belonged to
the Phelips family until it was sequestered in 1645. It was the
last Mr. Phelips who left money to Corfe Mullen, " partly for the
better maintenance of the curate, who has £10 per annum,
partly to provide a certain quantity of bread and cheese every
Sunday and beef at Christmas for ten poor children."

The Kingston Lacy road, on the other side of the river,
traverses the pretty village of Shapwick. Above this place is
the great fort of Badbury Rings, and it is worth while to visit
Dorset, if for no other purpose than to see this romantic spot.
The camp is best approached from Shapwick by the Roman
road which runs from Dorchester to Old Sarum. Badbury
Rings will be found on the grassy summit of an open down, the
only object in a wind-swept solitude. The fort, as seen from
the Roman road, stands up against the sky line as a heavily
entrenched conical hill capped by trees. It is made up of three
circles of immense ramparts—each with a fosse—rising one
above the other until over the highest crest there surges the
crowning plateau. The cone is steep, strange, and awe-
inspiring. It might be a grass-grown Mont St. Michael, or a
Mount Calvary approached by purgatorial steps. The circuit
of the outermost rampart is a mile. The summit, although
only 330 feet above the sea level, commands a view over the
Isle of Wight, the Purbeck and the Dorset hills, and there is
seldom a day in the year when there is not a sound of wind in
the pines.

There is little doubt but that this fortified city was founded

by the Celts, and was modified and added to in later times by
the Romans and the Saxons.   A row of round barrows of a
well-marked type will be found to the west of the fortress.

It is no matter of surprise that this spot has been made the
scene of many legends and many stories.   The country people
around believe that somewhere under the cap of pines and
oaks, or beneath the wave-like rings of entrenchments, there
lies buried a coffin of solid gold, still bright and wonderful.   A
more widely credited story tells that Badbury Rings is the
Mount Badon where King Arthur in 520 defeated the West
Saxons under Cedric, and so saved the West of England for a
time from the clutches of the triumphant invaders.

It was here, says Sir Lancelot of the Lake, that—

> " I myself beheld the King
> Charge at the head of all his Table Round,
> And all his legions crying Christ and him,
> And break them,; and I saw him, after, stand
> High on a heap of slain, from spur to plume,
> Red as the rising sun with heathen blood."

No place could be more fitting for a meeting between King
Arthur and his Knights of the Round Table than the breezy
summit of this wild ridge.   It is hard to be told, after wandering through this entrenched fortress, that King Arthur is a
myth, that Merlin and Vivien were not, and that Sir Lancelot
never wooed the faithless Queen.

There is another episode connected with Badbury Rings
which comes more definitely into the pages of history.   In
901—just after the death of King Alfred—Athelwald the
Atheling rose in rebellion against the new sovereign, King
Edward.   Athelwald swept down upon Wimborne and took
possession of that town.   King Edward advanced towards him
from the South, and encamped at Badbury Rings.   From this
hill fort he sent a messenger to Athelwald requesting him to
leave Wimborne at once, and generally to cease from troubling.
The message no doubt concluded with the assurance that, if

I

Athelwald did not do as he was told, the King would descend
upon Wimborne and destroy him.   To this the valiant Athelwald, who was prepared to wade through blood in support of
the cause he championed, replied, with much dignity and
heroism : " He would do one of two things ; he would live at
Wimborne or die there."   These are great words.   Athelwald,
however, did neither of these things, but under the cover of the
night he sneaked away and joined the Danes.   Thus it is that
there was no battle of Wimborne.

Athelwald, moreover, left his wife behind him when he

Wimborne Minster from the Meadows.

fled.   He had taken her out of the nunnery at Wimborne, and
to that institution he returned her when he resolved to play
the coward.   The nunnery, by the bye, had been built by
Cuthburga, a daughter of one of the Wessex Kings.   The
poor lady had been crossed in love, so she laid out this retreat
to soothe her heart, and within its sympathetic walls she died.

From Badbury the road passes by the beautiful park of
Kingston Lacy to Wimborne.   The manor of Kingston Lacy
once belonged to the Crown, and came at last by marriage to a
son of John Lacy, Earl of Lincoln ; hence the double name of
the place.   The manor, after certain vicissitudes, was possessed
by the Bankes family, one of whom built the present mansion
in 1660.

Wimborne Minster is a commonplace town squatting soberly in the meadows about the Stour. There is little to show that it had ever been—as Leland avers—"a very large thing." It is a characterless place, that, having set its face against any show of individuality, has become successfully mediocre. It looks its best when seen from a distance.

Its great and only feature is its splendid minster, which is visited in the summer by thousands of exuberant folk in

The Bridge leading to Wimborne Minster.

char-a-bancs and coaches. The church has two towers, one a glorious lantern tower of the late Norman period, and a western tower which dates from the fifteenth century. Not the least among the delightful features of this gracious building is its richness in colour. Owing to the different stones employed, the western tower is a column of soft greens and greys, while the Norman tower is aglow with the red of the Ringwood sandstone, the red of the autumn leaf blended with every phase of yellow, drab, and brown.

Within is a nave with Norman pillar and arches, a Norman clerestory, and other interesting features which have been dwelt upon in the endless descriptions of the minster. Few there are who do not know of the library of chained books ; of the orrery clock, which, even after the lapse of five centuries, still compels the sun to move round the dial once a day and the moon once a month ; of the ridiculous figure perched high up in the western tower, where he is convulsed every quarter of an hour, a figure that the tourists call a French gendarme and older folk a " centinel " or " jackman " ; and of the ancient chest hacked out of a single log of wood, very archaic and elemental, yet provided with no fewer than six locks. This chest probably contained the documents of some trust. The minster was, however, at one time possessed of treasures more remarkable than trust deeds. Among those detailed in the list provided by Hutchins are a piece of the Cross and of our Lord's manger, some of the ground where our Lord was born, some of the hairs of his beard, part of the thigh of the blessed Agatha, one of St. Philip's teeth, one of the joints of St. Cecilia, and some of the blood of the blessed Thomas of Canterbury, together with his hair shirt.

There are many interesting tombs in the minster. The supposed burial place of Aethelred, King of the West Saxons and brother of King Alfred, is marked by a curious brass placed over the stone in 1600. The beautiful monument to John Beaufort and his wife Margaret has been already described (page 99). The memorial to Sir Edmund Uvedale (d. 1606), erected by "his loving wife in doleful duety," is very ornate, although it was much defaced during the civil wars, when the legs of the recumbent knight were broken. The monument of the crusader, Sir Piers Fitzherbert, is a mere loose block of stone lying on the ground. It shows the battered torso of a human figure, and has the aspect of being a fragment of a fossil.

The tomb which most delights the tourist is that of Anthony Ettrick of Holt, the magistrate who committed the Duke of Monmouth after his capture at Woodlands. The coffin is brilliant and indeed gaudy with frequently renewed paint, for Anthony left to the minster twenty shillings a year to keep his sarcophagus in order. The minster has not faltered in this trust, for the wooden coffin is as gay as a gilded toy box. It is placed in a niche so as to be half way through the church wall. The legend is that this worthy man was offended with the people of Wimborne, and declared that he would never be

Wimborne Minster.

buried in the church nor out of it. This dreadful threat no doubt worried the citizens of Wimborne at the time, but Anthony's executors solved the difficulty by introducing the device of the niche, which is neither in the church nor out of it. Thus were the neighbours soothed, and thus were they spared the grief of losing their Ettrick. They were far-seeing, for the tomb—now the subject of a pictorial postcard—is of present profit to the town by attracting the curious.

This same Anthony Ettrick—the admired of the visitor in the char-a-banc—is said to have " grown very humoursome and

phlegmatic towards the latter end of his life." He therefore
had this handsome coffin made to cheer him, and deciding
that he should die in 1691, caused that date to be carved on
the panel. He lived, however, until 1703, and hence two sets
of figures are superimposed on the monument, to the great
comfort of the verger who discourses upon the melancholy
Ettrick daily.

Holt Lodge, the home of this epicure in coffins, is now a farmhouse. Holt village, a pretty hamlet near God's Blessing
Green, possesses in the form of a little thatched cottage as
picturesque a post office as will be found in England. Holt,
however, has long forgotten Anthony Ettrick. He has been
replaced by a greater hero in the person of Mr. Benjamin
Bower—greater because he weighed 34 stone 4lb. and was
" lively and active." His death in 1763 was due to his drinking a gallon of cider at a roadside inn to ward off a fit of gout.
It is particularly recorded that part of the wall of the room in
which he died had to be taken down before his body could be
removed for burial.

Monmouth's ash is most agreeably reached by road from
Wimborne, a distance of some nine miles. As the tree is not
easy to find, I would advise the traveller to take the Salisbury
road through Hinton Parva, and when short of the fourth
milestone to turn to the right by Hinton Martel and Chalbury,
and so come to Horton village. Here the road to Ringwood
must be taken. This road, a little more than one-and-a-half
miles from Horton Church, crosses a minute stream, at which
point a lane leads away to the left. If it be followed for
about a mile " Monmouth's close " will be found—with local
guidance—in the angle between Peat's Hill and Horton
Plantation.

This road is, as already mentioned, very agreeable. Hinton
Martel, an out-of-the-world hamlet of thatched cottages, has a
possession which is, so far as I know, unique among the
attractions of hamlets. In what may be called the street is a

circular basin, in the centre of which is just such a fountain as may be found in a suburban tea-garden or in front of a gaudy Italian villa. The fountain, of painted metal, tawdry and flimsy, represents a boy standing in one dish while he holds another on his head. No unhappy detail is spared : the ambitious pedestal, the three impossible dolphins, the paltry squirt of water, are all here. How this *café chantant* ornament has found its way into a modest and secluded hamlet there is no evidence to show. It would be incongruous even for a Jubilee memorial.

From Hinton Martel a deep Devonshire lane leads to the hill of Chalbury. The village, save for a few houses, has disappeared, but the faithful church still clings to the summit. It is an odd little building to be found here alone, very ancient and very simple; its windows vary from those of the Early English period to those of the ordinary dwelling-house. It boasts neither tower nor steeple. Within are high pews with doors, an old wooden gallery, and a little box for the clerk below the pulpit. There are iron pegs along the wall, handy for hats and cloaks, but they must be few who climb up to this meek church of the summit.

According to Hutchins, the air that sweeps over this hill is " clear and wholesome," while the view from its height is one of the most fascinating in the county. To the East are Ringwood church and the sweep of the New Forest. To the North are Monmouth's country, Wimborne St. Giles, and Cranborne Chase, the "long backs of the bushless down" and the wild heath. To the South are the water meadows of the Stour, the Purbeck hills, and the Needles. The only blot in the landscape is the nightmare tower of Horton, built for an observatory, and now happily falling into decay.

Close to Chalbury is Horton, a most unattractive village. It is possessed of a quaint church, however, which contains, among other monuments, an effigy of Sir Giles de Braose, who died so long ago as 1305. Here also is the tomb of Henry

Hastings, of Woodlands. He was the second son of the Earl of Huntingdon, and became the lord of the manor of Woodlands by his marriage with Dorothy Willoughby. He died in 1650, aged ninety-nine. It is to be hoped that Dorothy was not fastidious, for Henry Hastings could not have been a pleasant man to live with. According to Hutchins, " he was low, very strong, and very active, of a reddish flaxen hair ; his cloaths always green cloth and never worth, when new, five pounds." He was a keen sportsman. " The great hall was strewed with marrow bones, full of hawks' perches, hounds, spaniels, and terriers, with gamekeepers' and hunters' poles in great abundance. . . . In the parlour, the windows (which were very large) served for places to lay his arrows, crossbows, and stonebows." In this parlour was his oyster table, where he ate oysters twice a day all the year round. He seems to have had at least two books, the Bible and the Book of Martyrs, and to have kept pheasants' eggs in all his old hats. If Dorothy was a lady of dainty tastes, she probably avoided both the parlour and the great hall. From a portrait of Henry Hastings which exists it can be imagined that he was not at his best when busy at his oyster table.

From Horton it is easy to reach Monmouth's ash if the directions already given be followed. Before visiting the tree it may be well to recall how it came to pass that a royal duke was found hiding in a dank ditch near Horton Heath. The lad who came to be Duke of Monmouth was a son of Charles II. and Lucy Walter. Both father and mother were nineteen years old at the time of the boy's birth. Lucy is described by Evelyn as " a browne, beautifull, bold, but insipid creature." Her portrait at Knebworth shows her to be a pretty, silly-looking woman with large tender eyes. She died in poverty in Paris before she was twenty-nine. The boy was made much of by the King. When he was thirteen he was created Duke of Monmouth. At the age of fourteen he married a daughter of the Earl of Buccleuch. By the time he was nineteen he was in command of the Life Guards and a Privy Councillor. He was so petted by the King and the ladies of the Court as to become self-indulgent, spoiled, and conceited. His face was handsome but somewhat effeminate, for he had his mother's large soft eyes. He was a man of no force of character, and when his vanity was appealed to he was very easily led. He became involved in the Rye House Plot, and fled to the Netherlands in 1683.

On February 6th, 1685, Charles II. died, and his brother James came to the throne. Monmouth, as a son of the late King and a Protestant, resolved upon an attempt to seize the crown. He landed at Lyme Regis on June 11th, 1685, was defeated by the King's forces at Sedgemoor on July 6th, whence he fled for his life. He and his companions entered Dorset by Berwick St. John (page 41), hoping to reach Poole by way of Cranborne Chase and the New Forest. At Woodyates Inn (page 82) they abandoned their horses, and Monmouth disguised himself as a shepherd. The party now consisted only of the Duke, Lord Grey, and an officer named Buyse. The way to Poole was over very wild country, across bare downs and bleak heaths. The fugitives tramped as far as Woodlands, where they separated, and here Lord Grey was captured on July 7th. In their flight they would naturally seek the shelter of any high ground under the lee of which they crawl along. They would make therefore for such a ridge as that now known as Horton Plantation. Under the shadow of this ridge lay some cultivated ground called " the Island," and into this oasis of growing crops and rough pasture the two men stumbled, dead beat, and here they spent the night.

They were seen to enter " the Island " by a woman named Amy Farant, whose cottage was close by ; so in the morning the pursuit became very keen, for £5,000 was the price of Monmouth's body, dead or alive. Soon after sunrise Buyse was captured, and he at once owned that he had left the Duke but three hours. All the fields and the hedges in " the Island "

were scoured, crops were trampled down, bushes were torn
aside, heavy boots scuffled through every hollow, until at last
a militiaman named Parkin espied among the ferns and brambles of a ditch what he took to be the skirt of a brown coat.
He clutched at it, and found beneath the brown coat the
palpitating body of a man, terror-stricken and trembling,
bespattered with dirt and faint for want of food. This haggard,
ragged, hatless wretch was his Grace the Duke of Monmouth,
Knight of the Garter and Privy Councillor. He was in the
dress of a farm hand, but in the pockets of his coat were found
things which were never before discovered in the pockets of a
Dorset shepherd. These were the badge of the Order of the
Garter, recipes for cosmetics, forecasts from astrologers, and
numerous quaint charms to ward off evil.

The ditch was by a hedge in which an ash tree chanced to
be growing, to be known evermore as " Monmouth's ash," as
the field will ever be " Monmouth's close." The ditch is filled
with ferns, flowers, and brambles, just as it was, no doubt, in
1685. The original ash tree is gone, for the life of the ash is
but 200 years. It was described by those who saw it last as a
tottering tree, whose bark was scored deeply with initials and
names. The tall and vigorous tree which has grown in its place
would seem to be from fifty to eighty years old. The only
marks on it are the work of a woodpecker. The ferns in the
ditch are, no doubt, the descendants of the very ferns the hunted
man lay among, face downwards, biting the earth and listening
with a bursting heart to the slowly approaching footsteps. In the
dank gloom of that ditch he must have seen a vision of Tower
Hill, of the crowd around the scaffold, of the headsman's axe.
Standing to-day in Monmouth's close, it is easy to recall the
drama which was played here at seven o'clock on that morning
in July : the emptied trampled ditch, the frowning background
of fir-capped hill, the ruddy, grinning militiaman, holding up a
dazed man by the collar of his coat, the iron hand that grips
the damp lappet of rags, the nerveless hand of the would-be

king, shuffling towards a pocket to find a bribe, the hurrying of yokels from off the heath towards the couple under the ash, the long shadows of the morning sun.

The Duke was taken before the nearest magistrate, Anthony Ettrick, of Holt Lodge, and then sent to London on horse-back with his arms pinioned behind him.   He died with courage on Tower Hill, on July 15th, seven days after his capture, and at the age of thirty-six.   On the scaffold he felt the axe edge and begged the executioner to do his work well, and not to mangle him as he did Lord Russell. The headsman did worse.   He made five blows at Monmouth's neck before the head was severed from the body.   After the first blow the Duke, who was unbound, looked up, but never moved again. He had little affection for his wife, whom he married by arrange-ment.   All his devotion was bestowed upon Henrietta, Lady Wentworth, who was as attached to him as he to her.   She followed him in his exile in 1683, and was still abroad at the time of his execution.   The sorrow-stricken woman survived him only nine months.   He sent her certain charms which were found upon him at the time of his capture. When she received them she said, "Good God ! had that poor man nothing to think of but me ? " It would seem indeed that at the end he had nothing to think of but her, for his last words on the scaffold were in vindication of her purity of heart.

Before finally leaving Wimborne, I would commend to the traveller a pilgrimage to West Parley, on the Hampshire border. This little hamlet, which lies below the ancient British outpost of Duds Bury, is picturesquely placed on the banks of the River Stour. The road ends at the river, and so secluded is the spot that the tiny village seems to have crept away as far as it could go from the haunts of men.   The little old church has a wooden belfry and an ancient wooden porch.   The church-yard in which it stands is merely a child's wild garden.   In a glazed recess in the outer wall of the chancel is a common earthenware urn covered by a faded red cloth.   This urn, which was found buried in the church when it was restored, contains the heart of " the lady of Lydlinch," who endowed this modest shrine. The heart must have been large to have filled the urn.

I do not know the story of the lady of Lydlinch—and possibly it is known now to none. Lydlinch is a small hamlet hid away in the delectable valley of Blackmore. There is an old church in the village, near to the porch of which is a plain, moss-covered tomb. It bears this inscription : " Here lie the remains of a lady who gave to the rector of this church for ever one portion of tyths arising out of Duds Bury farm in West Parly and another out of Knowle farm in Woodlands." There is neither name nor date on the ancient stone.

I fancy that the lady's home was in West Parley ; that circumstances led her to end her days at Lydlinch, where her body was buried. She was well disposed to the people of Lydlinch, but her tenderest affection was ever for the little village by the Stour ; and here she willed that her heart should be sent, so that it might lie within sound of the stream in the child's wild garden that encircled the church of her girlhood.

CHAPTER IX

AN OLD-WORLD SEAPORT

On the outskirts of Wimborne is Canford Magna, once a manor that was really great. The village is now a model village, built according to a contract pattern. The houses, all alike, are all stamped with the same effusive coat of arms, as are the sheets of a quire of much-emblazoned note-paper.

The manor in times past was held by the Earls of Salisbury, the Earls of Lancaster, by John of Gaunt, by the Montacutes, and other famous families. It ended, as many other great estates have ended, by "coming into the market." The ancient house was pulled down, and the present modern building appeared in its stead.

There are many episodes of interest in the annals of the manor. It belonged at one time to a little girl of eight, named Ela, who was the sole heiress of Walter de Eureaux. The child, being regarded as especially precious, was hidden away privily in Normandy. At an auspicious moment she was brought over to England and presented to Richard I., who promptly gave her in marriage to William de Longespée, whereby he became lord of the manor of Canford. This William of the Long Sword was a son of Henry II. by Fair Rosamond. He was a fighter of no mean parts, whose love of adventure carried him away to the Holy Land. During his long absence a certain Hubert de Burgh set afloat the report that William de Longespée was drowned. He whispered this to the gentle Ela, and, after fumbling expressions of sympathy, solicited her in marriage for a relation of his. The lady of the manor would hear him not : her lord was not drowned, she said, and one day a ship would sail into Poole harbour on whose deck her husband would be standing, looking for her welcome ; moreover, even if he were dead, she would be never faithless to his memory.

In the fulness of time he of the long sword came home to find the loyal Ela awaiting him at Canford and to hear of the false tongue of Hubert de Burgh. The chronicles say that "he resented" the doings of this Hubert, and in those days resentment meant much and took strong forms. However, at an entertainment at the Castle of Sarum, Hubert contrived to poison the lord of Canford so that he died. This was in 1226. Ela, the widow, became a nun, and in the course of years an abbess. She died at Lacock in 1261, at the ripe age of seventy-four, and in the choir at Lacock [1] she was buried.

She and her husband had assisted in laying the foundation-stones of Salisbury Cathedral six years before he was murdered. It was to this Cathedral that the body of William de Longespée was brought from Sarum for burial. His tomb is still to be seen there, surmounted by an effigy of the great warrior, clad in chain-mail from chin to foot, with his long sword by his side, together with his shield bearing the six golden lioncels of his grandfather, Geoffrey of Anjou. A monumental slab in the cloisters of Lacock Abbey marks also the resting-place of the faithful Ela.

The church at Canford Magna has been lamentably mutilated. It is a small, low building of great antiquity, with a plain square tower and ponderous buttresses—an old-world village church, shrunken with years. To this simple and dignified little sanctuary have been added both an East and a West end in the loudest *nouveau riche* style. The additions are glaring, pompous, and aggressive, as well as painfully out of

[1] Lacock Abbey in Wiltshire.

sympathy with the quiet modesty of the aged building. It would have been more merciful if the gentle old church had been pulled down rather than subjected to these indignities. That the new porch of gaudy sandstone has been already scribbled over with names and initials, cut by the penknives of the profane, does not seem to be inappropriate.

The church is kept locked, so I am unable to say if the fol-

Poole Harbour.

lowing memorial, described by Hutchins, is still in existence. It is in the form of a brass plate to the memory of Ann Hillary, who died in 1653, and is thus inscribed :—

> " 'Tis not because this woman's virtue dies,
> That the brass tells us here Ann Hillary lies :
> Her name's long lov'd, she is in this commended,
> The poor cry out their Hillary Term is ended."

On the way to Purbeck lies Poole, one of the most interesting towns in Dorset, and one with possibly the most romantic and adventurous history. The town covers to its very edge a

small peninsula which juts out into one of the wildest of
English estuaries. It is just where the Great Heath comes
down to the Channel that Poole steps out to meet the sea.

It is an amphibious place, made up of huddled red brick
houses which rise—as the tide pleases—out of the ooze or the
water, so that from afar it is a mere island-clump of ruddy roofs
and masts standing between the heather and the blue sea. As
Leland says, "It standith almost as an isle in the haven, and
hangith by N.E. to the mayne land by the space almost of a
flite shot." That writer further adds, "And in this place is a
dike, and to it often cummith thoroughout of the haven water,
and here is an embatelid gate of stone to enter into the town.
There is a fair town house of stone by the kay. King Richard
the 3 began a pece of a town waulle at one end of the kay, and
promised large thinges to the town of Pole."

A fragment of the fair town house still stands on the "kay,"
and the water still comes to the city's edge from out of the
haven, but the gate has gone, and of the wall but few fragments
are now to be found. It mattered little that "King Richard
the 3" did no more than promise large things to the town of
"Pole," for the people of "Pole" were always singularly able
to look after their own interests. They had had a very hard
bringing up. If any marauders thought fit to visit the South
of England, it was inevitable that they should drop in at Poole.
The little sea town was burnt and pillaged times without number,
and had it not been that the heath and the forest were handy
for hiding, the "people of Pole" must have ceased to be. When
the terrible Canute came down upon Britain in 1015, it was at
Poole that he landed. Many times, both before and after this,
there must have rung through the village the horrifying cry
of "The Danes! the Danes!"

The Poole folk obtained their first charter in 1248, from
William de Longespée, son of the fair Ela of Canford, for
Poole was in the manor of Canford. From that day they never
ceased to ask for privileges, and they obtained many. Their

mayor had vast powers given him, and was indeed, by virtue of his office, an admiral. Were not the arms of Poole " a barry of 8, sable and vert, over all a dolphin naiant, argent, with besides three escallops of the first," and the crest a mermaid, with mane-like hair, holding an anchor in her right hand ? The burgesses acquired many indulgences and "acquittances both of body and goods from toll." They were adamant as to their rights. Thus in 1609 they insisted " that the liberties of the port are known, beyond the memory of man, to begin from Shag Rock, above Russell Point, and from Haven Point as far to the northward as a Humber barrel may be seen." In 1667 they rowed in solemn state, in forty boats, up the channel of Wareham to Attewell Lake. Here they found certain boundary marks, opposite to which they anchored, read aloud their charter with much emphasis, and claimed their liberties to extend so far.

They were never satisfied. They even induced Queen Elizabeth to make Poole a county incorporate, and by the will of that sovereign the county of Poole became separate from the county of Dorset.

It must be acknowledged on their behalf that they were always ready with ships and men—at a price—for as long ago as 1347 they provided Edward III. with four vessels and ninety-four men for the siege of Calais. They were not laggards too in the matter of entertainment. In September, 1665, Charles II., with the Duke of Monmouth and others, visited Poole, and were received with appropriate dignity. All the expenses were borne by Peter Hall, the Mayor, who " had the singular honour to attend his Majesty at dinner." "After dinner it pleased his Majesty to take collector Wm. Skutt's boat to Brownsea (steered by the said collector, and rowed by six masters of ships), where his Majesty took an exact view of the said island, to his great contentment."

The Duke of Monmouth, who went with the King on this water excursion, must have retained pleasant memories of

K

Poole. It was towards Poole that he was flying when he was captured in a ditch near Horton. As he lay there in hiding it is little to be doubted that he would have been ready to exchange the hope of a kingdom for the sight of William Skutt's rowing boat.

As to the King, his visit to Poole cannot but have carried his mind back to an episode of fourteen years before, about which the townfolk had never ceased to brag. On the evening of

Poole Harbour.

October 16th, 1651, a small coal brig named the "Surprise" sailed into Poole haven and dropped anchor. The loungers upon the quay took no notice of this, beyond to remark that "Tattersal was back again." Tattersal, the captain of the brig, traded between Poole and Shoreham with coal, but on this occasion he was one day late. When Tattersal rowed himself ashore he had a story to tell which had no concern with coals, but which soon gathered a curious crowd around him. He was late, he owned, yet he had left Shoreham on the morning of the day before; could they guess where he had been? No? Well, he had just come over from Fécamp, in France, where he had landed two gentlemen who had paid him £60 for the job. Sixty pounds, and he was no liar! Who were the two who had squandered £60 for a day's passage? Why, his Majesty King Charles and my Lord Wilmot, forsooth, flying the country after the battle of Worcester.

After the Restoration the rough little brig was brought up the Thames, was painted and decked up, and anchored off Whitehall. · Her name was changed to the "Royal Escape," and Tattersal, with a pension of £100, was still her master, for she was now entered in the Navy as a "fifth-rate." She survived this honour 140 years, since it was not until 1791 that she was broken up for fuel.

During the Civil War, Poole was so strong for the Parliament as to become the terror of the Royalist strongholds around. It was from Poole that the assault upon Corfe Castle was made, and whenever the garrison felt the tedium of affairs they went up to Wareham in boats and plundered that unfortunate and ever unsuspecting town.

In 1643 the Royalist Earl of Crawford laid siege to Poole, but as he could make no effect upon the place, he tried treachery. He was told that a Captain Sydenham of the Poole garrison "seemed inclinable to admit him to the town if he might have his pardon and a valuable consideration. . . . The Earl assured him that his terms would be complied with, and as an earnest sent him £40. It was then agreed that on such a night Sydenham should be captain of the watch and his men on the guard : The Earl to approach in the dead of night, the gate to be left open, and the Earl to cause a horn to be blown, as Sydenham used to do, for want of a trumpet, that the town, and a frigate lying near the gate, might not suspect them. They should then enter the town and seize the ship. The Earl so liked the method that he sent him £100 more, and promised him a major's commission and the ship."

The Earl, however, did not know his Sydenham. On a dark night in February the Royalist crept up to Poole with 500 silent men. He found the gate open, to his joy, and felt that he had done well at the modest outlay of £140 and a ship which was not his. His men passed through the gate breathlessly and with muffled steps, the horn was blown, and Poole seemed won. What next happened was not according to the programme or schedule. The gate chains were drawn up, the Earl's men, their minds aglow with dreams of plunder, found themselves trapped and fired upon by an invisible and jeering foe. Most of them were killed, the Earl escaped with difficulty, while Captain Sydenham sat in his room chuckling over a pleasant night and over two bags containing £140 in gold.

Poole was a little involved in Monmouth's rebellion, and did not escape the attention of Judge Jeffreys, as the following warrant, dated September 22nd, 1685, and signed by Allen Scutt, Mayor, will show. The warrant is directed to the "cunstable or tythingman of Upper Litchett" by the order of the Rt. Hon. George, Lord Jeffreys, Lord Chief Justice of England. "I doe hereby will and require you to take into your care and custody two quarters of the severall persons this day executed within this towne and county and herewith sent you by Charles Barfoot of Sturminster Marshall, husbandman, and to affix them on poles or spykes in the most notable places in Upper Litchett, and hereof fayle you not at your perills." The footnote to this order is interesting, there being no parcels post in those days : "The officer to pay 5/- for carridge."

Poole, in the course of years, flourished exceedingly, doing much trade with Spain, with the Mediterranean towns, with Newfoundland, and with South Carolina. In 1770 the customs amounted to £13,747, while the port owned no fewer than 230 sail, manned by 1,500 men. Two large hoys sailed every Monday to Portsmouth, returning on Saturday "sooner or later, as the wind serves." The mail-coach, carrying four inside passengers, arrived from London every day at twelve, and left for London the same day at four. There was also—

so bustling and reckless was Poole—a stage waggon for goods
to London every week.

Poole, however, has an interest above all this.   It is a place
which is ever picturesquely bound up with the romance of the
sea, with smugglers and pirates, with filibusters and men in
worsted caps, who could chat about marooning and keel-

The Quay at Poole.

hauling, who could swear in many tongues, and jingle in their
pockets " pieces of eight."   The " people of Pole " in the good
old days stood at little.   They had great enterprise, both in the
matter of adventure and iniquity, and if their records occasionally read like the Newgate Calendar of the sea, it must be
remembered that laws were very harsh and very readily
broken.

Smuggling was a vigorous and popular industry at Poole,
which was much favoured by local advantages.   The estuary
was traversed by intricate waterways, hard for a pursuer to follow ; from the lagoon rose certain bush-covered islands, while

about the shore were creeks and inlets handy for the beaching of boats. The town itself sprang out of the water; a boat could whisper at night under a bedroom window, a man could put out to sea without crossing a street, houses had good cellars, and the lanes of the old seaport were as perplexing as the channels in the haven. Moreover, all around Poole and its shifting harbour was the Great Heath, wild and trackless. No better place for hiding could be imagined, whilst, to make escape easy, the moor reached to the confines of the New Forest and of Cranborne Chase.

There must have been many a cache for hiding kegs and bales among the sandhills or under the bracken and long grass. In the Dorchester Museum can be seen the contents of a forgotten cache discovered at Bulbury, on the outskirts of the heath, and a good two miles from the sea. Here were found hidden an anchor of ancient pattern, with its chain matted by rust into a rugged lump, as well as certain axes and hammers which would be out of place on an innocent fishing-smack. Whoever buried these inconvenient pieces of evidence never came back again to claim them. There are probably other forgotten hiding-places still undisturbed on the heath, for many a smuggler was done to death in those days whose story died with him.

In the matter of piracy, too, Poole always held an eminent position. Indeed, one of the boldest and most successful of English buccaneers was Harry Page, of Poole, whose name the French conveniently reduced to Arripay. This worthy was the terror of the Channel. On one occasion he brought back to the humble haven of Poole no fewer than 120 prizes picked up in detail off the coast of Brittany. "He ravaged the coast of Spain, burnt Gijon, and carried off the crucifix from Finisterre." At last so daring did he become that the Kings of France and Spain thought fit to turn their attention to this native of the town of Poole. In 1406 they fitted out a joint expedition for the purpose of burning the noisome Arripay in his hole. In

pursuit of this intent, their fleet had the boldness to land at
Poole and to attack the pirate in his very lair.   It is needless
to say that the inhabitants sided to a man with their distinguished townsman.   There was no mean battle in the
streets and around the town, but the burgesses got the worst
of it, and, after a gallant defence, fled with Arripay to the
friendly heath.

Nothing came amiss to Poole.   When smuggling and filibus-
tering were effectually discouraged, there was still the excellent
sport of blockade-running and privateering to be developed.
The following passage from Hutchins's account of the town
shows how keen was the mariner of Poole to find new channels
for his particular talents as soon as old occupations had passed
away.   "About 30 years ago," he writes, "some attempts were
made by adventurers from this port to establish a trade to the
coast of Africa.   Several voyages were undertaken and the
returns made in slaves, who were carried to the West Indies
and Carolina."

Modern Poole is a prosperous place, of unimpeachable
respectability.   The new town, with its prim park, its electric
tramway, and suburban villas, is featureless, but the old town
about the "kay" is most fascinating.   Here, ranged in a
broken line along the quay wall, is a crowd of ships—not or
steamers, be it noted, but of picturesque sailing vessels.   The
steamers pass by in the Channel afar off, while the craft that
make for the haven of Poole belong to that vanishing fleet
about which clings the last of the real romance of the sea.
Here is the old-world sailing ship, the barque from Norway
with a stair leading to her railed poop, the lumbering brig
from the North, the piratical-looking topsail schooner, the jovial
ketch, the brigantine.

A fine show they make—a palisade of masts, with here
a square sail hanging limp, and here a jib set to dry—a tangle
of ropes and spars, of braces, stays, halliards, and purchases,
a network against the sky ; and below patches of white deck

showing up between dark bulwarks, between a medley of deck-houses and hatches, of coiled ropes and anchor gear, of galley chimneys and miscellaneous lumber. Some of these ships are the last of their kind, and when their staunch old timbers have rotted the end of a living tale of the sea will have been told.

Here in Poole harbour are to be seen the very "properties" of the old sea drama of England. The armed frigate is not in the haven, nor the tea clipper from the China seas, nor the full-rigged ship from across the line, but hugging the quay wall are the quaint coaster, the Channel tramp, the bluff "wind-jammer," the timber ship, the crafty sailing barge. Here are the "Morning Star," the "Harold and Jane," the "Pride," the "Black Cat," the "Two Cousins," the "Rose in June," the "Enterprise," with sailing ships from the Baltic, as well as from southern ports, bearing unfamiliar names.

The quay itself is a part of England of bygone days, is very redolent of tar, while squatting on a bollard, or on a heap of sails, or on a dinghey turned up for repairs, will be a tobacco-chewing mariner of the past who might have come off a privateer. No two houses on the quay are alike. Here, for example, is the ancient "Harbour Office," with a sundial on its front—placed there when dials were cheaper than clocks—with an arcade of pillars convenient to lean against, and a life-buoy hanging up in the shade. Under its gable end is a curious tablet with a portrait of Benjamin Skutt, who was Mayor of Poole in 1727. He is depicted as a fat, much overdressed, but contented man in a voluminous wig. Next to the office is the very homely "Steam Packet Inn," then comes a sail loft with ample dormer windows in the roof, then a ship chandler's with a cosy bow window for old customers. There are shops, too, from whose lintels swing jerseys and oilskins as well as pilot jackets and boots ; shops full of binnacles, rowlocks, signalling flags, and second-hand sextants, while everywhere is the picturesque litter of the harbour side.

On the quay is the " Town Cellar," " King's Hall," or " Wool-house," a low building of grey stone with stout buttresses, a pointed arch over its doorway, heavy roof beams, and Gothic windows. It is supposed to have been built in the time of Edward III. or Henry VI., and to have served many purposes. Originally it would seem to have been the church of the monastery of St. Clement's, founded by the Lady Ela of

The Quay at Poole, showing the " Town Cellar" and the Harbour Office.

Canford Manor.[1] Then in 1348, when the town was decimated by the plague, the monastery was abandoned and fell into ruins. It became a storehouse, where possibly Harry Page found it convenient to bestow the plunder from his 120 prizes. Later it was the place wherein the town stored such dues as were collected in kind, and thus it came by the title of the " Woolhouse."

The sea town behind the quay is made up of faded red brick houses with rugged roofs, which houses are disposed about a plexus of lanes and alleys leading all ways. In whichever

[1] *Proceedings of the Dorset Field Club.* Vol. IX., page 78.

direction a Poole street starts, it will come in time to the sea, while at the lane's end there is as likely as not to be seen a cluster of masts or a bowsprit. In these rambling ways are houses with copious bow windows and a superfluity of roofs, cottages very gaudy with paint, laid on no doubt by a colour-loving mariner, houses within high walls and flagged courtyards with capacious cellar flaps, of great worth when smuggling was in vogue. In the sea town also are still to be seen many of the fine old houses belonging to the wealthy merchant-adventurers of Poole. They date mostly from the seventeenth and eighteenth centuries, and are rich in carved door porches, fanlights, strong gates, and imposing balustrades. Certain of these buildings have a foreign look, as if their designer had lived long in the Netherlands, while in Hutchins's time "there still remained many old houses of timber and plaster in the Spanish taste."

The lanes of Poole have changed little since mahogany-faced men with pigtails hanging beneath their worsted caps and with monstrous earrings flapping by their cheeks lurched along with kegs of smuggled brandy on their shoulders. They affected petticoats in those days, and belts, stuffed with knives and pistols, from which swung a lethal weapon called a hanger.

The chief church of the town is peculiarly plain both inside and out, yet it once had great possessions. The same included " Two ferthyngs of golde, III gylte pens, a woman's hed harnys and shulders of sylver, a legge of sylver, and a burgym grose." What became of these curiosity-shop treasures the chronicle does not tell, nor is there any record dealing with the history of the woman's head harness.

In the church is a graceful wall tablet to Peter Joliffe, who died in 1730, aged seventy-two. He was the master of the hoy " Adventurer," of which the following deed is told. When cruising off Swanage in 1694, the hoy fell in with a French privateer which was dragging an unhappy Weymouth smack away captive. Joliffe attacked the French ship, forced her ashore at

Lulworth, where the country people promptly seized both vessel and crew, and set the trembling fishing-boat free. For this service Peter received a gold chain and a medal from the King.

At the west end of the churchyard there was at one time a large hillock of earth, beneath which lay buried, in a coffin filled with spirits of wine, one James Thomson, merchant. Of the mound now no trace exists, nor are we told whether the coffin was found to be still filled with spirits of wine when the hillock was levelled.

The fine Georgian town hall of Poole, the almshouses, which date from the time of Henry V., and which are now nearly all chimneys and roof, together with the solitary thatched cottage in the centre of the busy and very modern High Street, may engage the attention of the visitor to this quondam county.

The Poole estuary extends inland for some seven miles, a tortuous sea inlet encompassed on all the sides by the famished heath. The most impressive view of this remarkable tract of water is to be obtained either from the wind-blown village of Lytchett-Matravers on the North or from the height of Ballard Head on the South. From the latter hill the whole expanse of the inland lake can be seen from the sea gate to the green, rush-lined passage of the Frome.

It is a maze of waterways, of capes and creeks, of islands and shoals, of gleaming water, that here scoops a bay out of the heather-tinted sands and there flickers like a light between the trunks of a clump of pines. The shores of this sea labyrinth belong to the moorland, so that by the water's edge will be found a ruddy sand cliff, a garden of gorse, a biscuit-coloured beach, a waving flat of drowned grass, a strand of stones and fir trees. Go back ten centuries, and this Wessex estuary is still the same, the same as when up the fairway came, with thud of rowlocks, the long boats of the Danes, lined with glistening shields, while on the shore were burning huts and folk fleeing across the heath.

It is a melancholy lagoon, a tragical inlet, sombre and desolate at most times. Its sea seems lifeless, and the country lonely, so that even in the summer time the landscape looks as if the sun shunned it. On the brightest day, when the tide is rising, the sea pours into Poole and floods the harsh moor with blue. The water shines like metal; the heath is a stretch of brown velvet, splashed with magenta where the heather is in bloom, with apple green where the pools are hidden, with a slash of red where a sand scarp catches the sun. There are crescent-shaped beaches of gold, crowned by hillocks of purple, or approached by yellow lawns and chocolate-coloured hollows.

When the sky is overcast and the tide on the ebb, the lagoon is a flat of snaky channels and slimy pools; its islands are black as if their trees were charred, its grey waters stagnate over jade-green shoals, its mud banks seem to be puffed up by a baneful air. It is then that the place appears to belong to the primeval world, so that it would not be unfitting if monstrous saurians, with spiny backs, were to be seen wading in the dismal ooze. On a chill November day, when the rain drips from terrifying clouds upon the shuddering swamp and the dead tide is at its lowest, the estuary of Poole is no faint realisation of the Slough of Despond.

There are several islands in Poole harbour—a " Long Island " and a " Round Island," a " Green Island " and a " Furzey Island," together with an eyot known as " Giggers."

The largest of the isles is Brownsea, which is a mile and a half long and three-quarters of a mile wide. It came into being probably as Bruno's Island, but has been called, according to taste, " Brownecksea," " Brunkerry," and " Branksea." There was at one time on the island a " chapelle for an Heremit," but it fell into ruins, leaving no trace. Henry VIII. built a square block-house here to protect Poole, to which six men were appointed for the keeping of the watch. In the course of time this block-house grew into a castle with tower and barbican. In 1573 the island was valued at nine shillings per annum, but it rose to be more in value later, owing to the development of alum works by the then owner, the Earl of Huntingdon. The good and virtuous people of Poole were keenly distressed by the wicked profligacy of the Earl's agent.

A Glimpse of the Poole Estuary

His name was Mountjoy, and his unpardonable crime was that he would not go to church. Moreover, as the sensitive folk of Poole stated in their plaint, "he hath a brother, a very bad fellow, of an odious religion, who persuadeth the men to work on the Sabbath day."

Queen Elizabeth granted Brownsea to Sir Christopher Hatton. He made himself also offensive to the honest folk of Poole by claiming certain ferry dues, as well as the right to detain all shipping entering the port. Sir Christopher had the courage of his opinion as to these rights, for in 1589 the

barque " Bountiful Gift " failed to comply with the knight's
regulation on making the harbour, whereupon he opened fire on
the " Bountiful Gift," killing the captain, Walter Partridge, and
one of the crew. Among other notable owners of the island
were the Sturts of Crichel, who did much to improve and
beautify the place ; and Colonel Waugh, who built the church and
restored and enlarged the castle. The church was partly
panelled with oak taken from Crosby Hall in London. Finally,
after many vicissitudes, the much-restored and much added to
castle was almost wholly destroyed by fire in 1896, to be once
more rebuilt in the following year.

On the shores of the estuary are two spots of interest, Arne
and Ower. Arne is an oasis in the heath, close to the sea, a
small cultivated promontory rendered fertile by the laborious
importation of chalk to mix with the sand. In the time of
Richard II. the settlement belonged to the monastery of
Shaftesbury. There were then twenty-four tenants, all of whom
had " plumbi." The plumbum was a ticket which admitted the
tenant, upon one or more public days, to a dinner in the Abbey.
These dinners must have been a great and rare joy, for Arne
is as out of the world as a rock lighthouse. It is now a pleasant
little hamlet under the shelter of a hill covered with gorse, oaks,
and ash trees. Here is a very ancient chapel—the grey chapel
of Arne. The restorer has fallen upon it with little mercy, but
the Early English East window still looks across the haven to
the open sea.

Ower was at one time the port for the passage across the
harbour. It was a place of consequence, from whence was ex-
ported the stone of the Isle of Purbeck, as well as the china
clay dug out of the heaths. The New Forest timber used in
the building of Corfe Castle was landed here. Since 1710, a
period of nearly 200 years, the little port has been silent, yet
there are still traces of the quay and of the stout road that led
westwards. When the Purbeck stone was shipped at Ower,
there was an agreement made between the stone-owners and the

proprietors of the quay, dated October 24th, 1695, wherein it was agreed that the " acknowledgments " of one pound of pepper and a football should be paid to the stone company the day following Shrove Tuesday.   A pound of pepper and a football form a curious commercial instrument, of which the chronicler furnishes no explanation.

CHAPTER X

THE WALLED TOWN

THE road to Wareham is across the heath, through Lytchett Minster, where is an inn named the "Peter's Finger," with a painted signpost by the wayside to explain this unusual title.

Wareham must have been one of the very earliest of human settlements in Dorset. It is unique in this: that it is a fortified town, that it lies within the compass of its own entrenchments, and that the great ramparts which still shut it in cannot be less than one thousand years old. The town stands on a ridge between the rivers Puddle or Pydel on the North and the Frome on the South. On the East lies the Poole estuary, so that the only land approach to the place is from the West, where the entrenchments are the most massive and formidable.

In ancient days the sea came nearer to Wareham than it does now; the rivers were wider, and there was a great swamp stretching seawards from the foot of the ridge. Wareham was, indeed, a seaport of a kind. When Edward III. was preparing for the siege of Calais the town provided three ships and fifty-nine men for the fleet. A good deal of shipping came here, so the records say, and so the ample quay and the waterside store-houses still testify. The place, moreover, maintained an important salmon fishery.

It is probable that Wareham was originally a riverside strong

hold, built by the Bronze Age Celts, and comparable to the
fortresses of Poundbury, Duds Bury, and Crawford Castle.
When the Romans came they no doubt held and strengthened
the position, and gave to it many of the features which it pre-
tends to now.   The town, with its four streets at right angles,
follows the plan of such Roman towns as Dorchester and
Gloucester, and conforms to the arrangement of the Pretorian
Camp at Rome.   These Roman characteristics of Wareham
have been graphically dealt with by Mr. John Bellows,[1] who
states that the stronghold is "the most remarkable Roman
camp of the first century in Britain."

In Saxon times Wareham was among the great towns of

The Walls of Wareham.

Wessex.   Its history is one long, lurid account of disaster and
woe, so that it would need a Jeremiah to tell of all its lamenta-
tions.   Possibly no town in England has been besieged so often
and so readily, or has been so many times burnt and reduced to
ruins.   Placed near the sea, on the bight of a handy harbour
and at the mouth of an ever-fertile valley, Wareham in the in-
frequent intervals of peace was probably well to do.   Pirates
raided it as a matter of routine, and any ruffian of Wessex who
found time hang heavily upon his hands called together a
company of freebooters and started for the Frome mouth.

The Danes were exceedingly busy with this river-encircled
town.   They snatched it from the Saxons in 876, with the
result that for some century and a half the unhappy place was

[1] *Proceedings of the Dorset Field Club.*   Vol. XIII., page 115.

the scene of endless forays, of alarms and assaults, of carnage and burnings, and generally of battle, murder, and sudden death. Sometimes the Danes held the ramparts and sometimes the Saxons, until at last Canute came down upon the town with impetuous ferocity and made of the place a heap of ruins. As centuries went by the besiegers of Wareham must have taken comfort from precedent, for, with the exception of one siege which lasted three months, it would seem that no sooner was the town beleaguered than it fell into the hands of the enemy.

During the civil war of Stephen's reign Wareham had what would be called in schoolboy speech "an awful time." That terrible virago, the Empress. Matilda, possessed herself of the place for a while, but in 1142—in the very year when she escaped from Oxford Castle in her nightdress through the snow—Stephen took it, and, acting in accordance with ancient custom, reduced it to ashes. King John too had an unfortunate and inconvenient affection for Wareham. He came there often, to the distress of the burgesses, for he always brought trouble in his train.

During the great Civil War Wareham was held by the Royalists. The holding, however, was nominal as soon as it became a casual relaxation for the Parliament to lay siege to the place. Indeed, the garrison at Poole appear to have regarded the raiding of Wareham as a suitable occupation for "a week end." In 1646, when the Parliament was comfortably in possession of the town, a vote was passed that Wareham should be "slighted." To "slight" an entrenched place in those days was to pluck it down and level it with the ground. Fortunately, the work of slighting was either too heavy or too uninteresting to be proceeded with, so the ponderous walls of Wareham were spared.

The reputation of this town has been founded mainly upon its misfortunes. It is famous for little but calamities, so that, had it not been for its sieges, its sackings, and its burnings, the place would have been of small account. Wareham, the much-enduring, is the Mrs. Gummidge of Dorset towns, and it may be that its troubles have in latter years made it " contrairy." It would almost seem as if the habit of being burnt became established in the settlement, for in 1762, after a hundred years of peace, Wareham set fire to itself with such effect that nearly the whole of its houses were reduced to ashes.

There was at times a tinge of melancholy about the place, as well as an element of the morbid in its enjoyments. Thus in the reign of Edward I. Earl Gilbert pleaded for the confirmation of certain liberties which he claimed that " he and his ancestors had enjoyed time out of mind." The liberties which had afforded enjoyment for so many years to this distinguished family comprised " a gallows, infangthef,[1] bloodshed, hue and cry, view of frank pledge,[2] pillory, ducking-stool, assize of bread and beer, a weekly Saturday market, and a fair for two days on the eve of St. John Baptist."

Something of the uneasiness of life in Wareham in old days may be gathered from episodes in the life and times of the Rev. William Wake, the rector of the long-suffering town. The days of a country rector are generally assumed to be passed in dignity and peace. There are roses in the rectory garden at Wareham and a trout stream at the foot of the rectory orchard. In the time of the Civil War a certain Robert Moreton of Wareham received orders to fortify and garrison the place for the Parliament. On a pleasant Sunday afternoon he went to the town cross and made a declaration of the authority vested in him. He was on horseback, and a little crowd of gaping people, sadly alive to the meaning of proclamations, gathered about him. The saintly rector, who was a firm Royalist, came strolling by, listened to the man on the horse, and then, turning to his flock, begged them not to

---

[1] The right of the lord of the manor to try and punish thieves taken within the manor.
[2] A system of mutual suretyship.

give credit to his utterances.   Whereupon Mr. Moreton struck
the reverend gentleman over the head with the butt end
of a pistol, " somewhat to his detriment," the chronicle states.
The next day the rector was returning from taking the
air, from a meditative walk probably by the banks of the
Frome.   In the street he met Moreton, who asked the gentle
parson as to what he had said at the cross on Sunday.
Before the divine could reply Moreton fired at him with both
his pistols and so shot him in the head.   " One of the bullets
lodged in his forehead at the breaking of the hair, with which
he fell to the ground."   The cowardly Moreton then drew his
sword and gave the prostrate clergyman " two cuts over the
head, very large."   In due course the rector, having received in
all eleven wounds, was put in a chair by his friends and carried
home.   He was really rescued by a woman, for in the record
the reading is as follows : " Meantime one Susan Bolt, a
servant of Wake's, being in a field hard by fetching of
pease, came, and with her corn pike made at Moreton,
who rode from her and was by her pursued to his own
doors."

The rector, who is described as a " merry, true-hearted
parson," was after some days seized and cast into Dorchester
gaol, his property was sequestered, and his wife and children
turned out of doors.   During one of the many changes in the
course of affairs the pastor was set free, whereupon he
promptly joined the King's army.   He was at Sherborne Castle
when that place was besieged.   As soon as it fell he was made
prisoner, and with others was stripped naked and led through
the town.   From Sherborne he was sent as a prisoner to Poole,
" where the plague then was."   He was " exchanged " to Corfe
Castle, and was one of the garrison of that fortress during the
memorable siege.   When Corfe capitulated the rector was again
made a prisoner and was "barbarously dealt with." His adventures
continued, so that before the war was over he had been taken
prisoner no fewer than nineteen times.   His son—who was the

father of a famous Archbishop of Canterbury—did not disgrace the annals of the rectory. He was only eighteen times a prisoner, but could claim the greater distinction that he was twice condemned to be hanged, drawn, and quartered. When peace fell upon the land it is pleasant to know that the Rev. William Wake returned to his rectory at Wareham, to his roses and his fishing. He and his son must have had much to talk about over the parlour fire on winter's nights. It is to be hoped also that quiet came again to Susan Bolt, and that she was able once more to employ herself in the rectory field in the "fetching of pease."

The very last call to arms to which the poor, war-worn, battered town of Wareham responded was the most remarkable summons of all. Possibly no garrison ever sprang to its feet and manned its trampled ramparts in obedience to a cry more astonishing. It was to repel a phantom army, which was creeping upon the town like a deadly mist, that the men of Wareham rose and rushed into the streets, buckling on their swords and priming their pistols. The warning came at the close of a winter's day in this wise. Between Wareham and the sea is a height called Grange Hill. It is on the way to the old Celtic camp of Flowers Barrow, which crowns the white cliffs of Warbarrow Bay. One evening in December, 1678, Captain John Lawrence of Creech, his brother, four clay-cutters, with other simple folk, were struck with horror at the sight of several thousands of armed men marching over Grange Hill from Flowers Barrow. The brothers Lawrence and the clay-cutters ran for their lives to Wareham to alarm that often alarmed town. Wareham was prompt. Before the ghostly army could draw in sight three hundred of the militia were called out, the bridge was "barricadoed," and all the boats were drawn over to the north side of the river. Captain Lawrence and his brother, being convinced that the safety of England was imperilled, rushed post haste to London and "deposed the particulars on oath before the Council." The loyal county of Dorset, in the meanwhile, called together some thousands of armed volunteers.

Yet nothing came of it all. There was no invading army marching from Warborrow Bay. In the hurry of the preparations for defence no one seemed to have thought it well to walk over to Grange Hill and take a look at the direful force. The army that was moving that winter's night upon unhappy Wareham was a fabric of the brain. It is conjectured by some that the delusion was brought about by clouds gliding over the downs, or that the light of the setting sun threw terrifying shadows from the boulders and the gorse bushes on the hill. No doubt the harried folk. around Wareham had invading armies "on the brain," had from frequent alarms become frightened at their own shadows, and so were ready to fly to the ramparts to defend themselves from an on-rolling mist. Captain Lawrence and the clay-cutting visionaries escaped punishment for this inconvenient dreaming of dreams. The story deposed on oath before the Council would have been more readily excused had not the imaginative Lawrence declared that this grey host of formless men approached "with great clashing of arms." Such was the last call to arms that rang through the streets of Wareham, a trumpet blast that summoned the garrison to fight an army of shadows.

The Wareham of the present day is a little town of two thousand inhabitants, very pleasantly placed on a strip of green meadow between two trout streams. It stands on the edge of the Great Heath, at the end of the sea inlet, with only the Purbeck hills between it and the Channel. On all sides but the south the town is surrounded by its ancient walls ten centuries old. On the south quarter runs the River Frome. The walls are represented by immense banks, steep and formidable, smooth with grass, but broken here and there by gorse and brambles or scored by headlong paths made by the children.

Seen from a distance the town is most picturesque. A long

green rampart rises sheer out of the meadow; at the foot of the slope is a stream edged by rushes and peopled by white ducks; over the top of the bank can be seen the roofs and chimneys of a town and the tower of a church. A causeway leads across the meadow to a gap in the wall—this is the North Gate, which opens upon the long street.

The whole of the town is within the walls. Indeed, so much

The approach to Wareham by the North Causeway.

has the little place shrunken that it occupies but a part of the area enclosed by the entrenchments. The rest of the space is filled up by gardens and orchards. The summit of the wall makes an excellent promenade, much affected by children at all times and by young men and maidens on high days and holidays. From the crown of the rampart it is possible to look down upon the few houses which venture near the battlements, upon potato plots, upon pig-styes and courtyards, flower gardens and paddocks with cows. Those who know the town say that the lanes between the gardens are old streets, and that there were once houses along Mill Lane, Bell Lane, and Howard's Lane.

The north wall is the longest, but the west wall is the highest and the steepest. One part of this west rampart, looking across the heath to the Purbeck hills, is called the Bloody Bank. It is here, they say, that Peter of Pomfret was executed. This unfortunate man seems to have been a notoriety-seeker who in the pursuit of his ambition took to prophecy. He ventured to declare that the reign of King John would end on Ascension Day, May 23rd, 1213. This impolitic statement spread beyond Pomfret and reached the ears of the King, who was not so pleased at the announcement as were his subjects. King John carefully imprisoned this minor prophet Peter in Corfe Castle, to watch his development and to abide the event. The month of May came and went, but the reign of the King did not pass with it. To discourage prophecy in general and Peter's efforts in particular, the drastic King caused him to be dragged at a horse's tail from Corfe to Wareham, where was the only convenient gallows. At Wareham the prophet, now probably unrecognisable by reason of dirt and blood, was dragged about the streets to please the people, and then hanged from the Bloody Bank in sight of a yelling crowd, over whose heads he could see the heather-covered uplands of the moor.

Here too, after Monmouth's disastrous rising, were hanged— by the sentence of Judge Jeffreys—Captain Tyler, Mr. Matthews, and Mr. Holway. Their quarters were ordered to be placed on the bridge, and their heads to be nailed to a wooden tower in the town on the completion of the mandate.

At the south-west angle of the town a spot called Castle Hill marks the site of a castle built by William the Conqueror, and probably laid low in the castle-destroying reign of King John. Here died that Robert de Belesme who rebelled against Henry I. He was imprisoned in the castle for long, until indeed he starved himself to death, leaving behind him the reputation of being "the greatest, richest, and wickedest man of his age."

On the south side of the town—as already said—the wall is replaced by the River Frome. The south gate, like the north, is approached by a causeway over the meadows. Athwart the stream is a grey bridge of five arches, built in 1775. There is generally one man at least fishing from the bridge, while others loll over the parapet watching their shadows on the gravelly bottom of the river, or gazing seawards at the white sails beating up Poole harbour.

By the bridge is the quay—a wide, capacious square—which

The Quay at Wareham.

was crowded and bustling when Wareham did trade with the world. It is now deserted, except for two boys who are fishing and a pedlar who has fallen asleep in the sun from the fatigue of watching them. By the river's side, beyond the landing quay, are storehouses held up by determined buttresses as if at one time the walls were bursting with merchandise.

Overlooking the quay is the fine Church of Lady St. Mary. So near is it to the river that the reflection of its tower falls across the water. There is much of interest in the church besides the usual stone coffins and cross-legged effigies of knights in corroded armour. There are cryptic writings carved on the wall, which none can read aright; a leaden font belonging to Norman times, on each of whose six sides is a little featureless Apostle black with age ; a Roman altar of doubtful repute, and a cresset stone or lamp with five holes, in which wicks floated on oil.   This rude lamp must have given out an unearthly glimmer.   It was possibly used to light the cloisters at night, when the monks from the Priory went to the midnight mass.   Its five smoky flames would have fluttered in the wind,

The Lady St. Mary Church, from the River, below the Bridge.

casting fantastic shadows of cowled heads upon the echoing wall and the glowing pillars.[1]

There is a stone in the church with a Danish inscription to recall the time when the Norsemen held the town, and above all is there St. Eadward's chapel, built about the time of Henry III. to reproduce the little wooden chapel in which the body of Eadward the Martyr was placed after the murder at Corfe. Another chapel, small and vaulted, is formed within a buttress at the south end of the great east window, and is dedicated to St. Thomas of Canterbury.

[1] A lamp like to this will be found in the church at Wool

The town of Wareham is remarkably prim and leisurely. After all its turmoils, its raidings, and its burnings, it seems to have now fallen into a peaceful sleep. Its streets lie north, south, east, and west, and beyond them are the gardens and the wall. No two houses are alike ; some are of stone, some of plaster, some of brick. Few are older than the great fire of 1762. The little almshouse, with its fine old roof of stone slabs, its belfry and its cramped windows, was rebuilt in 1741. It was endowed in 1418, and, according to a tablet on the wall, was "founded, time immemorial, for six antient men and five women." The streets are described as " airy," and indeed so still is the place that at the time of the mid-day meal they may contain nothing but air, together with possibly one of the "antient" men from the almshouse.

Of the eight churches of the old town, but three remain. One is used as a school-room, one is the Lady St. Mary Church, and the third is a queer, ivy-covered little chapel on the walls. This last-named is the Church of St. Martin, in whose bare nave the voice of the preacher has not been heard for 170 years. The place is weird, empty, vault-like, and eerie with great age. There are traces of unremembered paintings on the wall, sand on the floor, heavy roof timbers hung with spiders' webs and grey with long-faded mould. The chancel is spanned by a Norman arch, while in the tower—with its single bell—is a Saxon window, and in the body of the chapel are other traces of pre-Norman days. The last time that the folk of Wareham came to the chapel-on-the-wall was to find a sanctuary there from the great fire. In this ghostly, dusty, vacant place they camped for weeks, while the embers in the streets grew black.

There is a solitary tomb in the church, to the memory of a surgeon, his wife and four children. He practised in Wareham for thirty-seven years, dying in 1791, at the age of eighty-one, from an " apoplectic fit." His wife succumbed in 1786 to "a typhus favour." How the doctor came to be buried in this forgotten place no record tells, for when he died the church had already been deserted for half a century. He and his family are here alone, and it is a matter of wonder that no one

The Chapel on the Walls, Wareham.

has seen through the chancel window, on some dreary night, the ghost of the surgeon lamenting his loneliness.

One of the most delightful walks around Wareham is through the Holme lanes, which are shaded by trees and make the most pleasant road to Lulworth and the sea. Holme is reached through Stoborough, a poor hamlet of a few houses, which was once so great a place as to boast a mayor and corporation. At Stoborough is the King's Barrow, in the heart of which was found the trunk of a mighty oak hollowed out. Within the tree was a skeleton, wrapped in deer-skins neatly sewed together. By the dead man's side was his oaken drinking cup. It would have been some such burial place as this, between the sea and the hills, that was in the mind of Louis Stevenson when he wrote this requiem :—

> "Under the wide and starry sky
> Dig the grave and let me lie :
> Glad did I live and gladly die,
>   And I laid me down with a will.
>
> This be the verse you grave for me :
> Here he lies where he longed to be ;
> Home is the sailor, home from sea,
>   And the hunter home from the hill."

To the north of Holme is Holme Bridge, which should ever be remembered in the annals of Dorset by reason of a most gallant and stirring episode. On February 27th, 1643, at this very bridge, a party of Royalists, under Captain Purton and his lieutenant, met a body of Roundheads numbering no fewer than 300—horse and foot. Captain Purton's force consisted only of twenty-five foot and twenty horse, but he nevertheless disputed the passage of the bridge and fought there for nearly five hours. By that time "the Captain and lieutenant were both shot, but they ordered their men to lay them on the brink of the bridge, where they encouraged the little band till, more of the King's forces coming to their assistance, the rebels fled, leaving forty dead and eight loads of hay and provisions. The Royalists had twelve wounded, but none killed : the lieutenant bled to death, encouraging his men with great cheerfulness." The spot where this sprightly soldier died has probably changed but little, for Holme Bridge was built early in the sixteenth century. Captain Purton and his lieutenant may well live in history with the "dauntless three" who held the bridge across the Tiber against the army of Lars Porsena.

CHAPTER XI

THE GREAT HEATH

THE Great Heath stretches from beyond Canford Magna and Poole in the East to within sight of Dorchester in the West. Northwards it comes near to Bere Regis, while towards the sea it extends to Winfrith and joins the heath land of the Isle of Purbeck. It has many names : " Gore Heath," " Decoy Heath," " Wool Heath," and the like, but it is, for all that, one wide unbroken sweep of moorland untrammelled by boundaries or divisions. This is the " Egdon Heath " made famous by Thomas Hardy as the scene of his tragic story, *The Return of the Native.*

The high-road from Wareham to Dorchester skirts he wild. It is one of the few level highways in the county, as well as one of the most delightful to travel. Another road to Dorchester crosses the moor to Bere Regis, and thence goes through more civilised country by way of Puddletown. Still a third road between the two towns keeps to the Heath all the journey through. It follows the Battery Bank, and, avoiding all haunts of men, comes at last to the small village of Tincleton. It is a lonely byway, rough enough, but is good in that it provides a view of some of the most picturesque parts of the Heath.

The river Puddle, or Pydel, crosses the moor boldly from North to South. The Frome, on the other hand, hesitates along its outskirts, and only now and then ventures into the savage country.

The Great Heath never lacks in interest. A week may well be spent in exploring its recesses and in visiting the villages which hang about its borders. The Roman road from Salisbury traverses its Western corner, while to the East is the long line of Celtic earthworks known as Battery Bank (page 70). Numerous barrows and tumuli are to be found scattered over the moor, some of the more prominent of which are the landmarks of the district. The huge isolated mound called Woolsbarrow is something more than a mere burial place. It is a natural hill, brown and bare, imperfectly fortified. On its gaunt summit are two or three starved trees which have been blown into rags and bones by the pitiless wind. The ramparts are irregular, except towards the West. It would seem as if the entrenching party had been surprised at their work, and had never come back to finish it. Of the purport of Woolsbarrow nothing is, I believe, known. I inquired about it of a countryman whom I met on the Heath, but he only committed himself to the opinion that it was "a fine lump o' dirt."

Among the most remarkable features of the Heath are certain deep hollows or pits, which are found about the centre of the great waste. The largest of these is Culpepper's Dish, near to Bryants Puddle. It stands high on the bare heath. The view from the plateau, at the end of which it is found, is remarkably beautiful. The "dish" takes the form of a conical pit of enormous proportions. The hollow in the ground is a perfect circle. The basin has smooth, symmetrical sides, lined with heather, while at the bottom of the steep-walled cavity is a little circle wherein a tree is growing. It can only be at high noon that the sun reaches the branches of this imprisoned thing. There is no way into nor out of the hollow, and no path down its slope. The dish might have been a monstrous die in which the cone of a volcano had been cast.

It has been conjectured that Culpepper's Dish was a semi-subterranean temple, or a place for burning bodies, or a cache for the hiding of stores. Local tradition is of no assistance, the archæology of the natives being limited to two propositions with regard to whatever is ancient, one being that it was made by the Romans, and the other that it was the work of "the monks and the friars." Culpepper's Dish they allot to the invaders from Rome. There is, however, no heaped-up earth around the pit, which is undoubtedly of purely natural origin.

A Road across the Heath.

The Great Heath, when surveyed as a whole, is a haphazard tract of sand covered with heather, bracken, and gorse, presenting highlands and lowlands, bald hills and dry, corroded glens. In some places life is so hard as to be nigh to starvation, while elsewhere are comfortable thickets of pines and firs, or green hollows where the rain has dribbled into pools. The largest of these ponds, the "Old Decoy Pond," is a patch of blue in the waste where wild ducks are tempted to rest for a while on their voyagings. Elsewhere the water has collected into sour swamps or shivering bogs.

The general aspect of the wild is morose and inhospitable, shrivelled with thirst, beaten and blown by the wind, and parched by the sun. It was into such a tract as this that the scapegoat was driven to wander until it died. It would seem as if a shadow rested on this homeless country, serving to make brighter the meadows and cornfields around it. As Thomas Hardy says, "The face of the heath by its mere complexion adds half an hour to evening : it can, in like manner, retard the dawn, sadden noon, anticipate the frowning of storms scarcely generated, and intensify the opacity of a moonless midnight to a cause of shaking and dread."

The tone of the moor is a russet-brown, splashed by the bracken with green and by the heather with purple. Under the summer sun marvellous colours appear, which break, as the clouds ride over, into infinite modulations. A far-away plateau may be Gobelin blue, and a near hillock bronze-brown. There may be here a bare slope of mushroom-coloured sand, and there a reedy marsh of parrot-green.

Beyond the burial mounds and the few buff roads which are hurrying across the waste, there is no sign of human interest on the Heath except this—one knoll, drab as a cinder-heap, stands up against the sky-line, and on its summit are three gaunt pines with outstretched arms, bared by the wind, which might be the three crosses on Calvary.

The Great Heath is a veritable part of that Britain the Celts knew, since upon its untameable surface twenty centuries have wrought no change. It is a primitive country still. The wheat, the orchard trees, and the garden flowers on its confines are products of civilisation, and are newcomers to the land. Here, still living, are the rough, hardy aborigines—the heather, the bracken, and the gorse—which settled on the heights when first they rose out of the sea.

Around the Heath are many interesting villages, which, by reason of their remoteness, are seldom visited. The most important of these is Bere Regis, notable on account of its

M

wonderful church.   Bere Regis was once the residence of
kings as well as a bustling market town.   It is now merely a
dull village adrift in a duller country.   Its long street, of
Quaker simplicity, has been at pains to strip itself bare of all
that is bright or picturesque.   Bere would seem to be enact-
ing a penance for its past frivolities, to have become a village
of sackcloth, and to have taken upon itself the vow of
silence.

In a field to the east of the church are trivial remains of a
building.   That building was the great manor house, and in
the bald field lies buried the tale of the town of Bere.   On
this spot Queen Elfrida owned a mansion whither she retired,
haunted and remorseful, after the murder of her stepson
Eadward at Corfe Castle.   That monarch of ill omen, King
John, had some kind of palace here, possibly a hunting box—
a Wessex Fontainebleau.   In the time of Henry III. the manor
was owned by Simon de Montfort, Earl of Leicester.   In
Henry the Eighth's reign it came to Robert Turberville, and in
the possession of the Turberville family Bere remained for
centuries.   It is to their manor house that the relics in the
field belong.   The first of the family was Sir Payne de
Turberville, who landed in England with William the Norman.
The latter end of the house is the theme of Thomas Hardy's
powerful novel, *Tess of the D'Urbervilles*, in which romance
Bere Regis figures as " Kingsbere."

The church is one of the most beautiful in the county.
Built of flint and stone, it possesses a handsome pinnacled
tower with exquisite belfry windows and canopied niches.   It
preserves evidences of many architectural periods, commencing
with Transitional Norman.   The Norman pillars in the south
arcade are noteworthy by reason of the humorous carvings
which some wag has graven on their capitals.   One figure aims
at displaying the horrors of toothache, while another represents
such humour as may be evolved from headache.   There is a
magnificent Norman font.   The pew ends show some bold

carvings, certain of which are of great antiquity. One, for instance, is dated 1547, while another is inscribed "IOH. DAV. WAR. DENOF. THYS. CHARYS." (John Day, warden of this church). There is a fine canopied tomb, stripped of its brasses, belonging to the Turbervilles, upon whose worn masonry falls the light from the Turberville window.

The glory of the church is its timber roof, which is gorgeous with the most elaborate carvings, with brilliant colours, and much gilt. Conspicuous among the rafters and the profuse ornament of the beams are twelve uncomfortable human figures, nearly life size, representing bishops, cardinals, and pilgrims, in the costumes of the time. These effigies are placed horizontally, like gargoyles, and project stiffly into the church with their faces turned downwards to the stone flags. They are gay with tints of red, blue, and yellow, and are so gaudy that they might be puppets from some Gargantuan toy shop.

Close to Bere is Woodbury Hill, crowned by ancient earth-works which take the form of a double rampart and fosse enclosing ten acres. Since the time of Henry III. a fair has been held on this hill, commencing on September 18th, near about the festival of the Nativity of the Blessed Virgin Mary. This fair was at one time the most important in the South of England, and merited the title of "the Nijni Novgorod of South Wessex." It lasted five days, which were thus divided: 1. Wholesale day. 2. Gentlefolk's day, given up largely to amusements, which included the eating of oysters and roast pork. 3. Allfolk's day. 4. Sheep fair day. 5. Pack-and-penny day, when unsold goods were disposed of cheaply. Although the fair yielded once £100 a day in tolls to the lord of the manor, it has now dwindled to an inconsiderable occasion which has long since ceased to dominate the markets of this part of the country.

Not far from Bere is a conspicuous Dorset landmark—the tower in Charborough Park. This tower—which at a distance

looks like a factory chimney—can be seen for miles. It was
built originally in 1796, was struck by lightning in 1839, and
unfortunately re-erected. It has been described as an example
of "the most distinctive and aggressive Strawberry Hill Gothic,"
and is mainly of present interest through its association with
Hardy's story of *Two on a Tower*. Charborough House
was the ancient seat of the Earles, who once held the manor
"by service of pouring water on the King's hands on Easter
or Christmas Day." In the unlovely church of Morden is a
monument to Thomas Earle—a solemn man kneeling in full
armour—who died in March, 1597. There are busts also of
two lads in costume, and of a girl with a ruffle about her neck.
These represent certain of his children, of whom the inscription
speaks as follows : "His sones wer 4 his daughters 2, of
whome John, Thomas and Dorithe ar desecid, and remayneth
now levynge Waltar, Christopher and Elizabeth."

A charming walk through Bere Wood leads from the Turbervilles' old town to Bloxworth, the daintiest hamlet on the fringe
of the Heath. The church is a perfect village church, a little
old building in grey, with a low, ivy-covered tower of sandstone.
The ancient wooden shutters to the belfry windows, bolted as
they are by immense bars of oak, are very remarkable. The
church has a Norman doorway, and appears to have been rebuilt in both the fourteenth and the seventeenth centuries. The
old manorial pew remains in all its exclusive glory, with its
venerable woodwork, its comfortable fireplace, and its memorials
to a long race of princely squires.

A notable possession of the church is a Jacobean hour-glass
and stand affixed to the pulpit. The stand is of wrought iron,
decked with the *fleur-de-lys*. The frame of the glass is of
roughly-cut wood, while the glass itself is in colour a faded
green. This timepiece ran for one hour, and calls to memory
the fact that, after the Reformation, preaching became obliga-
tory, while the hour-glass was an assurance that the worshippers
would not be robbed of their full due in the matter of exhorta-

tion. Unfortunately, the waist of the glass was broken some years ago, whereupon the glass-blower who repaired it closed the pipe between the two bulbs. The falling sand, which was watched with so much anxiety by generations of yawning yeomen and impatient lovers, has therefore ceased to run for ever.

A " Puddle" Village.

In the churchyard, near the tower, is a tombstone with this inscription :—

> " Here lyes that reverend orthodox divine
> Grave Mr. Welsteed, aged seventy nine.
> He was the painfull pastor of this place
> Fifty five years compleate, during which space
> None justly could his conversation wound
> Nor's doctrine taint, 'twas so sincere so sound.
> Thus having his long threed of life well spunne
> 'Twas cutt, November's tenth in fifty one.
> 1651."

A very famous rector of Bloxworth was John Morton, Cardinal Archbishop of Canterbury in the time of Henry VII. For a prelate, he led a most adventurous life, not without the usual episodes of imprisonment in the Tower and flight to

Flanders. He comforted Edward IV. when that King lay dying, and was the stoutest advocate of Henry's marriage with Elizabeth of York, whereby the red rose and the white became blended in the rose of Tudor. As Bishop of Ely he takes his part in Shakespeare's play of *Richard III.*, wherein occurs " the incident of the strawberries," thus described by Sir Thomas More, once a page in his household :—" And after a little talking with them, he (the Duke of Gloster) sayd vnto the Bishop of Elye : my lord, you haue very good strawberies at your gardayne in Holberne,[1] I require you let vs haue a messe of them. Gladly my lord, quod he, woulde God I had some better thing as redy to your pleasure as that." These are indeed ready words for a crafty plotter like the Bishop, who wished the Duke of Gloster to perdition, and who had no " better thing " in store for him—if he had his way—than the dungeon or the headsman's axe.

A clear, bright stream, libellously called the Puddle, runs, as already stated, across the Heath. On its way it gives to each of the many villages along its banks the unhappy cognomen of Puddle. The traveller who has crossed the Heath to Bloxworth and Bere may well return by the side of this rush-shaded river. Its course is marked by many trees, by many water-meadows, by endless flowers, so that it makes a path of generous green across a poor and famished country.

Tolpuddle, on the Bere to Dorchester highway, is a typical Dorset village of thatched cottages and gardens, very indulgent to ducks and geese. It takes its name from Thola, the wife of Orc, one of Canute's famous henchmen.

A pleasant lane leads thence to Affpuddle, an exquisite riverside hamlet, whose sleep has remained unbroken for the last hundred years or so. The old church stands by the river-side, in company with a mill whose water-wheel, if it splashed and moaned during service time, would drown the voice of the preacher. The shadow of the grey tower, with its battlements

[1] Still Ely Place, Holborn.

and pinnacles, falls across the thicket of reeds by the stream.
No more lovable village church than this is to be found in the
county. Its chancel is Early English, its font Norman, while
the richly-carved woodwork with which it is furnished dates
from the sixteenth century. On one seat, indeed, is the legend :
" Thes seatys were mayd in the yere of oure Lord God
MCCCCCXLVIII., the tyme of Thomas Lyllyngton, vicar of
thys cherch " ; the time, too, of Edward VI., and just one year

Affpuddle.

after the death of Henry VIII. The " seatys " used by yeomen
then are used by their descendants still. This little hamlet of
the past might well be the village of Alderburnham, of whose
church chimes William Barnes has sung—

> " They bells, that now do ring above
>   The young brides at church-door, O,
> Woonce rung to bless their mothers' love,
>   When they were brides avore, O.
> An' sons in tow'r do still ring on
> The merry peals o' fathers gone,
>   Noo mwore to sound,
>   Or hear ring round,
>   The bells ov Alderburnham."

In Hutchins's time life in this pleasant village was "extremely hard." There was much scrofula, as well as a prevalent fever, which he ascribes to the too early use of new cyder. In modern times the malady would probably be called typhoid fever, and be ascribed to imperfect sanitation.

Bryants Puddle receives its title from no less a personage than Brian de Turberville, who was lord of the manor in the time of Edward III. It is now only a very rudimentary, very pretty

Turners Puddle.

hamlet, which may certainly claim to be situated in what city folk call "the real country."

At Turners, or Toners, Puddle is a small church, simple and pathetically plain, standing by the river's edge at a bend where the stream widens into a rush-bordered pool. By the side of the childlike church is a lonely rectory, as unpretentious and as rustic. The houses of the hamlet have shrunk away from these two, as if in respect for their venerable companionship.

Quite to the west of the Heath is Woodsford Castle, one of the oldest inhabited buildings in England, since the most ancient part of it was erected in the reign of Edward III.

There is little of the castle now about this long, rambling,
thatch-roofed building, with its drab stone chimneys, its
broken off walls, and its bricked-up windows. Yet it was a
strong place enough when the Beletts, the de Bryans, and the
Staffords held it. It has changed owners but seldom since
Domesday time, for the Strangeways have been the Wardens of
the castle for the last 300 years. It is now an unkempt farmhouse, a place of three stories and many doors, with few of its
mullioned windows in a line, with here a Gothic light to recall
a chapel and there a mighty buttress hiding a turret stair to give
it claim to be a castle. The creepers which cover its great
walls make its greyness more pallid, while the fowls which strut
in and out of its arched doorway, where pikemen stalked on
guard, make its humiliation more abject.

At one time it was a square stone building, with a tower at
each corner crowned by machicolated parapets. There are still
in the farmhouse walls—5½ feet thick—arrow slits, vaulted
rooms, a chapel with a piscina, a haunted chamber, and a
kitchen with a fireplace 14 feet in span. There is a beacon
tower too, where stood the grate for the beacon fire, which
same, no doubt, lit raiders home across the stream or warned
the neighbours that there was trouble on the Heath.
Woodsford has indeed seen mighty changes. It once stood
like an alert warrior, with head erect, watching the passage of
the ford. Now the sentry has sunk to a bent and aged man
who squats by the river, whose helmet has been replaced by a
cotton nightcap, and whose rusty sword is a plaything for the
children.

On that high-road from Wareham to Dorchester which skirts
the south of the Heath are the ruins of Bindon Abbey. The
Abbey is in a wood by the river—a dank, melancholy wood, full
of shadows. All that remains of the holy house is an outline
of its chief parts, a ground plan made up of walls five to six
feet high, bases of pillars, indications of doorways and of
windows, all so covered with ivy and moss as to have become a

part of the green shades of the thicket. There are still
sombre walks among the trees, straight and stiff, that have been
tramped hard by centuries of meditative feet. When the wind
howls through the bare trees in winter this monks' walk
might be a ghostly path in Purgatory. In the summer the way
is dim, or dappled only by a few flecks of uninvited sun. Around
the Abbey in the wood are the monks' fish-ponds. They are
dark pools, so cowled with shade that the water is of mahogany
colour, and upon its unrippled surface the reflection of the
green bank is almost spectral. Here and there the sun,
dripping through the trees, makes spots of gold on the bottom
of the shallow pond and brings to light the dead leaves of
a century.

Bindon Abbey was founded for Cistercians in 1172 by
Roger de Newburgh and Matilda his wife. The place was
called Great Bindon, because the Abbey was first begun at
Little Bindon, on the east side of Lulworth Cove. In a cottage
at that spot there is still a Gothic window and a coved ceiling,
the sole remains of the humble church of the original Abbey.
The Abbey at Great Bindon fared well. Kings were gracious
to it, and many gave grants of land to the Abbot for the
health of their souls. The last Abbot surrendered to the
King in 1539. In 1664 the larger part of the Abbey was
burnt down. In 1750 the Great Gate fell.

An interesting relic of Bindon Abbey still survives in the
form of an altar-cloth possessed by the church at Wool. It is
now deposited in the Dorchester Museum. The cloth appears
to have been made from a cope, and to date from the fifteenth
century. It is a quaint and archaic piece of needlework, de-
picting the Twelve Apostles on a background of brown velvet.
There is little doubt that it played a part in the religious
processions at Bindon, and was much admired by the gaping
crowd. It is admirable still, although more than four hundred
years have passed since devout women with eager needles and
pious chatter bent over this very piece of dun velvet.

Near to Bindon Abbey is Wool, known to thousands as the station for Lulworth. It was once a pretty village enough, but the railway has contaminated it. Here by the river's brink and by an ancient grey stone bridge is the well-preserved Jacobean manor house of the Turbervilles, familiar to the tourist by reason of the place it holds in the story of *Tess of the D'Urbervilles*.

Farther along the highway is Ower Moigne, a shy, old-fashioned hamlet, "highly suspicioned" of smuggling in the days when the Free Traders hid their "stuff" in church towers ; of which fact the vicar was rendered only obscurely conscious by the appearance of a mystic keg of excellent brandy in the vicarage porch. Ower Moigne is now one of those many hamlets which have no apparent object in life.

The manor of Owers was long held by the Moygnes—hence the name of the place—and later by the Stourtons. The old Court, much modernised, still stands to the north of the hamlet, and can show even now some masonry which was chiselled in A.D. 1200. It was once moated and well supplied with loop-holes for arrows. The estate at one period of its history came to the Crown in the following manner. On a lamentable day in January, 1557, Charles, Lord Stourton, who then possessed the manor, invited to the Court one Hartgill and his son.

The neighbours rejoiced over this, for the Stourtons and the Hartgills had been long at variance. The two families, how-ever, had happily become reconciled, and the invitation to the great house was to seal the newly-established friendship. The Hartgills, as it came to pass, were not long to enjoy the hospi-tality of the lord of Ower Moigne. Some little while after their arrival, possibly at the end of their first jovial dinner, Lord Stourton "caused them to be knocked down with clubs." He then directed his servants to cut the throats of his uncon-scious guests, which they did. The night following this event at the Court was extremely busy, for his lordship and his men were occupied in the cellar digging a hole fifteen feet deep. At the bottom of this pit they deposited the Hartgills, father and son, replaced the casks, refreshed themselves no doubt, and then sank to sleep, breakfastless, on benches.

Murder, however, will out, even when buried fifteen feet deep, so on March 16th Lord Stourton and four of those servants who had been so active with clubs and spades were hanged at Salisbury. His lordship, when under sentence, pleaded for some indulgence from Queen Mary. The only indulgence she granted him was permission to be hanged by a halter of silk, " in respect of his quality." Thus it was that the ancient estate came to the Crown.

CHAPTER XII

THE ISLE OF PURBECK

THE Isle of Purbeck is no more an island than is the Isle of Thanet, nor was there ever a time when it was wholly cut off by water. The sea bounds it upon the South as well as by the East. On the North is the River Frome, but Westwards there is only the Luckford Lake. The "Lake" is a tiny stream which creeps out of the hills near Lulworth Castle, to end its timid career in the Frome above Holme Bridge. A schoolboy could jump across the "Lake," so that its pretence to form a channel between an island and a mainland is a mere matter of make-believe.

A view over the whole of the apocryphal island can be obtained from the summit of Creech Barrow. This is a graceful, isolated, cone-shaped hill near Wareham, so like in shape to a volcano that when the light-hearted tripper sets fire to the gorse and bracken which cover its sides the belief that there is a Vesuvius in Purbeck could gain ground. On the summit of the hill are the foundations of a watch tower which in the sixteenth century was tenanted by the Keeper of the Deer. The fine turf around the hunters' lodge is richly carved with the initials of tourists. This curious distemper which compels certain folk to cut their names upon altar tombs, Jacobean pulpits, and castle doors must be a survival of that impulse which urged their ancestors, the cave men, to carve figures upon horn and stone. From the summit of the hill is a view of the Purbeck Downs, from Ballard Head to Lulworth, while over their broad, smooth backs glitters the blue of the Channel. Due east too are the Needles and the Isle of Wight. In the same quarter are the Poole estuary, the cliffs and crude villas of Bournemouth, and beyond, drawn in faint grey, the Priory of Christchurch by the sea. To the North, among the generous

Corfe Castle from the Swanage Road.

green of water-meadows, a patch of deep red marks the roofs of Wareham and an unsteady line of silver the River Frome. Far away is the Great Heath, sombre and dull, while on the horizon, like the uplands of a phantom country, loom the heights of Salisbury Plain.

Of the two towns of Purbeck, Corfe and Swanage, nothing is to be seen from Creech Barrow. Corfe Castle—on the high-road between Wareham and the sea—is the most interesting place in this traditional isle. The village is ancient and grey, a dim, mumbling place of tales and gossip. It has

changed but little in the last century or so, and has remained
unspoiled, although the canker of red brick has begun to gnaw
at its vitals.   It is a wrinkled old place in the winter of its
age, lying at the foot of its Castle like a faithful hound.   Its
three little streets lead humbly to the Castle gate.   The keep
rises high above the village, and looks down upon it as a sacred
image would regard an adoring worshipper.   The small town
has ever been dependent upon the Castle, and is dependent
on it still, for it brings to the place hungry tourists in char-a-
bancs, with their holiday money in their pockets.

The quiet, ever cool-looking, ever beautiful village of Corfe
is all of one colour—a symphony in grey.   If ever it boasted
brighter hues, they have long since faded to one sober, ashen
tint.   It is a village of drab stone.   The houses, all old, are
for the most part low.   The roofs of crumpled slabs are
broken up by dormer windows, at which white curtains will be
fluttering, or are crowned by chimneys of dun brick.   Here
and there is a stone porch with a little chamber over, whose
diamond panes look up and down the street.   Even the
humblest cottage may boast a strong buttress or an ancient
outhouse of good masonry.   Stone-mullioned windows are
common, while gables and flagged courts have never been
démodé in Corfe.   Opposite to the village cross is the Town
House, with an especially fine bow window of many panes,
capped by a roof of rugged stone.   The inn has a porch with
a small room over it, like a miniature house.   This chamber is
held up, with no little dignity, by three stone pillars, which have
in their time afforded comforting support to the backs of many
carters while they drank their cyder.

There is every phase of grey in Corfe, although the monotony
of the colour never lacks relief.   Ivy, or some warm, homely
creeper covers the cold walls; white railings, a clump of
hollyhocks or of fuchsias take away the primness from the
door ; there will be jessamine over the porch, dark green moss
on the roof, and a tuft of yellow flowers growing in every

hospitable cranny. In gentlest contrast of all will be the soft cheek of many a blushing rose laid against the worn ashen stone. Near the north entrance of Corfe are the picturesque remains of an old building, once the residence of the Uvedales, while on the Swanage road is an E-shaped, gabled house, with a paved court full of flowers, which was at one time the manor house of the Daccombes.

The little town has had numerous vicissitudes. It was once a self-contained place with considerable resources, as a return made in 1796 serves to show. At that time Corfe could boast of two persons "of independent fortune," of eighteen farmers and sixteen shoemakers, of three breeches-makers, of a barber, a mole-catcher, a surgeon, a furze-cutter, and a hurdler, besides blacksmiths, painters, carpenters, and thatchers.

Curious people seem to have wandered in those days into Corfe, where they were hospitably treated by the Mayor and Corporation. Of such the town records show entries after this fashion :—

"1662. Gave two travellers, by the Mayor's order, 2d."

"1673. Gave to a traveller that came from Norfolk, 6d."

It will be noticed that the extreme remoteness of Norfolk demanded the addition of fourpence to the ordinary dole. Women, soldiers, and sailors were very kindly dealt with by the town of Corfe, as the subjoined make evident :—

"1668. Gave to a woman whose husband was in slavery, 6d."

"1686. Gave two seamen that were drove ashore at Chapman's Pool, two Shillings."

"1786. Paid to a Soldier that had one arm, one Shilling."

Foreigners also in doleful plight found their way into this out-of-the-way town, as the following will testify :—

"1682. Gave to 5 Dutchmen, by the Mayor's order, 2s. 6d."

"1686. Gave 10 Frenchmen 3s. 6d., which they spent at the George."

" 1786.   Gave to 3 Turks, by the Mayor's order, 1 shilling."

" 1786. Gave to an American, by the Mayor's order, 1 shilling."

Even sadder derelicts drifted into the pale town. In the church register there is this entry : —

" 1722. A strange woman was buried in woollen."

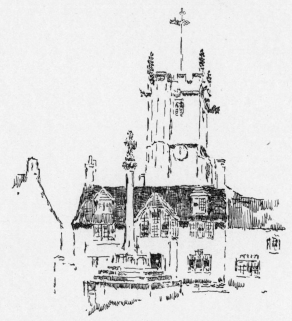

Corfe Castle: the Cross, the Town House, and the Church.

One would like to know the story of the strange woman, and how it happened that, with so many on the road, she came to the town alone and died there nameless and unknown.

Hutchins, writing at the end of the eighteenth century, describes the people of Corfe as of "supine disposition," as well as with "a propensity to idleness."   He goes on to say

N

that " the appearance of misery in the town is only too
striking." Yet the morality of Corfe seems to have been high.
The records of the " Court Peculiar" of Corfe Castle show
that the churchwardens once " presented " John Pushman,
Anthony Vye, and James Turner, for playing in the churchyard
upon the Sabbath day. At another time they " presented "
John Rawles for being drunk on the Sabbath, while on a
further occasion they charged James Turner and George Gover
with being " drinky " during the time of Divine service. It will
be noticed that the acute moral perception of the churchwardens enabled them to distinguish between offenders who
were vulgarly drunk and others who were merely " drinky."

The twentieth century Corfe is cheerful and prosperous,
and still sternly opposed to both the drunk and the " drinky."

The glory of Corfe is the ancient Castle, now a picturesque
ruin. Its position is most imposing. The Purbeck hills run
from east to west across the isle in the form of a long rampart
of smooth grass downs. In a sudden abrupt gap, or gate,
in this Titanic barricade stands the Castle upon the summit
of a precipitous mound. It rears itself against the light—a grim,
menacing figure, the guard of the pass, the silent sentry in the
breach. Beyond the breastwork of hills is the sea, and
here, in the only passage for escape, the Castle strides across
the highway.

The most impressive view of Corfe is to be obtained from
the other side of the downs—the side towards the Channel—
from the village of Kingston, for example, about the time of
sunset. Here to the south of the long hill is a plain, genial
and green, shut in like a garden. In the one savage gap in the
boundary wall are the tall Castle and dim houses of Corfe.
Through the breach and over the jagged towers can be seen the
country beyond—the hinterland. It is a land that is all dark,
a blackened heath bordering a dead pool, for so the estuary
looks when the light is failing. Here is a scene from Bunyan's
Pilgrim's Progress. Here is just such a murky country as

Christian looked back upon, with its pathless moor, its Slough of Despond, its ghostly Castle.

The story of Corfe Castle has been many times told, and needs but be lightly touched upon here.   Before the Normans came there was merely a hunting lodge on the guardian hill. A wall yet standing among the ruins—a curtain with rude herring-bone work, near the Buttavant Tower—may have been a part of this unpretentious house.   Here dwelt in 978, with her son Aethelred, the lovely Elfrida of Devon, widow of King Edgar.   Eadward, a son of Edgar by a former wife, was then King of England.   He was still a mere lad.   In this particular year 978 the young King was hunting in the forest about Corfe, and, becoming separated from his followers, and very weary, he bethought him of the hunting lodge and of the drinking of a cup of wine there.   It was " at eventide," so the chronicle says, that he reached Corfe.   Elfrida the Beautiful met him at the gate breathlessly, for there was a lurid vision in the depths of her soft blue eyes—a vision of the lad dead and her own son Aethelred King of the English.   She gave him a goblet, so the story runs, and as he drank the smile left her lips, the white hand that had fumbled in her bosom was raised aloft, and with a cry of terror she stabbed the rider in the back.   The goblet clattered on the stones, the frightened horse leapt down the hill, and at its foot, where the stream still runs, the King dropped from the saddle dead.

The body was found, and by Elfrida's orders was dragged into a cottage near by and covered over with " mean cloaths." The woman of the cottage was poor and blind, and, as it was now night, she was left alone with the terrible heap of " mean cloaths " on the floor.   She sat and watched by the dead. Before morning dawned a wonder happened : the squalid room became filled with a silvery light, which even broke through the shuttered casement on to the black road; sight came back to the sightless eyes, a glow as from the moon illumined the paltry

details of cupboard and shelf, and the watcher knew that
beneath the poor rags lay the body of the King.

It has already been told how the corpse of King Eadward

Corfe from the Castle Gate.

the Martyr was carried in time to Wareham, and later to the
hill town of Shaftesbury (pages 2 and 154). The church
of Corfe dedicated to the murdered King stands nigh to the
spot where the cottage was.

At what date the present Castle was built is unknown.

Certain it is that there was a strong keep here in Stephen's time, which was held by Baldwin de Redvers for the Empress Matilda and was besieged by the King in vain. In the time of John it was not only a royal castle, but also a royal treasure house and a state prison. King John blighted the place by his esteem, filled its dungeons with the unhappy, and kept here not only his miserable money-bags, but his crown. What malignant hate and fiendish cruelty could do was done within the walls of Corfe. Those prisoners were fortunate who were merely starved to death in a windowless pit, and were so spared a glimpse of the sun on the open heath and of the blue sea hurrying across the sands into Poole haven.

One of King John's most interesting captives was Eleanor, the Damsel of Brittany. She and her brother Arthur had substantial claims to the throne, so Arthur was done to death and the Damsel came a prisoner to Corfe. She was confined for many years in the Castle, and was removed later to Bristol, where the poor soul died after an imprisonment of forty years. It would appear from the "Close Rolls" that the Damsel was liberally treated while at Corfe Castle. In 1213 there was ordered for her a tunic and supertunic of dark green, one good cap of dark brown, furred with minever, one hood for rainy weather, and also a saddle with gilded reins. It is evident from the last two entries that the Princess Eleanor had some degree of liberty. "Moreover, once when the Damsel was ill, a doctor—Master J. de Beauchamp—was sent all the way from London to attend her. He was paid three marks—about £2—but this was partly in compensation for his horse, which died on the journey back."[1]

During the Civil War, when most of the strong places of Dorset were held by the Parliament, Corfe Castle remained loyal to the King. At this time it was in the possession of Sir John Bankes, who was away with Charles at York when, on a certain day in 1643, Sir Walter Erle, the Parliamentary

[1] *Old Dorset.* By J. H. Moule. London, 1893. Page 175.

leader, laid siege to the place. The Castle in Sir John's absence
was held by Lady Bankes, who had retired to Corfe with her
children, her men-servants, and her maids, before her husband
took his journey to the North. Upon the many stirring incidents of this memorable siege it is unnecessary to dwell. The
brave and ingenious woman, although encompassed on all
sides, although attacked by "a demy cannon, a culverin, two
sakers," and other ordnance, both from the church tower
and the adjacent hills, never yielded an inch. Her little
garrison of maids, footmen, and house servants was threatened,
coaxed, and tempted, but Sir Walter and his captains piped to
deaf ears. From the seneschal to the scullery-maid they remained true to their gallant mistress. Every engine then known
to the art of war was brought against Corfe, every military
expedient was tried, but the stout Castle walls and the tireless,
courageous woman defied them all. The last enterprise of the
besiegers was the most curious of any. Some hundred and
fifty mariners were brought from Poole to Corfe, attracted by
the assurance that £20 would be given to the first man who
scaled the walls. As a further security for success, the com-
placent mariners were made, if not drunk, at least, in the language of Corfe, "drinky." Under the influence of some firkins
of "hot waters" they girded themselves for the task. It must
have been a fantastic spectacle to behold—the creeping, reeling
crowd, hiccoughing under the burden of scaling ladders, baskets
of petards, and bags of grenadoes, ruddy with vinous valour and
occasionally bursting forth into song or into the fulminating
blasphemy of the forecastle. Now, the green slope leading to
the Castle walls is very steep as well as very slippery. It is
hard even for a sober man to climb, to say nothing of a man
who is both "drinky" and encumbered by implements of
war. The alcoholic host advanced, and possibly reached the
foot of the wall, but the kitchen-maid who was in command of
the Plunkenet Tower met the essay by pouring down upon
the panting mob buckets of hot ashes. Now, a glowing

ember dropped down the neck between the skin and the shirt is no thing to meditate upon. The accident is best healed by sliding incontinently down the slope into the wet ditch. This the mariners did. At the Gloriette Bastion the gardener would be in charge, who would hurl down stones and rocks of great weight, while possibly her ladyship's maid, with white lips, would scatter a few gunpowder bombs gingerly among the swollen-faced crowd. Anyhow, the attempt spluttered out like an over-fed candle. The mariners were glad enough to crawl back to the shelter of the church, where they could tend their cut heads and broken shins, and boast of the havoc they would have wrought had it not have been for the hot cinders or the fifty pound lump of stone. On that very night—a night in August—the siege, which had commenced in May, was abandoned, and the sturdy lady and her women had leisure to make merry over reminiscences of red coals, boiling oil, and squealing men.

A second siege, of a less romantic type, ended, in February, 1645, in the capture of the Castle, not by force of arms, but by the base treachery of an officer of the garrison. In the following month a vote was passed in the House of Commons to "slight" the indomitable Castle of Corfe. This order was carried out with no delay, but with some difficulty, for the fortress was not a place to be easily levelled with the ground. It was, however, reduced to ruins. As it was left by the wreckers in 1645, so is it now.

The Castle is still magnificent. Its masonry, in spite of mining and blasting, has proved to be almost indestructible. It is easy to follow the details of the fortress by the aid of the plan drawn in 1586 by Ralph Tresswell, Sir Charles Hatton's steward. From afar off the defiant keep looks like a white, wind-worn, storm-splintered crag on a mountain peak. The gate leading to the outer ward is reached by a bridge over the moat; grass covers the parapet where once tramped the alert guard, while one tower of the gate is cleft by a fracture like the

Corfe Castle.

crack in a skull from a battle-axe. The great walls around the
Castle still stand, with their line of towers or barbicans. There
is still the embrasure with its arrow slit, through which so many

eager eyes have peered, and the low stone coping, made smooth by the rubbing of leather-covered shoulders and bent backs. The Gloriette Bastion has gone, but the Buttavant and Plunkenet Towers even now look defiantly down the pass.

A long path leads up hill across the outer ward to the inner gateway. How many poor souls have toiled up this road on their way to the dungeons by the northern wall! This up-hill path is a veritable Via Dolorosa, the last steep step on a weary road. Behind them as they went were the free downs and the open sea ; in front, death by torture or starvation ; on either side hideous towers and grinning men. Now and then they would have caught a glimpse of a woman's kind face among the crowd, with pity in her eyes and the words " God help you ! " on her lips.

The keep, tall, stiff, and imperious, crowns the fortress. Its gigantic walls are planted upon a mass of rock. Its faded pinnacles have for a background only the blue sky and the white clouds. In the base of the King's Tower are small chambers and vaulted ways which give a vivid idea of the Castle as it was. High up towards the heavens are windows, doorways, and passages laid bare by the ruin, and accessible only to birds. No human being has passed through these entries or gazed from the windows since the scared inmates fled before the tramp on the stair, or since the looters hurried through the emptied corridors. High up on the wall is a fragment of a winding staircase open to the sky. He who trod it last trod it 260 years ago. There is a great fireplace near the windy parapet, like a niche in a sheer cliff, which may yet contain the ashes of the last fire that Lady Bankes's maids lit in it. The Buttavant Tower, the Queen's Hall, and the Chapel, reached through a maze of ruins like tumbled rocks at a cliff's foot, are well to see.

We may now leave Corfe and go southwards. Mention has been made of Kingston, a village near Corfe. It is a pleasant place, lying in a dip on the summit of a hill. The fine tower of its modern church—built in 1880—is one of the landmarks of the Isle of Purbeck. There is in the village an older church, as simple and commonplace as the other is sumptuous and imposing. In this meagre building will be found memorials to John, first Earl of Eldon, and to his wife Elizabeth, Countess of Eldon. These very high sounding titles cover the remains of two very simple folk—John Scott, a poor lad who made his way in the world, and Bessie Surtees, his humble sweetheart. The romance of the lives of these two is of an old-fashioned type. John Scott was born in Love Lane, Newcastle, in June, 1751, of "obscure but respectable parents." When he was twenty-one years old and still very poor he ran away with Bessie Surtees and married her. At the time this rash act nearly ruined him, but it proved in the end to be a fortunate step, for his lifelong and pathetic devotion to his "Bessie" atoned for many defects in his character. He took to the law, and by his stupendous abilities raised himself to the position of Lord Chancellor. Thus Bessie's needy lover became an Earl, and left behind him a fortune of over half a million pounds. He purchased the estate at Kingston, where, at the age of eighty-seven, he died, and side by side in the now empty church the daring lad and his trusting Bessie rest together.

Quite near to Corfe also is Barneston Manor, now a farmhouse in a roadside orchard. It derives its name from a Saxon thane named Bern, who held the manor at the time of the Conquest. The little old homestead provides an example of the domestic architecture of the thirteenth century. A window in the north gable of the house was fashioned at a time when glass was not used in casements. The open windows then were closed in bad weather by shutters, and at Barneston the bolt holes for such shutters are still to be seen in the stone.[1] In the front of the house is a fine stone-mullioned bay window of the Tudor period, with no fewer than

---

[1] *Proceedings of the Dorset Field Club.* Vol. XXII., page 60.

sixteen lights filled with diamond panes in both the upper and the lower sections.

The largest town in Purbeck is Swanage, a very popular seaside resort, on the margin of a blue water bay and under shelter of the great white cliffs of Ballard Head.   All around the town are stone quarries, for from time immemorial Swanage

Swanage.

has been the centre of the stone trade of the Isle of Purbeck. There can hardly be a cathedral in the South of England, or a self-respecting church, castle, or manor house, that owes not some beauty in mason's work to " Purbeck marble " shipped from Swanage.   The place therefore has always been well-to-do.   Hutchins, in his time, was struck by "an appearance of affluence, especially on Sundays, in the inhabitants of this town."   There was, and possibly still is, a very ancient Company of Stone-cutters here.   The manner in which the elders of the company admitted the apprentices was both simple and convivial. "At the annual meeting," says the record, "the apprentices take up their freedom. They appear in court with a penny loaf in one hand and a pot of beer in another, and upon paying 6s. 8d. their names are entered in the register."

In Domesday Book the town was called Swanwic, which name it long retained, for in the reign of Henry II. it is recorded that "the men of Roger de Poles of Swanwich answered half a mark for seising wronfully a great or royal fish." Swanage, as I knew it some thirty-five years ago, was a queer little town with a rambling High Street and a jumble of picturesque cottages of Purbeck stone, whose rough roofs were much given to gable ends and dormer windows. In those days it could still claim to be the "quaint, old-world village" that Charles Kingsley loved. Now it is the scene of a feverish struggle between rival builders, who fight to cover the land with copious red brick in as little time as possible. What can be done to spoil a character-istic village the founders of Swanage the Up-to-Date have done. The curve of the sandy bay is swept by a long brick coal-shed, and is palisaded by the unlovely backs of unashamed houses. It only needs a gasometer on the beach to complete the sorry *renaissance*. Old Swanage has gone; the features which made it unique among the Southern sea towns have been swept away, so that in a few more years it will be indistinguishable from the host of "developed" red-brick coast resorts on the shores of England. Its stretch of sand, its blue bay, its rolling downs, and its healthy site are still happily left to it.

Swanage devotes itself body and soul to a hearty multitude called by the townfolk "the steamer people" and by the less tolerant "the trippers." They come to old Leland's "fishar towne" in their thousands, so that in August the beach is as "jolly" and as "ripping" as Hampstead Heath in holiday time. Probably none in these islands deserve a holiday more thoroughly than do the "steamer people," for when they are not "tripping" they are busy with every kind of useful work. None enjoy a holiday so well. If they are a little over-exuberant, a little destructive and untidy, and if they have caused the land to be planted with notices that "Trespassers will be Prose-cuted," their untrammelled enjoyment must excuse much.

For the delectation of the steamer people Swanage has made most liberal provision. On the cliff's edge is Durlston Castle, a stronghold of the Bank Holiday period, in which are combined the architectural features of a refreshment buffet, a tram terminus, and a Norman keep. Close to this is Tilly Whim, reputed to be a smugglers' cave, but in plain fact a disused quarry. It is approached by a dark, sloping tunnel, in the descent of which the women scream, while the men support them copiously. Every available surface in this smugglers' haunt is carved with the names or initials of steamer people, while the ground is littered with their bottles, their egg-shells, and their paper bags. The enterprising developer of the estate about Tilly Whim has a fine literary taste. He has named every stone seat after some famous poet, and has engraved in many places improving sentiments upon slabs of local marble. Thus, in one spot he implores the steamer people to "Look round, and read Great Nature's open Book," while in the cave, where the quarrymen fashioned kitchen sinks, he breaks out into Shakespeare in the following depressing strain :—

> " The cloud-capp'd towers, the gorgeous palaces,
> The solemn temples, the great globe itself,
> Yea, all which it inherit, shall dissolve ;
> And, like the baseless fabric of a vision,
> Leave not a rack behind."

Certain unwonted features in Swanage are due to the circumstance that two quarrymen of the town, by their industry and talents, raised themselves to the position of great paving contractors in London. They were ever mindful of their native village, and showed their tender regard by bestowing upon the place a few of the miscellaneous oddments which must find their way into a great contractor's yard. Thus along certain roads about the town will be found iron street posts inscribed, " St. Anne's, Soho," and " St. Martin's-in-the-fields." In the

High Street is the entire stone façade of the Mercers' Hall, Cheapside, moved bodily to Swanage in 1882, balcony, doorway, puffy cherubs holding garlands, and all. This piece of the veneer of London has an odd effect in the "fishar towne." By the brink of the sea is an elegant Gothic clock-tower, very finicking, dandified, and townish. It came from London Bridge, where it had been erected—at the cost of many pounds —as a memorial to the great Duke of Wellington. As it was obstructive to certain improvements, it was handed over to the contractor, who, true to early memories, sent it to his beloved Swanage. Amongst other litter in the London contractor's yard there would seem to have been some cannon-balls. The faithful paviour evidently had some difficulty in working these in for the adornment of his birthplace. Cannon balls suggest battle, but there had been no battle at Swanage. King Alfred, however, is supposed to have defeated the Danes in Swanage Bay in the year of our Lord 877. Naturally enough, the contractor erected a pillar on the Marine Parade to commemorate this proud if dim event, and placed the cannon-balls on top of it. To some these missiles may appear inappropriate, as gunpowder was not invented until more than 400 years after the assumed engagement.

There are just a few relics of old Swanage left to show how charming a place it was before the red villas and the rows of featureless lodging-houses swept down upon it. In lanes about the church are old drab houses with picturesque backs, dormer windows, and most ample roofs. There is a mill-pond, moreover, closed by low walls and reached by a slope of wide steps. The cottages around this Pool of Siloam are a part of Kingsley's "quaint, old-world village." There is a stone prison, too, no larger than a bathing-machine, with a very ancient door, studded by iron knobs. Between the door and the roof of coarse tiles is this inscription : "Erected for the prevention of Vice and Immorality by the Friends of Religion and Good Order, A.D. 1803."

There are two ancient farmhouses near Swanage—Godling-stone and Whitecliff—which are worth seeing. Newton Manor House is here also. It was once owned by the jovial family of Cochrams. Their habits may be gathered from the fact that when the foundations of the house were recently disturbed in the course of building a new drawing-room " some

The Road to Studland.

scores of old squat Dutch gin bottles " were brought to light.

A very pleasant path across Ballard Down leads from Swanage to the beautiful village of Studland. This quiet little place lies on a flat where the chalk cliffs end and the sand dunes of the Poole inlet commence. It is a medley of country lanes, lost among trees, with a few thatch-roofed cottages dotted about in a wild garden of brambles, ferns, and gorse. There is nothing methodical or regular about Studland. There is no definite hamlet, no village street, no centre, no beginning, and no end. It is merely a casual, unarranged sample of rural Dorset brought, in all its luxuriant greenness, to the very water's edge. In the maze of this shady oasis are, besides cottages, an exquisite Norman church, orchards and gardens, and cows in fields. There is no "sea front" to Studland, no pretence to a quay. Blackberry bushes and bracken come boldly to the astonished beach, but the brown, creeper-covered cottages hide snugly away in the thicket. Studland indeed declines to be maritime. It turns its face from the sea to bury it among its myrtles and fuchsia bushes.

The strand at Studland is a pretty compendium of seaside scenery on a miniature scale. It has no real cliff, but merely a sandy bank covered with bushes—a hummocky slope colonised by many rabbits. In the centre of this would-be cliff is a reddish-yellow headland which divides the beach into two tiny bays. It is a bright, gallant promontory, although a softish boy would come to small harm if he fell from the summit of it. Where the bank gives out the very fields and woods are in touch with the wavy line of sea-weed cast up by the last spring tide. To the East are sand dunes, with tufts of rustling grass, heather in blossom, a reedy mere, a long sickle-shaped sweep of fawn-coloured sand. To the West are steep chalk cliffs and rounded downs, while inland is that outpost of the Great Heath which has here crept to the brink of the Channel.

There are two roads to the sea at Studland, both very rough. One, after stumbling and staggering through the sand and furze bushes, ends on a plateau of grass which fringes the beach. The other winds through a wooded glen, so full of shade as to be a very cloister of leaves. The sky is shut out by the over-lacing boughs, while at the end of the green tunnel is a disc of blue sea such as one may glimpse from the porthole of a ship.

Sad to say, Studland is by no means an unsophisticated village. Any simplicity it may present is rather on the surface.

A crowd of char-a-bancs and wagonettes will crowd its lanes in the summer, a thousand initials will be found carved upon its sandstone cape, while an ample refreshment room permits the tourist to have tea " at separate tables " on the beach. The red brick epidemic, moreover, has seized upon it mercilessly.

The beautiful Norman church is happily unspoiled, and is alone worth a visit to Dorset to see.   It is a small, sturdy,

Studland.

wizened church, altered but slightly since the Normans left it. Built in or about 1180, it is dedicated, as may be imagined, to the patron saint of sailors.   The archaic font, shaped like a bread-pan, is coeval with the church.   To it have been brought squealing Norman babies who lived to adore Richard the Lion, babies who served under the Plantagenets, the Lancastrians, the Yorkists, the Tudors, and the Stuarts, as well as the babies of twentieth century stockbrokers whose wives were staying for a while in Studland.   The church, with its quaint pack-saddle roof and grotesque corbel heads, is one of the most

o

interesting village sanctuaries in England, as well as one of the most perfect.

In the beautiful churchyard there sleeps at least one restless soul, for here was buried, in 1869, Sergeant William Lawrence, of the 40th Regiment of Foot. He served in the war in South America in 1805, as well as through the whole of the Peninsular War from 1808 to 1813. He was engaged in the battles of Rolica, Vimiera, Talavera, Ciudad Rodrigo, and Vittoria. He was one of the volunteers for the forlorn hope in the assault on Badajos, where he was most severely wounded. Finally, the gallant soldier fought on the field of Waterloo. During the occupation of Paris by the Allied Armies William Lawrence found leisure to marry Clotilde Clairet, of Germain-en-Laye. After all this turmoil he and his French wife retired to the silent shades of Studland. Here Clotilde, hugging memories of Paris, died in 1853, sixteen years before her sturdy husband. There are elderly people in Studland now who well remember the hero of Badajos.

CHAPTER XIII

A STRETCH OF THE COAST

I DOUBT if there be around England a more picturesque stretch of coast, for its length, than that which borders the sea from Swanage to Weymouth. Certainly there is no shore which presents so many contrasts and variations in so few pleasant miles. In this sea line are cliffs of jagged rocks, sheer as a bastion wall, as well as green lawns which creep lazily to the water's edge. There are wide, open bays, and fissured sea-echoing chines. There are round coves, inlets reached through arched rocks, level sands, and moaning caves. There are beaches of shingle, of pebbles, of colossal boulders, and of the clay of crumbling banks ; precipices of every colour, from the white of chalk to the black of the shale ; and walls of stone streaked with tints of yellow, buff, or red.

After leaving Swanage the coast is drab and savage, the cliffs erect or scooped out in places by quarries. There is no beach. The rock rampart, cracked by sinister rents, rises from the sea above evil-looking ledges and hollow sea halls. At Dancing Ledge a sheltered bay has been fretted in the cliff. In the place of the beach a flat, acre-wide slab of rock slides into the sea, like the slope in harbours for the hauling up of boats. The sea swirls smoothly over the glacis, as it were feeling it with blind hands, and then falls off by the far end into a pool of foam. An iron ladder leads down to the ledge, which is a place slippery with death in a rising tide.

Winspit, two miles westward, is a lonely, tragic spot. It is here that a valley comes down to the Channel, to a cleft in the cliffs so narrow as to be like a Titanic hatchet cut. In this gap is a beach of boulders wedged in between high walls. On the strand are a boat and the wreck of another. Just above the creek, where the grass begins, is a cottage in a garden. The place is a solitude. There is ever a moan of the wind in the gap, while from the cottage windows can only be seen the sky and the downs. This harsh place, with the castaway house and the boat in the gorge, may pass for a scene from some drama of the toilers of the deep. It is near here that the "Halsewell," East Indiaman, was wrecked in 1786, with the loss of 168 lives.

In the museum at Dorchester is an old hour-glass, a sturdy, rugged thing of stout wood and thick green glass. It runs for four hours, and was used to time the watch on the "Halsewell." When that vessel foundered this hour-glass was washed ashore entirely unhurt, while human beings were mangled beyond recognition on the rocks.

Inland from Winspit is the queer, dun hamlet of Worth Maltravers, built wholly of stone, but boasting a few trees. The landscape around it is reduced to two elements only— bare grass and the sea. In the burial ground of the beautiful Norman church lies one Benjamin Jesty, who died in 1816, and who was "the first person who introduced the cow-pox by inoculation, and who from his great strength of mind made the experiment from the cow on his wife and two sons in the year 1774." The epitaph says nothing of the greater strength of mind shown by his wife and her two sons in submitting themselves to this hazard, nor how it came to pass that the iron-minded Benjamin did not first try the experiment upon himself.

A little way beyond Winspit Gap is the promontory of

St. Aldhelm's Head.   Standing boldly out into the sea, it faces
the Channel with a bald cliff 350 feet in height.   At its foot is
a most inhospitable shore of rocks.   Upon the summit of the
promontory is hardy grass, so scoured by centuries of wind that
it has become as smooth as a sand drift.   There is a sense
of defiance about this strong cape, a suggestion of a clenched
fist outstretched in the tideway to challenge the elements.   It is
a solemn place too when a sea mist makes it a mere point
among the clouds.   To walk then to the cliff's edge and look
over is to come to the very edge of the world and gaze into
the steamy void of space.   On a sunny day a superb view of the
coast opens up from the headland.   To the East is the hard
sea wall, to the West are capes and valleys, green downs and
sandy bays, shut in by the far-away island of Portland.

On the summit of St. Aldhelm's Head is a tiny Norman
chapel, square and low, built of walls so thick that there is
little space within.   For over 700 years this humble sanctuary,
which but for its Norman door might be a gun casemate, has
withstood the wind and the rain.   On the summit of its vaulted
roof is a platform now surmounted by a cross.   Here stood,
they say, in olden times the cresset whose flames gave a
warning glare as well to the armed galley as to the homing
fisher's boat, and lit on its way the swift caravel and the lumbering galleass.   The chapel inside is almost dark, for there is
but one narrow window slit in the east wall, so that when the
door is closed it is hard to see even the solitary pillar that
holds up the roof.   A service is held here on Sundays for the
coastguardsmen of the station on the Head.

This St. Aldhelm's Chapel is a chapel of the sea, a sailors'
chantry, a tabernacle of the winds.   It stands near to heaven ;
its tiny cross can be seen far over the sea ; it is within a step
of nothingness.   On a summer's day, when the Channel is an
oily blue and the downs are hazy with heat, the voice of
the preacher is apt to be interrupted by the whimper of circling
seagulls, while in the winter it is more often the shrieking of

the wind and the lashing of the hail that drown the chant of the evening hymn.

Under the shelter of the headland is Chapman's Pool, a small round cove, where a dip in the downs opens to the sea. In an ancient report, dealing with the defences of England, it is spoken of as "a creek where two or three boats may land, but not dangerous for any great attempt of the enemy." Chapman's Pool is merely a haven for fishermen, although none live by the harbour side. On the beach are tarred boathouses and huts, lobster pots and miscellaneous ships' gear. At anchor in the haven are two or three piratical-looking fishing smacks. The place is sombre by reason of the hue of its cliffs. They are smoke-coloured, varying in tint from cinder-black to a funereal blue. Such cliffs as these may fitly encircle a charred bay in the Underworld or a cove by the waterless oceans of the moon.

Close to Chapman's Pool is the Glen of Encombe where is the Earl of Eldon's seat. I am unable to speak of this valley, because, owing to the atrocious conduct of the "trippers," the road through it has been very properly closed by the owner. One who has seen this green chine tells about it in the following fashion : " Think of all the beautiful road scenery you have ever seen or heard of, and you will not have seen or been told of anything more beautiful, in its especial kind of beauty, than this sequestered road down into Lord Eldon's retreat. "[1]

The traveller who follows the coast now passes the fine hill of Swyre Head, and so comes to Kimmeridge. The downs here are in long rolling lines, like terrific sea combers about to break upon a shoal. On the slope of one of these is the hamlet—a cosy place of thatched cottages in a clump of trees. A rough road leads to a bay surrounded by low, earth-coloured cliffs. But for a ridiculous tower, a life-boat shed, and a coastguard station, made up of unpleasantly formal houses, the place is as desolate as it is dingy.

[1] *The Hardy Country*. By C. G. Harper. London, 1905. Page 95.

The only remarkable features about the spot are certain evidences of a long-forgotten commercial activity. There was once at Kimmeridge a large cobb or pier, which was destroyed by a gale in 1745, together with a platform " for two cannon in time of war." This bald bay hardly suggests a place where many thousands of pounds sterling were once ventured and lost. Yet in the days of Elizabeth Sir William Clavel made a harbour here for the exploiting of alum, to his great detriment. Kimmeridge could boast too of great glass works, which flourished for a while and then ended in shabby ruin.

Finally a company of Frenchmen, with superior acumen, determined to develop the shale of the district, which the dull islander had apparently overlooked. They shipped the stuff to Paris for the making of gas, grease, and lamp oil. The fastidious Parisian, however, would have none of it. He said that it smelt horribly and was beyond endurance, so that he would rather sit in darkness and forswear grease for ever than take to him the oils of Kimmeridge. A *débâcle* therefore once more blighted the unresponsive bay, with the result that the French adventurers shook the unclean dust of Kimmeridge from their feet and, returning sulkily home, sat around little tables in *cafés* and cursed the coast of Dorset and its stinking shale.

There are still to be seen in a corner of the cove the ruins of their abandoned pier, the rails they laid down from the quarry to the sea, and on those rails the skeletons of the trucks which were to help them to fortune. Grass and weeds have nearly obliterated these remnants of a quay, which when last tenanted rang with the valediction of French oaths. Here are still relics of the harbour of the forgotten—a stone slip for boats, rusted windlasses, rotten cables, half-buried anchors, shreds of tattered sails, and nets which are dropping into dust; a veritable Davy Jones's Locker, or such a haven as may be found on some pirate's island long centuries abandoned.

Here also are old boats drawn up to die. The tar upon them

has fused into solid drops, or has burst into black blisters. Holes stare in the timbers, through which grass is springing, while in the bottom of one old, shapeless craft lies quite a miniature garden. The men who sailed these boats had no heart to break them up. The little buffeted ship that had many times stood between them and death must find a quiet haven within sound of the sea. I wonder how long ago it was that some white-haired fisherman hobbled painfully down to the harbour to see for the last time his smack, the " Polly," so named after his young wife, dead more than fifty years since. He caresses " her " with his hand, while in his thoughts the fond woman in the churchyard and the crumbling boat are never separable.

About the ruins of the port of Kimmeridge the nettles have grown, many blackberry bushes flourish among its stones, and under the shelter of its dwindling walls are unheeding thistles in flower.

From this curious place comes the " Kimmeridge coal money." This misunderstood coinage consists of round plates of " jet," from $1\frac{1}{2}$ to 2 inches in diameter, which appear to have been treasured at one time as articles of value. These discs are neither money, nor are they of coal. They are of Roman handiwork, are fashioned from the bituminous shale of the bay, and represent the refuse or cores from the lathe. The ancient turners made strange things out of this shale, including great beads, little cups, amulets, and rings. The worthless disc that held the work of art in the lathe was thrown aside, to be cherished in the course of years by the unwitting as " coal money."

Some two and a half miles west of Kimmeridge is Worbarrow Bay. This bay, which stretches from the isolated beacon-hill called Worbarrow Tout to the rocks of Mupe, is not only the most beautiful on the Dorset shore, but one of the most pictur-esque in England. It is a bold, virile sweep of coast, dominated by the towering cliffs of Ring's Hill and Bindon, very gentle where the green gap and tiny beach of Arish Mell meet the sea, and very savage where the Mupe's rocks rise out of the tideway. The sheer cliff under Bindon is of pure white slashed with green, and is capped by the downs. The precipice of Ring's Hill springs from the beach to the height of 560 feet—a pale, terrific wall, made less dazzling by being tempered with ashen-grey. On the summit of the rock face, and at its very edge, is the Celtic

Lulworth Cove. The Entrance and Look-out.

camp of Flowers Barrow, with its triple line of ramparts and ditches, where men have dug up the bones of those who came from over the seas, together with their urns and their implements of bronze and stone. On either side of these immense precipices are lower cliffs, radiant with colour, for they are streaked with yellow, with carmine, with Pompeian red, with the tint of rust, with the brown of dead leaves. This shimmer of colour rising above the white line of foam on the beach makes of Worbarrow a bay of rainbows.

It may interest boys to know that at the easternmost point of

Mupe Bay is a genuine smugglers' cave. I remember aged fishermen at Lulworth who forty years ago told me heart-stirring stories
of this retreat, and of feats with barrels which they and their
forefathers had wrought therein. The place is best reached by
following the coast from Lulworth and by descending the cliff
the moment the bay is reached. The cave is by the foot of
the precipice, at a spot where a little channel has been cleared
between the boulders for a boat to land. It is a low-browed
cavern, quite of the accepted type, and in every way appropriate
to the long-haired mariner who wore a petticoat above his heavy
boots and tilted a red worsted cap on his head.

West Lulworth itself is the next point along the coast, where
is the famous and romantic cove known to so many holiday-
makers and "steamer folk." It is a white-walled sea pool
scooped out of the very heart of the downs. The entrance to
it from the Channel is a mere breach in the cliff, which here rises
straight from the sea. Perched on a pinnacle on the eastern
side of the entry is the coastguard's look-out, while in a dip on
the other side are the scanty remains of the first Abbey of
Bindon. The tide pouring in through the neck fills the pale
cove with blue. Each wave spreads out into a widening circle
as it nears the beach, so that the water viewed from the heights
is rippled by concentric rings like the lid of a flat sea shell.

The cliffs that shut in the cove on the land side are steep and
terrible. On the beach at the foot of the highest precipice is
a board with this inscription on it :—

"This marks the spot whereon
E.H.L.
Aged 11 years,
Fell from the summit of the cliff,
a descent of 380 feet,
September 7th, 1892.
She miraculously escaped without
sustaining lifelong injury.

S.T.S.L."

Any who look up from this spot to the fringe of grass which crowns this appalling wall will never for a moment credit that a child can have fallen from a height greater than that of St. Paul's Cathedral without having been mangled to death. I did not actually see the poor girl fall, but I was on the beach when she was brought to the coastguard boat-house, where I was able to attend to her terrible injuries. She came down with her

Lulworth Cove.   The Cliffs and Boat Beach.

back to the cliff. Her clothes were torn into strings, and it would appear that the catching of her garments on the rough face of the precipice, together with the circumstance that certain slopes and ledges were encountered in her descent, help to explain the incredible fact that she escaped with her life, and still more happily without permanent ill effect. Those who are curious about coincidences may be interested to know that at the time the alarm reached my cottage I was reading a book written by her father. He was himself not staying in Lulworth at the time, nor had I previously made his acquaintance.

The village of West Lulworth lies along the foot of the blunt-ended Bindon Hill, in a valley curving to the sea. It was years ago as picturesque a hamlet of thatched cottages as could be imagined, with its spring of clear water issuing from the hill, its mill-pond where a great sheep washing was held once a year, and its mumbling old mill. Now numerous red brick villas and lodging-houses have done much to rob it of its ancient charm. The queer old church too has long since been pulled down. It stood by the roadside in that part of the village known as "Up along" to distinguish it from the maritime end of the single street, which was called "Down along." It was a very small, ancient church. Its dwarfed tower was so low that it would have been no desperate feat to jump from the top of it into the graveyard which was heaped about its foot. I remember well the singing gallery and the pews, which were so high that when I and the other children sat down the whole congregation vanished from our view. It was not considered reverential to stand upon the seat, so those of tender years saw little. We, however, heard much, because the music consisted of a violin, a bass viol, a flute, and an instrument called, I believe, a serpent. This orchestra occupied the singing gallery, and I recollect that the players were both slow and deliberate, and that when they commenced the wrong tune they were loudly rebuked by the clerk. I always felt it a privilege to reach the church in time to hear the tuning up of the instruments, which was an awe-inspiring affair attended by whisperings.

The lads of the village, with red faces and vivid neckcloths waited outside the porch in a giggling crowd until the bell ceased tolling, at which moment they lurched in with great clatter of hob-nailed boots. I have no doubt that the village maiden found the passing of the porch on Sundays no small ordeal. The farm labourer always came to the service in a picturesque smock frock, which has now almost ceased to be a feature of English costume. When he reached the door he took off his shapeless felt hat and pulled a lock of hair over his forehead with an expression of devout humility. I recollect the introduction of the harmonium and the disbanding of the players in the gallery. It may be surmised that the new instrument was regarded as of questionable orthodoxy, and that its notes grated upon the ears of the village folk. Both geese and ducks have, to my knowledge, waddled into the church during Divine service, and have made some progress up the aisle before they were discovered and driven forth by the indignant clerk. To a child sitting in a high pew, both their entry and their exit were to be appreciated only by signs and sounds, helped by fuller information gained from the fortunate youngsters who occupied the open seats around the font. When the days were hot the windows of the church were thrown open during the hours of worship, and through one of the little casements—visible over the pew top—it was possible to see the apple-trees of an orchard, with apples on them. Through the windows also came the sound of bees, the tinkling of the sheep-bells on the downs, and the muffled laughter of ungodly boys who had escaped church-going.

Leland, in his memorable journey through England, came to this inviting spot. " I saw," he says, " on the shore a little fishar towne caullid Lilleworth, wher is a gut or creke out of the se into the land, and is a socour for smaul shippes." The ancient holders of the manor were the De Lolleworths. In Domesday Book the place is called Lulworde. It had many lords in early years, but came in 1641 to Humphrey Weld, of Hatfield, Herts, in whose family it still remains. In Hutchins's time the Weld who possessed the manor possessed also the "lordship, with its rights, royalties, court leet, view of frank pledge and court baron, value £8 10s. and 24 capons per annum." This seems a great deal for so modest a sum, but possibly county councils and urban rural authorities have absorbed some of these mysterious powers. There was once in the cove a little stone harbour, surrounded on two sides by a pier.

A line of seaweed-covered rocks, laid bare at low tide, still shows where this humble marine work was laid down. In Hutchins's book will be found a picture of this miniature harbour, which none now recollect.

The cliffs about Lulworth are singularly picturesque. The look-out itself is on the summit of a very narrow splinter of precipice, which cuts into the sea like the ram of a battleship. Westward of the look-out, a great pocket has been dug out of the land, at the bottom of which is a beach of boulders, which the waves can reach only through an arch in the rock. This place—called Stair Hole—is practically a lofty cavern, the roof of which is open to the sky.

The coast from here to Osmington is extremely beautiful. Beyond the sandy sweep of Oswald Bay, with its majestic precipices, is an archway, tunnelled through a sharp rock cape. This is the Durdle Door of the photographer, of the pictorial postcard, and of endless water-colour sketches. Westward, again, is a stretch of drab cliffs which ends in the all-dominating headland of White Nose. After that the coast level drops into Ringstead Cove, and at Osmington reaches the flats which carry the sea line round the last curve of Weymouth Bay.

The only settlement between Lulworth and Osmington is Ringstead, now reduced to two or three ancient cottages, which, littered by lobster-pots and nets, are in a state of listless dotage. Yet Ringstead has a place in the Domesday Book. That part of the village known as East Ringstead was destroyed by pirates. The church has long since vanished, all but a chancel arch of the thirteenth century, which will be found incorporated in an unconscious cottage.

Inland from Lulworth cove is the delectable village of East Lulworth, lying contentedly in a wooded hollow at the foot of Flowers Barrow. It is a scattered hamlet of engaging thatched cottages and old-fashioned gardens, facing all ways, for each has been placed as some man's heart desired it. Here is Lulworth Castle, a solid, square building of much solemnity, with

a rounded tower at each angle.   It is a little like an old
French *château*, and is at the best a heavy mass of masonry
planted in a clearing in a wood.   Within sight of it is the more
ancient Celtic Castle of Lulworth, Flowers Barrow, and between
the old stronghold and the new is interposed nothing less than
the history of the world.   The castle of stone was erected at

Lulworth Castle.

the commencement of the seventeenth century.   A Weld built
it, and Welds live in it still.   In the Civil War it was garrisoned
for the King, but was seized and held by the Parliamentary
soldiers, who treated the place ill and left little lead upon its
roofs.   Several Kings of England have stayed within its walls.
James I. came hither to escape the plague raging in London.
Charles II. visited the place in the guise of a royal pleasure-
seeker, while finally George III. and his family, during their
sojourn at Weymouth, honoured the castle with a visit in the
capacity of "trippers."

Opposite the Castle is a bewitching dip in the coast called Arish Mel Gap, where is a rounded beach and a spring of ice-cold water. Seen from the high-road, the gap appears as a triangle of blue sea with its base in the clouds and its point in a green dell. Its sides are formed by the slopes of the downs and by a fringe of trees. When a white sail is crossing the azure gap the picture of this embrasure in the hills is complete.

Inland from Ringstead, in a hollow leading nowhither, is the long-forgotten village of Chaldon Herring, in whose church is a remarkable font of plain stone, shaped like a glass tumbler, and reputed to be Saxon. On a ridge above the village stand in a line five round tumuli, affectionately called " The Five Maries." Those who may fail to be interested in the font must needs be impressed by this wild and romantic burial ground. The men of the bronze age had grand conceptions of what a place of burial should be. Such a spot, to be to their thinking, must be found on a wind-swept hill, on the sky line, as near to heaven and in as little touch with earth as can be ; clear before the sun, bare to the rain and the sea mist, and in a solitude where could fall the silence of the dawning world. Such a spot is here around the " Five Maries "—the five little grass-covered mounds. The view from this lonely ridge is marvellous, stretching as it does far to the North over the valley of the Frome and across the Great Heath, and commanding a sweep from East to West which is lost on both sides in immeasurable distance.

The road from Lulworth Cove to Weymouth enters the Wareham highway at Winfrith, and, leaving it again at Warmwell Cross, comes to the trim and decorous hamlet of Poxwell. This place, the Pockswelle of Domesday Book, possesses a delightful manor house, built in 1654 by the then owners, the Hennings. It is an agreeable relief to a singularly stiff modern church by its side. The house is an ash-grey building with stone-mullioned windows gleaming through ivy, a roof of chocolate-coloured tiles, tall chimneys, great gables, and a hospitable porch with a chamber over it. A bright moss has splashed the old masonry with patches of gold. The manor stands among trees, with for a background a green hill. About it is a garden wherein is a gateway with a porter's lodge over it. This queer little guard-room has a pointed roof of red tiles toned down by yellow lichen and an abundance of ivy. It also boasts a pinnacle on each of its angles, as if it were a casket

Poxwell Village.

of stone. The simple wooden wicket which closes the archway and defends the garden is of most obsequious modesty. The window of the tiny chamber is always opened wide, as if whoever dwelt within loved the air.

On a high down just beyond the village, and in full view of Portland and Weymouth Bay, is a stone circle made up of fifteen rough grey stones. This circle of unknown antiquity has only a diameter of 14 feet, yet it is protected by a rampart and ditch on the side towards the sea. It is little more than a yokel's Stonehenge, the effort of a humble village, a work as innocent of pretension as a model of the Great Pyramid built out of pebbles by a boy on a beach. It would be curious to know how it came to be. If the poor folk of British Poxwell built on this bleak down their own tiny temple in imitation of that at the great capital near Sarum, it would be well if they could have foreseen that, thousands of years after, their stones would still be found exactly as they had placed them. Three of the stones of the Poxwell Stonehenge are fairly large, but

Poxwell Manor House.   The Garden Gate.

the others could have been carried by any lusty lad in this camp of small ambitions.

Osmington, the next place on the coast road, is an indifferent village, which is rapidly assuming suburban characteristics. The detached portion by the sea, called Osmington Mills, is a popular tourist resort, strongly recommended by every char-a-banc driver in Weymouth. In the only still rustic quarter of Osmington is the church, which, although rebuilt, has preserved an ancient inscription carved very rudely in stone. This writing on the wall gives, with the abruptness of a telegraphic message, an account of human life. It reads as follows :—

> "MAN'S LIFE.
> MAN IS A GLAS : LIFE IS
> A WATER THAT'S WEAKLY
> WALLED ABOUT : SINNE BRING
> ES DEATH : DEATH BREAKES
> THE GLAS : SO RUNNES
> THE WATER OUT
> FINIS."

In the churchyard of this town of St. Osmund's is the veritable ghost of a house. It consists of a faint wall, with the pallor of moonlight upon it, in whose height are stone-mullioned windows emptied of their casements like eye sockets in a skull. Its masonry is partly covered by patches of dead ivy, which are as shreds of brown cere cloth upon a corpse. This dead, phantom-like thing is all that remains of the manorial hall of Osmington.

A little beyond the village there breaks upon the eye what the guide books call " a fine view of the White Horse." The White Horse is a figure of Titanic proportions carved out of the chalk upon the slope of a grass-covered hill. On the horse is a white rider with a cocked hat and unreasonable spurs. It is none other than his Majesty King George III. The monarch is less imposing than the animal, which is very stout and is provided with a tail so wide and straight that it looks like a chalk road descending the hill.

Still nearer to Weymouth is the once pretty village of Sutton Poyntz, tucked away in a nook in the downs. It is the "Overcombe" in Thomas Hardy's story of *The Trumpet Major*. The place, however, has sadly changed since John Loveday had his mill there. There is yet a mill in the village, but it is as unpicturesque as only a modern mill can be. There are yet thatch-roofed cottages of stone by the side of a

P 2

mill-pond, the stream from which is crossed by an artless little bridge. That part of "Overcombe" is well. At the end of the village, however, the Corporation of Weymouth has erected waterworks of exceptional ugliness, while opposite to the mill-pond are popular tea gardens of recent growth, where char-a-bancs from Weymouth (for the fee of one shilling each) bring hundreds of hearty folk, who clamour for "shrimp and

The White Horse, near Osmington.

lobster teas," pelt the ducks in the pond, and "rot" the dignified villagers with unintelligible jests.

On the green, basin-shaped hill over against Sutton Poyntz is Chalbury, one of the fortified towns of ancient Britain, with near it the remarkable necropolis of Rimbury. Here the traveller will find himself in an utter solitude among the downs, for the driver of the char-a-banc knows not of Chalbury. The camp is some 300 feet above the level of the sea. It commands a view of Weymouth Bay and of the frowning fortress of Portland, with its dull gun casemates. Since man took to protecting the shores of England, things have changed mightily. Here, from this quiet hill top, can be seen the first effort at defence and the last—the rampart of earth, held by clubs and flint-tipped arrows, and the bastion of stone and steel, commanded by a hundred-ton gun. The camp looks down too upon the beach, where the frail war canoes landed their half-naked company of clubmen and archers. In this very bay are ironclads of the latest type, monstrous and terrible, while on the strand trim bluejackets are stepping ashore from a petrol launch.

The works enclosing the old camp are very simple. Within the compound are traces of many pit dwellings, which if reconstructed would compare with the last great hotel and the last row of villas in the new Chalbury-by-the-sea known to all people as Weymouth. At the south-west foot of Chalbury is a spring called "The Boiling Rock," which no doubt some few thousands of years ago supplied the hill town with water.

The great burial place of Rimbury, where innumerable kistvaens and urns have been unearthed, lies on the south-east spur of the town hill. The way to this city of the dead is by a sombre valley, narrow and silent, which winds slowly upwards into the heart of the hills. The slopes of the valley are bare of even a gorse bush, for the solemn road looks only upon banks of grass and stones. Many a funeral procession has crept up this valley of the shadow of death, the dead chief lying on a bier covered with deerskins and held aloft by poles of unhewn pine borne upon the shoulders of his stalwart sons. Behind the bier would come the weeping women wailing the death song, and the notes of their coronach would be heard by the shepherds across the downs and by the fisher boats in the bay.

CHAPTER XIV

THE joint town of Weymouth and Melcombe Regis is incommoded by its exceptional popularity, which is well deserved and is vouched for by a crowd of many thousands of visitors every summer. The town lies upon a flat at the end of a glorious bay which has been compared with the Bay of Naples, but which resembles that bight in the Italian coast in no essential. The charm of Weymouth Bay is due to its great size, to its symmetry, to the majestic sweep of its shore, to the variations of colour in its sea walls, as well as to the deep blue of its waters. Before the town a level stretch of sands leads eastwards to the ruddy heights of Redcliff Point and the shores of Ringstead. Beyond that buried village the coast soars upwards to the downs of White Nose, becoming brighter and brighter as it rises, until the promontory itself stands out as a gleaming cape. To the East of this point the shore fades into the mist of the far-away, one spectral headland after another looming out of the haze until the land breaks off at the jutting splinter of St. Aldhelm's Head.

To the West of the town is the severe military ridge called the Nothe. It belongs to the older town across the harbour, is faced with stone, and is very solidly armed. The Nothe has always been the guardian of Weymouth, from the time when it served to protect the town from the quarrelsome islanders of

Portland. The view from this strong place is good to see, for it commands the island on the one hand and the fine curve of the sea town on the other.

The town in which the visitor disports himself is of no antiquity and of no especial interest. It is merely what it professes to be—a popular twentieth century holiday resort, a place of lodging-houses and hotels, and of villas for the "retired." Its equipment in this particular is complete, from the fine Esplanade, with its shelters, bath-chairs, and goat-

Weymouth.

chaises, to the Jubilee statue of Queen Victoria and the Jubilee clock. The town is not given over-much to terraces or rows, quadrants or squares. One pleasant characteristic of the place is due to the fact that the houses along the sea front are irregular and of infinite variety, conforming generally to the haphazard style observed in old seaport towns.

The picturesque parts of Weymouth are about the quay and in the older settlement across the harbour. This harbour, which leads to the backwater behind the town, is spanned by a bridge, from which can be seen the old cobble-stone quay, the crowd of sketchy ships and of blue-jerseyed loafers, together with ancient warehouses of faded brick belong-

ing to the time when Weymouth was a place of commerce.
Here, about the harbour side, or huddled together in narrow,
absent-minded lanes, are cosy old houses with round bow
windows of many panes, comfortable lodging-houses, such as
pilots "use," where a telescope can often be seen projecting
from an open casement, and where reefer jackets and oilskins

Weymouth from the Nothe.

half fill the narrow hall.   The landladies of these genial
quarters must be of that stout and rosy type in which Charles
Keen and John Leech especially delighted.   The shops, too,
in this quarter belong to the days of the Georges, are small
and low, are often entered by dropping down a step or two,
and are without counters, since what you want is fetched out
of the window.   One venerable house near the quay has a
cannon-ball embedded in its gable end, an uninvited relic of
the siege of 1644—one of the many assaults to which
Weymouth was periodically subjected.

In the early days of this seaport there was no bridge across the harbour to join the two towns of Weymouth and Melcombe Regis. In Leland's time the traffic was carried on by means of a boat attached to a swinging rope, "so that," as the traveller says, "in the ferry boote they used no ores." In 1597 a wooden bridge had been built here to meet the increasing business of the port, of which fabric it is stated with pride that it possessed no fewer than seventeen arches.

The beginnings of Weymouth were very small and most discouraging. If ever it made any little progress or reached any degree of comfort, coarse persons—usually French pirates—fell upon it and laid it low. Yet it manfully took its part in the affairs of the country during the intervals between its raidings and burnings. Among the ships serving under the Lord Admiral in 1588 were the "Catherine" and the "Heath Hen" of Weymouth, both of sixty tons, as well as the "Golden Rial Lion," a princely vessel of no less than 120 tons burden, which was probably a really "rial" ship and the pride of the Channel. Yet when Leland came to Dorset all he could say of Weymouth was that it had "certain liberties and privileges, but ther is no mair yn it." The town had a very unhappy time in the Civil War, when no less a sum than £20 12s. 6d. was expended upon its fortifications. Endless and indecent squabbles took place between Weymouth and Melcombe as to the profits derived from the harbour which divided the towns, and these disturbances only came to an end when the two villages were made one. They continued, however, to send four members to Parliament, disregarding the fact that the number of the electors was reduced to two hundred.

In 1763 a new era dawned for Weymouth. In that year the foundations of its fortunes were unconsciously laid by an unknown medical man at Bath. It came about in this manner. At the date named one Ralph Allen, of Prior Park, Bath, philanthropist, fell ill. He consulted a doctor, whose name has remained unrevealed, and who advised the sick philanthropist to adopt a treatment so extreme and so strange that it savoured of madness. This consisted of the heroic measure of bathing the bare body in the open sea. Ralph Allen selected Weymouth for the carrying out of this desperate remedy. Here he had a " machine " constructed for the purpose of the prescribed ritual, which engine is claimed to be the prototype of the bathing machine of the present day. From his course of treatment, watched with much concern and amazement, the inventor of the bathing machine " happily received great benefit."

In due course he induced H.R.H. the Duke of Gloster to visit the scene of his restoration to health. The Duke was so pleased with the place that about 1780 he built a house on the Esplanade, known as Gloucester Lodge, and still surviving as the Gloucester Hotel. In the wake of the great man followed pump rooms, assembly rooms, coffee taverns, and billiard saloons, so that the fortune of Weymouth was secured. A relic of the effort of the townfolk to please " the quality " remains in the " Baths," a pretentious building with a façade of Ionic pillars, in one of the main streets. In 1787, just twenty-four years after Ralph Allen acted upon his doctor's daring advice, a writer reports that " Weymouth is rapidly growing more considerable from the vast concourse of polite company by which it is now frequented for sea bathing."

The polite company not only indulged in bathing, but they also adopted the elegant pastime of collecting shells and seaweed. These pursuits were not a little to the comfort of the inhabitants of the town. A historian of the county, dealing with this topic, makes the following note : " The late Duchess Dowager of Portland, whose rich and splendid cabinet of shells will long be the theme of naturalists, was particularly successful at Weymouth, but," adds the writer, " her Grace was often shamefully imposed upon by the fishermen whom she employed to drag."

The glorification of Weymouth was completed in 1789, when George III., his Queen, and the three Princesses visited the

Weymouth Harbour.

town and established themselves at Gloucester Lodge. They
left Windsor Castle at 7 A.M. on the morning of Midsummer

Day in three carriages, and travelled by way of Bagshot, Winchester, Southampton, and Lyndhurst. They broke the journey

Weymouth. The Bridge over the Harbour.

in the New Forest, where they remained some few days to refresh themselves. A full account of this summer holiday is given by the observant Fanny Burney. Sea bathing even in 1789 was a measure by no means to be lightly undertaken.   The King was advised by his physician, Dr. Gisborne, to prepare for the ordeal of the ocean by special observances, the chief of which consisted in using a warm salt bath in his room, with appropriate caution.   In due course his Majesty was sufficiently hardened to dip boldly in the open Channel in the month of July.   " The three Princesses also bathed frequently, and were much delighted with their ablutions."

The royal family took decorous trips upon the water, always returning in time for dinner, which took place at four in the afternoon.   So pleased were they with the town that they remained there eleven weeks.   The citizens of Weymouth were not lacking in expressions of devotion.   They dogged the footsteps of the royal folk every moment of the day, calling out "God save the King!" with the monotony of a minute gun, and pressed their noses against the window panes when the exalted company were dining.   "The preparations of festive loyalty," Miss Burney writes, "were universal.   Not a child could we meet that had not a bandeau round its head, cap, or hat, of 'God save the King.'   All the bargemen wore it in cockades, and even the bathing women had it in large coarse girdles round their waists."   They did more than this, as the following subtle attention will show. "Think," says Fanny Burney, "of the surprise of his Majesty when, the first time of his bathing, he had no sooner popped his royal head under water than a band of music concealed in a neighbouring machine struck up 'God save great George our King.'"

His Majesty's happy patronage of Weymouth led to the erection by a grateful people of a monument to commemorate "his entering the fiftieth year of his reign."   The memorial consists of a statue of the sea-bathing king, surrounded by the emblems of royalty as well as by a miscellaneous collection of flags, shields, implements of war, and books.   It is an object of ridicule to the easily amused, and can only claim to be of interest as a sign of the times.

Near to Weymouth is the ruin of a block-house called
Sandsfoot Castle, erected by Henry VIII. in the year 1539,
when the country was in daily fear of an invasion prompted by
the Pope. It stands upon a green flat by the sea, into which
it is gradually tumbling. In Leland's day it was "a right
goodly and warlyke castle," but time and the tourist have reduced it to a mere windy shell of corroded stone.

Sandsfoot Castle.

The "isle" of Portland seen from the mainland—to which it
is connected by the Chesil Beach—is a dismal heap of stone
standing out into the sea, with the ravenous, ship-destroying
"race" tearing in front of it, with Deadman's Bay, the scene
of a thousand wrecks, to the West, and a fatal shoal, well called
the "Shambles," upon its Eastern side. The azure bay enclosed by its mighty breakwater is ever full of black, unwieldy,
unshiplike vessels of war. There is a dour solemnity about
the place, about its wall-like cliffs piled up at the base with a

slope of fallen stones, about its greyness, its chilling isolation, its melancholy story.   It is not to be expected that beauty will be found upon a rock which is in part a fortress, in part a quarry, and in part a convict prison.   Indeed, the wan, colourless " isle " has no more pretence to charm than has the barrel of a dismounted cannon.   Viewed from the Nothe, it has something of the outline of Monaco, yet at close quarters no two peninsulas could be less alike than this place of stones and the green, palace-capped headland in the Mediterranean. Spion Kop, as seen across the veldt from far south of Ladysmith, will put any Dorset man better in mind of the Portland of his native county.

The way to Portland is by Wyke Regis—a village on a hill— whose lofty church tower is a familiar beacon to the man of the sea.   Around the church are two churchyards of very exceptional size, crammed with tombstones.   There are reasons for the existence of this immense necropolis.   At one time Wyke church was the mother church of Weymouth ; thus it is that many of the dead come from inland.   Moreover, in this God's Acre is gathered no small part of the harvest of Deadman's Bay, the scene of some of the most terrible of wrecks. Here lie Cornet Burns of the 26th Regiment and Lieutenant Ker of the 46th, with twenty-six soldiers, a few of the great company who were washed ashore dead from the transports " Venus," " Piedmont," and " Catherine," lost in the West Bay, November 18th, 1795.   Of the bodies thrown up by the sea on or about that day no fewer than 208 were buried on the Chesil Beach where they were found.   In one grave in this woeful cemetery lie 140 of the passengers and crew of the " Alexander," East Indiaman, wrecked in the bay in 1815.   Here also are the resting places of eighty out of three hundred drowned in the loss of the " Earl of Abergavenny " on the Shambles in the winter of 1805.

Among the tombs is one of a famous smuggler who perished

in the pursuit of his calling, and whose epitaph runs as follows :—

> " Sacred to the Memory
> of
> WILLIAM LEWIS
> who was killed by a shot
> from the *Pigmy* Schooner
> 21st of April, 1822.   Aged 33 years."

In some lines of poetry which follow this simple statement the unfortunate William is made to exclaim, " Repent all ere it be too late," as well as to refer with some confidence to the Judgment Day.

The road from Wyke Regis to Portland is by the attenuated ridge of the Chesil Beach which connects the so-called island to the mainland.   This road is some two miles in length, and for monotony and tediousness it cannot be surpassed.   To a tired pedestrian on a hot summer's day the glaring penitential path is little less than a torture.   The road appears to have the power of extending itself without end, like a treadmill placed horizontally.   The way has no variableness nor shadow of turning.   It is ever pebbles, pebbles, pebbles.   The only relief are the telegraph poles which border this road of the Wandering Jew, and which furnish the blessed diversion of something to count.

Portland is an abrupt peninsula of rock, some four and a half miles long and less than two miles in width.   Its sides are steep except at the point which is thrust forth into the Channel. Its summit is flat, and can nowhere be reached without a climb. Years ago the " isle " was merely a sheep run, where pasture was found for hardy black-faced sheep, which were well esteemed, and whose descendants still haunt the bleak plateau.   No really characteristic Dorset dinner is even now complete without " Portland mutton " on the menu.   In Hutchins's time the number of sheep on the island was 3,000 and the population

2,000.[1] There was a little arable land, as there is still, while much care was devoted to the growing of sainfoin.

The natives were as hardy and as well defined a race as were the sheep. They had little traffic with the mainland, where they were regarded as recluses of unpleasant habits. The Portlanders not only kept to themselves, but were exceedingly jealous of strangers ; they married only with their own folk, and possessed curious laws and still more curious morals. They are spoken

Portland, from the Main land.

of—with some surprise—as being well-informed and as exhibiting no poverty. On the subject of this exclusive community Leland writes, " The people ther be politique inough in selling their commodities and sumwhat avaritiose." It is patent from this and other evidence that the Portlanders were no fools. Their one village was Chesilton—hence the name Chesil Beach—while the approach to the place was by a ferry over the Fleet. The island was ever wind-swept, barren and sour, treeless and ill supplied with water.

It is the same island still. As in Leland's time, " there be

[1] The present number of inhabitants is over 11,000.

very few or utterly no trees in the isle." The southern part of the rock, near the Bill, retains its primitive condition unchanged. Here in melancholy fields marked off by stone walls are the little sturdy Portland sheep. Elsewhere are a few plots of ground where depressing phases of agriculture are being carried out, and where patches of corn and of potatoes are grown under protest. There is not a tree to be seen from the summit of the island, for the flora of the Portland plateau consists of harsh grass, a few teazles, and an occasional starving bramble bush.

The islanders eked out their uneventful lives as shepherd-fishermen until the day when Inigo Jones discovered the stone of the place and pronounced it good. He made use of it for building the Banqueting Room at Whitehall, and soon enough the fame of the poor island spread. The natives thereupon began to thrive, as they had never thrived before, upon the very dust of their native land. They ate into its vitals. They dug it up and sent it away in blocks by brigs and schooners and in trucks. St. Paul's Cathedral was largely fashioned of stone brought up from Dorset. Indeed, so many great and important edifices in the capital were constructed out of the island quarries that it begins to be a question whether there is not as much of Portland in London as remains at the end of the Chesil Beach. Every year more and more of the island is carried away on trolleys, yet, like the burning bush, it remains unconsumed. This exporting piecemeal of a territory which was known to the Romans as the country of Vindilis is indeed a strange thing.

With the passing of years Portland became an important military station. The great fort was raised, barracks were built, and all the unlovely productions of the War Office flourished callously upon the ugly rock. In 1848 a final effort to make of Portland a colossal trophy of the miseries of civilisation was attended with success, for a convict prison, capable of housing 700 convicts, was founded here. There are mediæval dungeons which are picturesque, and modern prisons which have some pretence to stateliness, but the builders on Portland wished to show to the world the blank unattractiveness of gaol life, and in this good purpose they have succeeded well. Thus it has come about that to the taste of some Portland "is one of the most ugly sights to be seen in the world." [1]

The chief town of Portland is Fortune's Well. The name suggests a glen full of trees and dripping ferns, where timid maidens come to learn of the future by peering into a pellucid pool. Portland encourages no such mawkish fancy as this. The capital is like the island—ugly. Its ugliness is vaunted with so little shame as to be nearly immodest. There is, however, something virile about its plainness, for, in a stern, Cromwellian mood, it spares the spectator nothing. The houses of stone and slate condescend to no weaknesses in the matter of style or decoration. The church has about it a sound, convincing ugliness. The town is built upon the side of what the inhabitants call a hill and others a precipice. On the level of one man's roof is another man's cellar. A bedroom window looks down not only into the backyard of its own house, but into a dozen strange backyards, each a street's height lower than the other. The chief feature of any prospect in Fortune's Well are slate roofs. On the west side of the steep High Street are narrow lanes which drop suddenly over the cliff, houses and all, and in this way vanish from the eye. There is just one thing of mockery at the entrance to the town—a public garden and a band-stand.

To the north of Fortune's Well rises the great fort of Verne, with its bastions, its earthworks, and its ditches—an imposing crown to the island, upon whose highest point it stands. On the plateau are many fragments of villages, all gaunt, hard-featured, and treeless. Where there should be grass there is dust, and where a garden a quarry heap. The houses are of

[1] *County and Town in England.* By Grant Allen. London, 1901. Page 33.

stone, are small, and for the most part possessed of as little
architectural ambition as would be presented by a row of pack-
ing cases made of oolite.   The chief church—St. George's—
is at Reforne, and is said by a competent writer to be " built
in an indescribable quasi-classical style of eighteenth century
architecture, midway between Wren and a Byzantine basilica."

There are still some very picturesque old cottages on the

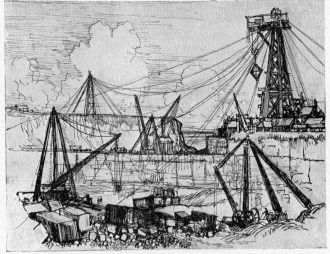

The Quarries at Portland.

island, which belong mostly to the early part of the seventeenth
century.   They will be found at Easton, Weston, and Chesil (or
Chiswell).   Small as they are, they display stone-mullioned
windows with dripstones, cosy porches and fine gables, and
often enough very sturdy buttresses.   To many a date is
attached, while they are notable as the only buildings in the
island roofed with the humble thatch.   There is a great fascination about these little houses, as well as about the Spartan flat
on which they are placed, regardless of shelter, shade, comfort,
or view.

As already stated, the larger part of the island is occupied by stone quarries, and these too by their gigantic ugliness possess some attraction. Here is a garden of stones with roads deep in dust or deep in mud : the grass is grey with dust, the horses, that in teams of eight or ten drag stone-laden trolleys through the waste, are grey too with the powder of stone. A faded traction engine rumbles by, crunching the stones and blackening the air, driven by earth-coloured men, who are shaken as they pass by the fearful vibrations of the machine. There are deep pits of stone, tanks of oolite, walls of white masonry laid bare by the pick, terrific slopes of loose rubble sliding down into the cool sea.

Over a wide chasm, with sides as clean-cut as those of a graving-dock, fantastic cranes rise up into the air. They wave Titanic arms against the sky, which might be the tentacles of some leviathan insect, or weave threads of wire over the abyss like the strands of some unearthly spider's-web ; smoke rises from gasping engines, while now and then a block of stone glides hissing across the void like a fearsome bird. All round are heaps of litter, piles of wind-blown dust, patches of scarred earth, and deserted pits which are becoming covered with a green mould. To intensify the allurement of this curious scene, the air is made to tremble now and then by the firing of a gun in the fort or in the harbour, the boom of which is re-echoed sulkily from the sea cliffs.

The prison is of great interest to the tourists, who make up parties to visit Portland, "to have tea and see the convicts." These convict-teas are timed to give a view of the prisoners as they are leaving work in the evening. This is a morbid diversion. The prison quarries are a dismal matter of stiff walls, set with many sentry-boxes and armed sentries, together with depressed companies of men in yellow jackets, knee-breeches, and Glengarry caps, slashed with the broad arrow.

Of the many miseries of a long imprisonment in Portland, I think that the keenest must be felt in the bright days of summer

by those who are working on the heights of the island. They
can look down upon one of the fairest scenes in England ; upon
the curve of the Chesil Beach, with the waves sweeping up the
pebble slope ; upon the green hills across the Fleet ; upon the
glorious bay of Weymouth and the radiant coast that lies east-
ward of it. They can see excursion parties arrive at the little
station, and scatter themselves over the island ; they can hear

Pennsylvania Castle, Portland.

their laughter above the roar of the surf ; they can see families
picnicking on the beach, fathers and mothers with their children,
and catch a glimpse even of the noisy bathers at Weymouth,
and of happy couples rowing on the bay. At night in their
solitary cells these sounds and sights must burn into their very
souls.

The strangest thing about this sour island remains to be told.
There lies on the east side of it a tiny, green-wooded dell, which
for charm and picturesqueness can hardly be surpassed. This

is the cove of Church Hope. The glen is narrow and full of
shade, a most gentle hollow in the cliffs opening to the sea.
On the summit is Pennsylvania Castle, a modern castellated
house, built in 1800 for John Penn, governor of the island, and
grandson of the founder of Pennsylvania. It is surrounded by
a luxuriant garden, in vivid contrast with the rest of the barren
and dusty rock. The trees in this genial nook were planted

Church Hope Cove, Portland.

by the said John Penn. At the bottom of the dell is a small
cove of shingle, where a wet beach glistens among a waste of
rocks and brambles. There are some tarred fisher huts on the
shore, together with a few boats, lobster-pots, and nets.

Close to the margin of the cove are the ruins of the old
parish church of Portland. It came to an end through a landslip, and of it little remains but ivy-covered walls, an arched
doorway or two, and certain venerable tombs buried among the
grass of the churchyard. One gravestone bears the date 1692.

The eternal quiet of the place is broken only by the sound of the sea.

Upon a crag on the other side of the cove stands the still gallant-looking keep of Rufus Castle, or Bow and Arrow Castle, as it is usually known. This pentagonal tower of ashen stone is of rude construction, and is connected with the side of the cliff by a stone bridge. The castle is reputed to have been built by William Rufus. Its chief interest consists in the window embrasures, which are closed by stone slabs, perforated in the centre by a hole for the archer. The keep provides a vivid picture of the castle defended solely by bows and arrows and by stones hurled from the walls. History records that in 1142 Robert, Earl of Gloucester, seized this keep for the turbulent Empress Matilda.

There is another castle on the island, called Portland Castle, a block-house built by Henry VIII. in 1520, to prepare for a surprise from the French. It passed through the usual experience common to Dorset strongholds during the war between the Royalists and the Parliament, and yet remains in better condition than any. It is chiefly notable on account of the following inscription to be found in a closet over the gun-room :—

> " God save Kinge Henri the VIII of that name, and
> prins Edwarde, begottin of quene Iane, my ladi
> Mary that godli virgin, and the ladi Elizabit so
> towardli, with the kinges honourable covnselers."

The "godli virgin" mentioned in this pious prayer is better known in history as " Bloody Queen Mary."

Before leaving this part of the county there are a few places near to the town of Weymouth which are worth visiting. To the North of the popular seaport is a backwater over one-and-a-half miles in length and half a mile wide at its broadest. It is much frequented by swans, and at the time of high water is a gleaming sheet of water. Into it runs the River Wey, which one would suppose to be a stream of as high intention as the great lake. It proves, however, to be a very modest rivulet, which, with much sparkle and cheeriness, finds extinction in the mere. It enters the backwater at Radipole, a charming hamlet in a green chine, where it appears to be hiding from the awful advance of the villas of suburban Weymouth. The church, once the mother church of Melcombe Regis, has a curious bell steeple with three cusped arches. Near at hand

Bow and Arrow Castle, Portland.

is a gabled manor house of drab stone, which has lost few of its ancient characteristics.

Higher up the stream is a deserted spa—the once popular Nottington—to which the quality from aristocratic Weymouth flocked to drink the waters. These waters, which have been the subject of not a few learned discourses, were advised for "eruptive complaints, scrophula, and loss of appetite." For the last-named malady they were no doubt in much request. The pump room still exists, looking sadly out of place among bald fields. It is an octagonal building of three stories, with something of the aspect of an enormous dove-cot. It no longer rings with the laughter and jests of the seekers after appetite, nor is it gay with silks and furbelows, for circumstances have changed it into a laundry. This part of the county is in the hundred of Culliver's Tree, or, as the boys like to call it, Gulliver's Tree. The origin of the name is interesting. The correct title of the hundred is Culvardestre—that is to say, Culvard's terræ or lands. Careless scribes have turned Culvard into Culliver and his terræ into a tree.

Buckland Ripers near by—the quondam seat of the de Ripariis or Rivers family—is of note by reason of the fact that its church is the best hidden in Dorset. Lying in a dip among the downs, it will need a patient man, with leisure and a precise map, to find it. The settlement now consists of a farmhouse and a cottage. The church has the architectural features of a school-house, yet bears over its porch the date 1655.

The village of Upwey—the Upper Town on the Wey— affords an extraordinary instance of the value of a happy, if meaningless, title. Upwey is one of the places of pilgrimage for the Weymouth holiday-makers. They come here in hundreds, mostly in coaches and wagonettes. The reason for their coming to Upwey is a spring there with the fascinating title of the "Wishing Well." It is to see the Wishing Well that the romantically minded pay their shillings for a seat in the crowded char-a-banc.

The well, as I remember it some forty years ago, was a spot of faint interest; its powers were ill-defined, and there was no particular ground for assuming that a wish expressed at Upwey would have especial advantage. The place is pleasant enough, in spite of the crowd, the swings, and the tea-gardens. A spring issues from the foot of a wooded bank, and, hurrying away under an avenue of trees, vanishes at the mill. A seat placed under two ridiculous stone arches has been erected for the benefit of the tripper. For the benefit of the villager, on the other hand, the following ritual has been introduced, which has proved to be more lucrative than a mere gazing at the waters.

The wisher receives a glass of water from the custodian of this Fons Bandusiæ, he drinks it with appropriate giggling, empties the glass by throwing the water over his left shoulder, and, most important of all, makes an offering of money to the keeper of the well. Folk of all kind go through this formula for the attaining of supposed ends—old men and maidens, young men and children. It is a curious spectacle for the twentieth century, even if it serves no more than to illustrate the magic of a pleasing name. The well is commonplace enough, but the name is charming. A like discrepancy between an object and its title is afforded by the "Golden Horn" at Constantinople, which is less picturesque than Wapping, and by the "Isles of Greece," which are the most scraggy and featureless of islands.

The village itself is very prettily placed under the shelter of the downs, but is slowly taking on the characteristics of a suburb. One of the earliest lords of Upwey was Ranulph de Baieux. In the time of Henry III. John Baieux left two daughters as his sole heirs. The King granted the marriage of one of them to Elias Rabayne, an eminent man of the period, who under colour of that grant carried the other daughter over the seas, so that he might seize the whole estate. The result did not come up to the expectation of the crafty Elias, for his estates were forfeited to the King as a punishment for his covetousness.

The old church of Upwey has been restored without being spoiled. It is of the type common throughout Dorset. A little of the ancient oak wainscotting remains, as well as a carved pulpit of the time of Charles I. In the chancel are three figures of saints in mellow wood, with which holy men are said to have decorated a still earlier pulpit. Among the three St. Peter is conspicuous. In one hand he holds the keys, in the other a book. He is clad in a furred cloak, which is coquettishly looped up so as to show his breeches, stockings, and smart shoes.

CHAPTER XV

THE LAND BEHIND THE CHESIL BEACH

THE Chesil Bank is a magnificent beach of pebbles, which swings in a stately curve from the foot of Portland to Burton Bradstock, a distance of from seventeen to eighteen miles. For about half of the way it is separated from the mainland by the reedy waters of the Fleet, the home of many hundreds of swans. Between the Fleet and the sea the beach stands up as a bank, steep and smooth, with a deadly slope towards the Western Bay. No sea rampart can surpass it in bluster, in massiveness, in truculence. It stands alone defying the tide. The Fleet is a mere moat or ditch behind it. Since England was an island the pebble beach has been an outpost of defence against the invasion of the sea. In a westerly gale it is a place terrible to behold. The sea roars and thunders against it with a sound that can be heard inland for miles. The ice-smooth combers crash down upon the glacis with the force of battering rams; the beach is torn at by the receding wave as if the straitened foam were a myriad of claws.

Once only has the sea made a breach through this curtain of stones. This was on a day in November, 1824, when the waves hammered a gap in the battlements and flooded the swannery at Abbotsbury to the depth of 22 feet 8 inches, as a pole erect in a field testifies to this day. At Fleet it swept away the greater part of a village and all but the chancel of the church. Farther eastwards an ordnance sloop laden with stores was being driven by the gale towards the fatal beach, when an enormous wave seized hold of the ship, lifted it up, and carried it to the very top of the bank, where it was left, to its astonishment, high and dry. The sailors, who had had all hope battered out of them, stepped over the bulwarks on to the beach, and walked, wet and amazed, into Portland, where they were greeted by some as liars, by others as men who had come out

Chesil Beach from near Abbotsbury, and looking towards Portland.

of the jaws of death. As they crawled into the first tavern in the town, and, above the howling of the wind and the rattling of casements, told how their sloop had been lifted by the sea out of the West Bay and deposited unhurt on the top of Chesil Beach, the men in jerseys who were sheltering round the fire must have stared at them open-mouthed. The doubters were perforce convinced when in the course of days the sloop was launched down the far bank into the Fleet, and was brought round to Weymouth Bay by this unfamiliar overland route. The sloop was a craft of ninety-five tons, by name the "Ebenezer," and in the fearsome voyage only two on board were drowned.

Incredible as it may appear, the exploit of the "Ebenezer" was outdone fifteen years later. In 1839, in the month of October, some ten ships were driven ashore upon the Chesil Beach. Nine of them were pounded into matchwood, while the tenth—a craft of 500 tons—was lightly thrown by a sea over the beach from the West Bay and floated away, but little the worse, into the smooth waters of Portland Roads. Let any who walk the road from Weymouth to Portland mount to the summit of the beach and ponder over the feat accomplished by this vessel, for on her passage she would have crossed the isthmus now traversed by the highway as well as by the line of the London and South Western Railway Company.

Probably no part of the English coast has seen more numerous or more fatal wrecks than has the Chesil Bank. The numbers of lives lost here are to be counted by thousands, for it has been to the seaman a veritable beach of death. When the sea gives up her dead it will be a host uncountable who will crowd the steep sides of the amphitheatre of Deadman's Bay.

The great beach too is haunted by stories of wreckers, of ships lured ashore by misguiding lights, of drowning men murdered, of gasping sailors robbed and pushed back into the sea to die, of booty washed ashore, of awful revels when men drank from derelict spirit casks until they lay purple and dead on the pebbles. In the winter of 1748 "The Hope of Amsterdam" was wrecked on this lamentable strand with a cargo of £50,000 in gold. "The shore then was a scene of unheard of riot, violence, and barbarity." A crowd swarmed about the water's edge grubbing for gold, tearing up the shingle with their nails, fighting over gleaming coins like starved wolves, and in the black of the night robbing and strangling men with glutted pockets. For ten awful days the mob held the beach in defiance of the representatives of law and order, while the terrace of the Chesil Bank might have belonged to a circle in Dante's Purgatory

Viewed on a calm summer's day from the heights above Abbotsbury, the Chesil Beach is but the gentlest, sleepiest curve of fawn-coloured shingle, lying lazily between the blue waters of the Fleet and the line of white foam on the margin of the treacherous bay.

One curious feature of the Bank is the very regular manner in which the pebbles diminish in size from Portland to Burton. So definite is this that a local fisherman landing upon the beach at night can tell from the size of the stones at what particular point he has come ashore. This index, it is said, was of much service to the uncertain smuggler who was bringing his goods to land in the dark. The reason for the diminishing scale in stones depends upon the wind rather than the tide. The shore is very fully exposed to the west wind, but is sheltered from the east. The west is the stronger breeze, and carries, by means of the waves it makes, the larger pebbles eastwards, so that the stones of greatest size are to be found under the shelter of Portland. Thus it comes about that the note of the beach varies in its course, changing from the whisper of sand to the hissing of shingle and then to the hollow rattling and rumbling of down-dragged pebbles.

The country that lies behind the Beach is somewhat bare, being backed by bleak downs. Quite close to the edge of the Fleet Water are the remains of the village of East Fleet, the greater part of which was washed away in the memorable storm of 1824. A wooded glen leads down to a gap in the grass bank, behind which the hamlet stood and through which the sea poured. Here are a few picturesque thatched cottages surrounded by trees. Through the gap one can look over the sleepy backwater to the towering bulwark of the Chesil Bank. Beyond the pass and near to the brink of the mere are the village graveyard and the chancel of the ancient church. This solitary chancel of grey stone, with its roof of stone slabs and its ivy-covered buttresses, is all that remains of the church of Fleet. The nave and tower were destroyed in the gale. The chancel is now but a mortuary chapel of the De Mohuns, the ancient lords of the manor. Here on the wall is a fine memorial in brass to Margarita Mohun, who died in 1603, leaving nine sons and eight daughters, as well as a tablet to Maximilian Mohun, Armiger, who was buried here in 1612. A more enchanting resting-place can hardly be conceived than is afforded by this lonely graveyard by the bay. There is ever about it the smell of the sea, and even on the calmest days the babble of the waves along the beach haunts this hollow of dead fishermen.

Farther west is the dismal village of Langton Herring, on a windy ridge. This Long Town of the Herring family was held in 1613 by the Prince of Wales, and, according to Hutchins, is held by him still. The historian further adds that in old days " some tenants paid rent to the Prince, others to Lady Wharton, between whom strays, felons' goods, etc., are equally divided ; but the Prince ought to have of every swan's nest built on the manor, or the beach opposite to it, one ground berde cygnet." Whether his Royal Highness still receives his proper share of felons' goods, as well as the ground berde cygnet, I am unable to say.

The chief place along the coast is Abbotsbury. This is a fat, comfortable, well-to-do village, very pleasantly situated among the downs, which close around it on all sides, except towards the East. It is a pretty village, moreover, clean and trim, filled with delightful houses and cottages belonging to the sixteenth and seventeenth centuries. All are of stone ; many are picturesquely thatched, or are roofed by rough tiles. There are houses with heavy buttresses, with stone-mullioned windows and worn dripstones ; houses with fragments of church carvings in their walls, or a section of a Gothic arch plundered from the ruins of the Abbey. Some are evidently the domestic build-ings of the Abbey, which have been turned into farmhouses and cottages, and have lost little by the change. The ancient manor house, with its many gables, its rugged roof, its old

porch with a quaint chamber over it, and, above all, its fine
stone stairway leading to an entry, is most charming.

The Benedictine Abbey, which was the glory of Abbotsbury, was founded in the reign of Canute by Orc, a steward of
the King, and his wife Thola. It was a place of great size and
importance. At the dissolution it came into the possession of
Sir Giles Strangways, in whose family—that of the Earls of
Ilchester—it still remains. The swannery was there at that
period, and can still claim to shelter the largest colony of swans
in the kingdom, the birds numbering over one thousand. It is
a place of quiet creeks and reedy pools, of rush-covered capes
and wandering islets, where wild-fowl settle in clouds. Here
are to be seen those subtle " decoys," which are more familiar
in Norfolk, and which offer such mean hospitality to the migra-
tory bird.

Of the Abbey but few fragments survive. One gatehouse
and an archway are still standing, the lines of a cloister and the
foundations of many pillars can be traced, while all over the
village are carved blocks of stone built into the walls of humble
habitations. The most remarkable relic of the Benedictine
house is the barn. This grand old building is of enormous
size ; one-third of its length is roofless, the rest is covered by an
ample thatch. Immense buttresses hold up its walls, as if to
suggest that there was a time when they might have bulged
under the pressure of such heaps of corn as could have filled a
church to its roof beams. It has a noble arched gateway, fit
for a palace entry, through which a waggon piled with tottering
sheaves could pass, with space to spare. Its gable-ends and its
pinnacles show that he who raised it aloft was the architect, not
of farm buildings, but of abbey chapels. Near to the doorway
is an octagonal staircase turret, which would look strangely out
of place by the side of the corrugated iron barn of modern
times.

Abbotsbury suffered much at the time of the Great Rebellion, when both the Abbey house and the parish church were

R

garrisoned for the King by Colonel Strangways. In September, 1644, Sir Anthony Ashley Cooper, at the head of a Parliamentary force, came down upon the gallant village, and after much lurid fighting took the church and burnt down the house. The following is his account of the episode, as furnished to the Parliamentary Committee for Dorset :—

"HONOURABLE.

"Yesterday we advanced with your Brigade to Abbotsbury, as a place of greate concerne, and which by the whole council of war was held

The Tithe Barn, Abbotsbury. The Chapel of St. Catherine in the distance.

feasible. We came thither just at night, and sent them a summons by a trumpeter, to which they returned a slighting answer, and hung out their bloody flag. Immediately we drew out a party of musketeers, with which Major Bainton in person stormed the church, into which they had put thirteen men because it flanked the house. This, after a hot bickering, we carried and took all the men prisoners. After this we sent them a second summons, under our hands, that they might have fair quarter if they would accept it, otherwise they must expect none if they forced us to a storm. But they were so gallant that they would admit of no treaty, so that we prepared ourselves for to force it, and so fell on. The business was extreme hot for above six hours. We were forced to burn down the outgate to the Court before we could get to the house, and then our men rushed through the fire and got into the hall porch, where with furze faggots they set fire to it and plied the windows soe hard with small shot that the enemy durst not appear in the low rooms. In the meantime one of our guns played on the other side of the house, and the gunners, with fireballs and granadoes and with scaling ladders, endeavoured to fire the second storey, but that not taking effect our soldiers were forced to wrench open the windows with iron bars and, pouring in faggots of furze fired, set the whole house in a flaming fire, so that it was not possible to be quenched, and then they cried for quarter, but, we having lost divers men before it, I gave command that there should be none given, but they should be kept into the house ; but Colonel and Major Sidenham riding to the other side of the house gave them quarter, upon which our men fell into the house to plunder and could not be by any of their commanders drawn out though they were told the enemy's magazine was near the fire and if they stayed would prove their ruin, which accordingly fell out, for the powder, taking fire, blew up all that were in the house."

Of the Strangways house, thus gallantly defended, nothing now remains but one ivy-covered wall.

The church is little altered externally since this fiery day in 1644, and is a very stately building, with a stolid, square tower. It is surrounded by relics of the old Abbey, as well as by stone coffins, about which legends are told. In the venerable porch is a stone coffin-lid, rudely carved with the quaint figure of a holy man, holding angularly a book and a pastoral staff. Over the west door is a still more remarkable and weather-beaten figure, representing the Trinity. The fine wooden pulpit shows in its carving two bullet holes made on that day in 1644 when "the business was extreme hot" and thirteen men were dodging behind the pillars of the nave. In the chancel is a curious plaster ceiling, placed there by the Strangways in 1648, where coats-of-arms are casually blended with angels. The east window is blocked by a fantastic altar-piece, erected in 1751, which is strangely incongruous and unhappy.

One gracious presence in the church should not be over-looked. Among the old stained glass in one of the windows is a woman's head, reputed to be that of St. Catherine. The glass is so old and so faded that the colours have come to be little more than a sun-tinted grey. The woman's face is wonderful to look upon, delicate, ghost-like, infinitely tender. It belongs to the time of the long-ago, for the gentle eyes seem to gaze through the mist of half-forgotten centuries. The lovable lady is much absorbed; her hands are clasped, there is a wimple about her shapely head, and around it shimmers a yellow halo. Many a village lad in the church must have adored the little saint in the window, and carried with him the memory of her features until others, less unsubstantial, blotted the picture from his mind. This fair St. Catherine was turning the same soft eyes into the church when the musket bullets whistled across the nave in 1644, and her cheeks must have glowed with red when the flames shot up from the Abbey House.

Conspicuous on the crown of a hill, to the south-west of the village, is the sturdy chapel of this very saint, St. Catherine. It is small, measuring only 45 feet by 15 feet, and is an admirable example of the simplest architecture of the Perpendicular Period. No timber enters into its construction. Every part of it, including the panelled ceiling and the roof, is of stone. The walls, massive enough in themselves, are supported by stout buttresses, while at the north-west angle is a look-out tower. This chapel, built during the first half of the fifteenth century, has withstood for 400 years every gale that has hurtled across the West Bay. Like the chapel on St. Aldhelm's Head, it has been a chantry for sailors, a sea mark to craft heading for the coast, as well as a look-out for the folk of Abbotsbury whence they could watch for the enemy.

Very near to Abbotsbury—in a hollow among the downs— is the village of Portisham. It is a somewhat dull settlement, although cheered by a clear and rapid rivulet which chatters down the street. It boasts of an ancient and handsome church with a battlemented tower, a Jacobean pulpit, a panelled cove ceiling, and many venerable monuments. Among the memorials is one, on the outer wall of the church, to William Weare (1670), an enthusiastic Royalist, whose property was sequestrated in the Civil War, and who is made to complain in somewhat sarcastic rhyme of the injustice imposed on him. He was the brother-in-law of Sir Thomas Hardy's great-great-great uncle. The Weares and the Hardys had been for generations prominent farmers in the district. Mary Weare, who died in 1675, is commended in the following words cut upon a plain tablet :—

> " Vnderneath lies her whose actions pend
> The perfect copie of a friend
> Whose good meek hart did always shun
> Shvch things as ovght not to be done
> Rest then for ever rest alone
> Thy ashes can be tovched by none."

This Mary of the "meek hart" would appear to have been a sister to the William Weare who suffered so severely for his loyalty to the Crown.

In this village Thomas Masterman Hardy, Nelson's captain, spent the early years of his life. He was born at Kingston Russell [1]—some three and a half miles distant—in 1769. In 1778, when the lad was nine years old, his father and mother moved to Portisham, to a little house which had been long in the possession of the family. Here the future admiral lived until he was old enough to go to sea. In November, 1781, at the age of twelve, he joined H.M. brig "Helena" as "captain's servant," the captain being Francis Roberts, of Burton Bradstock. Burton Bradstock is but a few miles distant along the coast and in that town is still to be seen a comfortable thatched and ivy-covered house, called "The Grove," where Captain Roberts of the brig "Helena" lived.[2]

At Portisham will also be found the house which was for

[1] See page 250.
[2] *Three Dorset Captains at Trafalgar.* By Broadley and Bartelot. London, 1906. Page 160.

many years Hardy's home. It is a small and very plain building of two stories, with a stone slab roof, a stuccoed front, and
modernised windows. In the garden across the road and
facing the house is a sun-dial brought from Kingston Russell
and bearing this inscription :—

"JOSEPH HARDY, ESQ
Kingston Russell. Lat. 50° 45
1767
Fugio fuge."

This Joseph Hardy was the father of the future sea captain.
To the end of his days Thomas Masterman Hardy retained
the fondest regard for Portisham or, as he always called it,
" Possum." His letters, published in the interesting volume
above referred to, are full of references to " Possum." He had
a great appreciation of everything that came from Dorset,
whether it was "sea cale," mutton, cheese, or beer. His
anxiety, when he was away with the fleet, about certain con-
signments of beer seems to have been often quite acute. He
claims that Dorset beer was "the best ever drank," and that
to be wholly commendable it must come from " Possum."
His first letters written from the " Helena " show that his
education was not quite complete when he took to the sea.
He states therein that he " was going to wright to Father," but
was prevented by incidents connected with " the chesing of a
Privateer." He at the same time complains that " the close
Mr. Bagter sent were to large."

Portisham lies too low to command a view of the sea,
although in a south-westerly gale the roar of the breakers on
the Chesil Beach can be heard in the village. From the hills,
however, which tower above the little place a grand expanse of
the Channel lies open, and there can be small doubt that young
Hardy climbed often enough to the highest point to look over
the sea, by which, from his nursery days, he seems to have been
fascinated. This highest point is on Black Down, whose

summit is some 770 feet above the sea level.   It is here that
a monument to the great admiral has been erected. The down
is bare, wild, and desolate, a wind-swept waste of bracken and
heather.   The monument is not imposing.   Afar off it may be
mistaken for a factory chimney, and when seen nearer at hand
it bears a strange resemblance to a telephone receiver placed on
end.   The spot, however, is appropriate.   It commands that
English Channel Hardy did so much to defend ; there is never
a day when a British battleship cannot be seen from its summit ;
it is a land-mark for sailors ; it stands above the village of
" Possum " the well beloved ; and, more than this, the sturdy
pillar has been raised—so the inscription on its side declares—
" on his own land."   " Dear Hardy," as Nelson called him, died
in 1839 ; the monument was erected in 1844, and those who
knew the great seaman best will own that no place could have
been more fitting for Hardy's tower than the crest of the Black
Down.

On the next height on the Portisham side of the monument
is a cromlech called the Hell Stone.   Hel in the Northern
mythology is, I believe, the Goddess of the Dead, and this
spot was no doubt the burying place of some chieftain of
the late Stone Age.   It consists of nine upright stones support-
ing, for a roof, a single flat rock of great size.   Thus was
formed a small cabin or hut, which became the habitation of
the dead man until such time as he could join his kinsmen in
the other world.   The door of the stone sepulchre opens
towards the sea, towards the sun at high noon.   Originally the
stones were buried under a long barrow, the earth of which
has been washed away by centuries of rain.   For years the
place was a shelter for shepherds, who might well have blessed
the spirit of the unknown king from whose tomb they looked
out upon the storm.

To the west of the Hell Stone, at the entrance of the Valley
of Stones, is another dolmen with the inappropriate name of
" The Grey Mare and Her Colts."   The Valley of Stones is a

mysterious glen among the downs, on whose grassy slopes
many huge grey stones are scattered. Lower down the hollow
are clumps of trees, under the cover of which the strange valley
curves out of sight. If it was along this vale that the dead
were borne for burial, then no processional road could have
been more awe-inspiring. The tribesmen might have gathered
on the lonely heights and watched the shadows below the
trees for the first sight of the slowly-moving company. It is
said that the stones were once covered by a barrow 54 feet
long, 25 feet broad, and 5½ feet in height, and that the sepulchre
was rifled and broken up years ago by men incontinently
searching for treasure. The stones are in a poor field entirely
overgrown and choked with thistles—a bitter, heartless garden
of Gethsemane. The boulders themselves are on a mound,
where they are almost hidden from sight by nettles.

The view from this place of burial has one remarkable
feature. To the North, the South, and the East are only to be
seen the bleak downs. Far away to the West the coast turns
inwards, and here is an unexpected glimpse of the sea, of a
blue bay breaking on a beach at the foot of pallid cliffs.
There is no sign of the open Channel, which is wholly shut out
by the hills. The land-locked cove is so distant, so faint, so
phantom-like in the azure mist, that it looks like the shore of
another world, a moonlit bay, marvellous and unsubstantial. I
think that the stones must have been placed here for the sake
of this gentle prospect, so that the dead man's spirit could ever
feast upon the comfortable land, upon the happy bay in the
circle of the pitiless heights.

The highway from Abbotsbury to Swyre commands probably
the most beautiful scenery to be obtained from any coast road
in the county. The way climbs the steep ascent of Tulk's
Hill, and passes westwards over open downs dotted with gorse.
From the summit can be seen the whole sweep of the shore
from Portland to beyond Lyme Regis, the line of the Chesil

Beach, the blue Fleet, the tree-begirt village of Abbotsbury, the yellow-red cliffs by Burton Bradstock, and the magnificent headland known as the Golden Cap.

Swyre lies in a sheltered gap which opens upon the sea—a small, humble, and uninteresting settlement. A little inland is the picturesque village of Puncknowle, where are many pretty cottages of stone, roofed with tiles or thatch. Here once lived that Colonel Shrapnel who was the inventor of the shell which bears his name. Puncknowle at the time of the Domesday Book was held by "Hugh the son of Grip." It later became possessed for many generations by the family of the Nappers or Napiers. Those who are imaginative have here a favourable spot for a story of hidden treasure. The story would be based upon the fact that in 1791 a farm labourer turned up with his plough a jar which contained no fewer than 1,200 coins. They are described as being "almost entirely decayed by time." The money can hardly have represented the hoard of a miser, and if it had been buried in troublous times by the great family of the village, it is scarcely to be believed that the place of hiding was not known to some. There would at least have been some legend of hidden gold to be handed down from father to son. It is probable therefore that this was the booty of some sea rover who beached his boat at Swyre, and, going off to seek further adventure, was either murdered for the secret or was wrecked on the Chesil Beach on a less fortunate venture.

The church of Puncknowle is curious and interesting. It has a small, low tower, a Norman chancel arch, and a peculiar font, shaped like a kettledrum and decorated by knotted ropes and very archaic heads. The place is full of monuments to many generations of Napiers. One old stone records the death of a Napier in 1597, while over the door hang the gauntlets and spurs of another member of the family. As a protest against the extravagant laudations common to epitaphs of the time, one ancient stone bears the following curt inscription :—

> " Reader when as thou hast done all thou
> canst thou art but an unprofitable servant,
> Therefore this marble affords no roome for fulsome
> flattery or vaine praise."

Hidden in a garden behind the church is one of the daintiest and most beautiful of the manor houses in the county, a marvel of ancient dignity and peace. It is trim, symmetrical, and very old. A steep and lofty roof of stone slabs surmounts it ; quaint stone-mullioned windows with tiny panes look into the garden, upon which opens also a porch with an arched doorway and a chamber over. This ancient homestead is far away from beaten tracks, but any who follow the coast road should turn aside to see it, so as to learn what an English home was like before the days when the small house mimicked the mansion, and when the flaunting villa was not.

Farther inland, between the sea coast and the Bridport road, is the lazy valley of the River Bride. The stream is small, winding, and weed-grown. It bubbles out of the chalk hills at Bridehead, a wooded corner of soft green at the end of the valley, a spot so secluded and so beautiful that a hermit's cell must once have found shelter here. Farther down the valley is Kingston Russell House, the birthplace of Sir Thomas Masterman Hardy, who was born here on April 5th, 1769, in the same year as Napoleon Bonaparte and the great Duke of Wellington. Here also died, in 1877, John Lothrop Motley, the historian of the Dutch Republic. In spite of these associations, the house, which now stands derelict in a field, is falling into ruins. It was at one time the stately home of the Russells, and on the pediment which surmounts the classical façade the arms of the family are boldly carved. Doors and windows have been taken away and replaced by brickwork, the oak wainscotting has gone to Woburn, ivy is creeping over the fine grey stone and weeds over the wide flight of steps before the entrance hall, while within is the lamentable chaos of heartless neglect and decay.

From the Russells of Kingston Russell rose the Earls of Bedford. The circumstances under which plain Squire Russell became a peer are curious, and are graphically set forth by H. J. Moule in the following manner :—

"In 1506 Philip, Duke of Burgundy, and his wife Juana were sailing down Channel to claim the throne of Castile, one of the kingdoms into which Spain was then divided, and of which Juana's mother, Isabella, had been queen. A bad storm came on, and they put into Weymouth. Now, the Sheriff of Dorset then was Sir Thomas Trenchard of Wolveton.[1] He seems to have known that the King, Henry VII., had reasons for wishing to seize any occasion for bringing influence to bear on the Duke of Burgundy, or King of Castile, as he already called himself. Down to Weymouth rides Sir Thomas : his Grace of Castile must by no means leave England till duly welcomed by his brother of England—his Grace must honour his poor house of Wolveton by abiding there till King Henry could hear about his guests ; and his Grace of Castile and the Lady Juana rode along the Roman road and through the gateway at the end of South Street, Dorchester, and out at West Gate, at the top of High West Street, and so away to Wolveton. A stately house is Wolveton at this day, and much of it is the very same—the gate-house, for instance—that King Philip entered, with Sir Thomas bowing and making dignified apologies. It was all very courteous and respectful. One small difficulty, however, was that, Sir Thomas knowing no Spanish, and the King no English, they found it passing awkward to make each other understand. But Sir Thomas be-thought him of his clever cousin, over there westward at Barwick[2]—Squire Russell—Farmer Russell the neighbours called him. He had been in Spain and he talked Spanish well, and was now living at Barwick, farming his own small estate. Over to Wolveton he was fetched to interpret. Interpret he did, and made himself so useful to King Philip that he took the squire to London when King Henry fetched the foreigners up to visit him. Now King Henry always knew a clever man when he saw him. Farmer Russell died first Earl of Bedford and Barwick and Kingston Russell, and much Dorset land belongs to his descendant, the Duke of Bedford, at this minute."[3]

---

[1] Close to Dorchester.

[2] Barwick or Berwick is in the Bride valley, near to Swyre.

[3] *Old Dorset*. By H. J. Moule. London, 1893. Page 185.

The village of Kingston Russell can hardly now be said to exist. In the days of Edward I., Nichola, the wife of Nicholas de Morteshore, held the manor for her life "by service of counting the King's chessmen and putting them in the box when the King had done playing with them." There must be some pleasant unremembered story belonging to this granting of the manor. The service was strangely small for so great a recompense. Possibly the fair Nichola played chess with the Prince before he came to be King, and it may be that the game was a cover for some love-making, and that the Plantagenet saw more of the lady's blue eyes and smiling lips than of knights and pawns. Possibly also there was some tender wrangling as to who should put the chessmen away in the box, and that Nichola did it so prettily that the prince vowed that no one should ever do it for him but she. He was a man of his word, whose favourite motto was *Pactum serva*, "Keep your promise," so the lady, or the memory of her, was present " whenever the King had done playing," and in token of many rosy hours he granted her this King's Town among the Dorset hills.

High up on the north slope of the Bride valley is Chilcombe. All of the village has vanished except the church and the manor house. They stand together in an utter solitude in the sunny niche of a hill whose summit is covered by the earthworks of a British camp. The view from the green ledge is singularly beautiful. The long forgotten settlement takes the form of a tiny square. On one side are the church and the ancient house, on another a venerable thatched barn, while on the third and fourth sides are a picturesque waggon shed and farm stables. There are many famous town squares, but none can surpass the square at Chilcombe in simplicity. On the knoll above this relic of a village is a clump of trees, from which can be seen the Channel.

The tiny church is possessed of a queer bell gable, of curious Gothic windows, and the traces of a Norman door. It has too a most archaic font, a piscina, a tablet to a John Bishop who died in 1682, and the arm-chair of another of the family, with " R. B. 1642 " engraved on its blackened oak. This chair stands in the chancel, in a position it has no doubt occupied for over 260 years. The most curious thing in this exquisite sanctuary is the reredos of deep yellow wood, strangely carved with figures to represent the crucifixion, the scourging of Christ, and Christ rising from the dead. It was obtained, they say, from one of the ships of the Spanish Armada, which was cast ashore on the Chesil Beach. It is a long cry from the Spain of the Armada days to this secluded church on a Dorset hill-side. The mansion—now a farmhouse—is an elegant building, with the inscription " 1578, John, Elnor Bishop," over the north door. The building has obviously been much altered since John and Elinor came there to live, but the sight of it serves to carry the mind back many centuries.

To the west of Chilcombe is the height known as Shipton Hill, which has a most remarkable resemblance to an enormous ship lying on the summit keel uppermost.

By Burton Bradstock the Bride finally enters the sea, or rather enters the ground, for it does not pass into the West Bay by any visible or orthodox channel. Henry I. gave the Priory of Bradstock to the Abbey of St. Stephen at Caen to redeem the regalia—" the crown and other ornaments "—which his father on his deathbed had recklessly presented to that house. When the foreign monasteries were suppressed the Priory came back to England and was attached to the Church of St. Stephen in Westminster.

Hutchins states, with scientific solemnity, that in June, 1757, a mermaid had the misfortune to be thrown ashore at Burton Bradstock. This romantic individual, being no less than 13 feet in height or length, was evidently a giantess of the species. Her upper or better half had a human form, while her extremity was that of a fish. The head of this unhappy creature was partly like that of a man and partly like that of a hog. Her fins resembled hands. She had a masculine jaw-bone, and forty-eight teeth in both the upper and the lower jaw.

The village is exceedingly pretty, possessing many delightful old houses and cottages with thatched roofs. It lies in a hollow protected from the sea, and opening through a hesitating gap upon the end of the Chesil Beach. The diligent holiday-maker has discovered this spot, and has sown therein the seeds of deterioration.

CHAPTER XVI

BRIDPORT TO LYME REGIS

BRIDPORT is a wholesome, homely, county town, with an air about it of substantial simplicity. It has no more pretence or assurance than has an honest yeoman's wife in homespun. It has made no effort at history making nor at the heaping up of annals. It boasts of no antiquities and of no particular past. It played but a languid part in the Great Civil War. Sometimes it was held by the King and sometimes by the Parliament, but there was no unseemly wrangling about the tenancy. Bridport always aimed at peace. The town did certainly make some show of fortifying itself in 1642, but as only ten pounds were expended on military works, it would seem that the warlike action was due merely to an amiable wish to be neighbourly and a little in the fashion.

Ancient records state that on June 13th, 1685, Bridport was "surprised" by three hundred of Monmouth's men under Lord Grey. The term must not be misunderstood. Bridport was probably as interested in the arrival of Lord Grey and his troopers as are the yokels of the village when a battery of artillery rattles down the road. The people of Bridport were no doubt " surprised," but not offensively. There were more gaping mouths and staring eyes, I believe, than violent feats of arms. It is true that there was an unfortunate fracas at the

Bull Inn, at this time as the following epitaph in the parish church records :—

> " In Memory of EDWARD
> COKER, Gent., second
> son of Capt. Robert
> Coker, of Mapowder.
> Slayne at the Bull
> Inn in Bridpur^t Ivne the 14th
> An. Do. 1685, by one Venner,
> who was an officer vnde^r
> the late Duke of Mvnmvt^h
> in that Rebellion."

Bridport. The Town Hall.

It is true also that Lord Grey and those with him were routed after some sharp fighting.

One other little event lies stored away in the memory of Bridport. When Charles II. in his flight from the country had failed to find a boat at Charmouth, he turned northwards, in order to make again for his hiding-place at Trent by

Sherborne.[1] He was attended by Colonel Wyndham and Miss Juliana Coningsby. The King was disguised as the Colonel's servant, while Juliana rode pillion behind him. Lord Wilmot and a man named Peters were following at some distance. When the party reached Bridport they put up at the George Inn. The town was unfortunately full of troops at the time, and while Juliana was anxiously watching at the tavern window for the coming of Lord Wilmot, the King was pushing his way—in the character of a dutiful groom—through a crowd of Cromwellian soldiers in the inn yard. As soon as Wilmot arrived the fugitives made off from Bridport by the Dorchester road. They took a turning to the left just beyond the town. This was fortunate, inasmuch as those who pursued them followed the high-road into Dorchester.[2] The turning taken by the King is known as Lee Lane, and is just such a narrow, insignificant byway as would appeal to a hunted man. At the corner of the lane is a stone in the hedge upon which is inscribed the statement that:—

"KING CHARLES II
ESCAPED CAPTURE THROUGH THIS LANE.
SEPT. XXIII., MDCLI."

The greater part of the George Inn was pulled down long ago. What remains of it is incorporated in a chemist's shop nearly opposite to the Town Hall. Behind this building are traces of the inn yard where Charles parleyed with the soldiers who were hot in his pursuit.

Bridport the unpretending is a lovable town, whose roofs of red and grey have a tree-covered hill for a background. Its streets are wide, no two of its houses are quite akin, a stream runs to the west of it, while around the comfortable settlement, except on the side that turns to the sea, is a circle of green heights.

The Town Hall, of pink brick and drab stone, with its cupola,

[1] See pages 264 and 316.   [2] See page 283.

S

its clock, and its weather vane, is in every particular the orthodox municipal building of a typical county town. The parish
church also is soberly parochial, and of the standard pattern.
In the South Street, on the way to the sea, is a stout grey
building, with stone-mullioned windows and a fine porch with
a room over it. This was at one time the Castle Inn, and it
needs only the Exeter coach in the road and a stout landlord
in a white apron at the door to recall the old tavern of two
centuries ago.

Another building of interest is the infant school, because it
so well fulfils any conception of what a seat of learning for
country infants should be like. It is an ancient thatched cottage
with a thatched verandah, where the infants can take the air
when resting from their studies. The playground is an old-
fashioned garden by the side of a stream. This charming little
academy is the village school of a child's idyll. It and the
Castle Inn are the two most delightful features in the town.

West Bay, the harbour of Bridport, is probably the queerest
seaport in any part of the British Isles. As it is approached
the country dies away, the trees vanish one by one, until at last
there is only a green flat left, which slides into the heaped up
shingle of the shore. The waterway to the port is a mere
gully hacked through the beach and marked by two wooden
piers of the ruggedest type. About the black timbers of the
pier the sea is ever banging and fussing as if it has some
grievance against the structure. The tiny harbour is nearly
full, inasmuch as it contains a schooner and a ketch, besides
sundry rowing boats.

That West Bay takes itself quite seriously as one of the
seaports of England is made evident by the fact that about the
harbour is a quay—somewhat grass-grown certainly—provided
with mighty rings and bollards to hold the leviathans of the
deep. A railway runs also to West Bay to bring back the
merchandise. It may here be said that any ship the size of a
schooner has to be dragged into the harbour by ropes, and has

to be coaxed between the piers with as much care as is needed
to bring a cumbrous piece of furniture along a narrow passage.
The essential hamlet of West Bay is made up of disorderly old
houses of the humbler type, which are arranged with no more
method than if they had been emptied out of a dice
box.   Among the more seaward of these are picturesque
thatched cottages which have stumbled on to the very beach,
and are standing there, knee-deep in shingle, with their backs

West Bay, Bridport.

turned to the ocean, and with a suggestion that they were
wondering how they had ever managed to get there.   West
Bay boasts of an inn of quite the jolly harbour-side type, but
the port has not yet developed anything that can be called
a street.   West Bay as an irresponsible haven for shipping is
pleasant enough, but there is another feature about the tiny
place which is lamentable.   There is evidence that it is making
pretence to be a seaside town and a resort for the holiday-
maker.   To this end swings and roundabouts appear now and
then on the solemn quay.   A block of dwellings has been
dumped down in the unoffending hamlet, where a " terrace "—

although in itself architecturally admirable—looks as out of place as an iron girder in a flower garden. More than this, along the beach has been built the rudiment of an esplanade, duly furnished with shelters of the type approved by Margate and Ramsgate. As a village of the incongruous, West Bay has probably no equal in the British Isles. So long as it was content to be a nursery-tale harbour it was charming enough, but West Bay as a "seaside resort" is a pitiable mockery.

The view of the coast from the end of the pier is remarkably fine. To the East are the sheer, orange-coloured cliffs of Burton Bradstock, and then the curve of the Chesil Bank tailing off into the faint island of Portland. To the West the cliffs as far as Lyme are most picturesque and irregular. They are all crowned by smooth downs. Between the port and the gap at Eype is the great West Cliff, whose walls are yellow and drab. Thence to the sea town of Chideock are Ridge Cliff and Doghouse Hill. A little short of Lyme rises up the Golden Cap, a grand headland 600 feet high, tipped, when the sun shines upon it, with gold, and draped below in grey and solemn blue.

Close to Bridport is Bradpole, a village of which the historian says little but that "its situation is very watry." It was in this uninteresting place that the Right Hon. W. E. Forster was born. The house of his fathers is a plain farmhouse of the simplest type. Growing against one side of it is a great pear tree, while behind lies a fair garden within walls. It may be safe to surmise that with both these addenda to the homestead the youthful Forster was well and practically acquainted.

The adjacent village of Loders is noteworthy by reason of its picturesque church, the architecture of which is mainly of the Perpendicular period. The church is under cover of the fir-capped hill of Waddon, which is the landmark of the district. The church possesses a battlemented porch, by the side of which is a curious staircase tower; the winding stair within it leads to a chamber over the porch. This chamber, which is empty, has two old college windows, and bears a resemblance to a quaint room above the church porch at Pulham.[1] The windows look upon a churchyard full of flowers, and if this was ever a priest's room, the good man had reason to be content with the prospect which met his eyes whenever he looked up from his missal.

The first place along the coast road is Symondsbury, a pretty enough village of thatched cottages and many trees, by the side

Chideock.

of the River Simene. The highway thence to Lyme is extremely hilly, and indeed can scarcely boast of a single level stretch. It passes through a fine country commanding views of the hills of Pilsdon and Lewesdon, of the heights of Lambert's Castle, and of the houseless Vale of Marshwood. In each dip between the great hills which make waves of the road is a townlet or village.

The first of these is Chideock, an unspoiled old-world village in a hollow of green fields. Most of its cottages are ancient, and are still made beautiful by thatched roofs, while among

[1] See page 329.

them are houses of greater pretence and a hint or two of the suburban villa. The handsome old church is comfortably in keeping with the village. At the time of the Domesday Book Chideock was held by the King. In the reign of Edward I. it was possessed by the Chidiocks, an ancient family whose mansion was for long the glory of the place. This noble house stood to the north of the village, where its foundations can still be traced in a field. The mansion or castle was a focus of strife at the time of the Great Rebellion. It was many times taken and retaken, until at last it was "slighted" in 1645 by the order of Colonel Ceely, the commandant of Lyme. As late as 1740 considerable ruins of the old house were still standing, for in that year "Messrs. Bucks took a draught of the same." In the "draught" taken by Messrs. Bucks can be seen the shattered relics of a massive square building with a tower at each corner, with fine Gothic windows and a princely gateway. Of these ruins not a vestige now remains.

One and a half miles beyond Chideock a narrow lane turns away to the left towards the sea. The lane is not only narrow, but precipitous in parts, as well as very rough. It leads to the site of the village of Stanton St. Gabriel, a village which was lost and forgotten centuries ago. The unsteady road ends at a farmhouse in a valley open to the sea. A footpath making for the beach comes at last—under the shadow of Golden Cap—to a "level mead" between a wood and the blue waters of Charmouth Bay. In this lonely spot was the village of Stanton St. Gabriel, which would seem to have crept as far away from the bustle of the world as it could go. All that remains here of the timid settlement is an ancient farmhouse, in a state of musty decay, and a cottage.

Close to the farm and encumbered with its litter are the ruins of the village church. Of the tiny sanctuary four grey, ivy-covered walls survive, together with a porch, two arched door-ways, and certain windows. Within the enclosure is a waste of brambles and thistles. The oppressive silence of the roofless

aisle is broken by the cawing of crows and by the splash of the
waves on the shore.   The east end of the church is the least

Charmouth from the Lyme Road.

ruinous.   Here is clearly shown the site of the altar, while just
in front of the altar is a wild rose bush in blossom.   It would
seem as if the spirit of the last bride who knelt upon the chancel

steps still lived in the blushing petals which the sea wind scatters over the stones.

Charmouth, like Chideock, lies in a valley between two round hills. Through the floor of the vale bustles the River Char. The town has one long street, which, leaving the stream, essays to climb laboriously up the hill towards Lyme. The beach has been the scene of sanguinary battles between the Danes and the Saxons. In 833 the Northern pirates came down upon Charmouth in thirty-five ships. King Egbert marched into the valley to meet them. The Danes effected a landing and drove the King inland. So desperate, however, was the fighting that they failed to follow up their victory. They felt that they had had enough, and so at sundown they took to their boats and sailed away. Precisely like results followed the raid made upon the coast by the Danes seven years later. They were then met by King Ethelwulf. He too was beaten back ; but the Danes were filled with no desire to meet him again, so, returning to their galleys, they nursed their wounds and mourned their dead in the solitude of West Bay.

Charmouth was the scene of one of the most stirring episodes which marked the flight of King Charles II. after the battle of Worcester. Charles found himself, after many vicissitudes, in Colonel Wyndham's house at Trent. He arrived there on September 17th.[1] Colonel Wyndham at once set to work to find a ship to carry the King across the Channel. He rode to Lyme with this purpose, and was there recommended to Stephen Limbry of Charmouth, who owned a coasting vessel of thirty tons, and was prepared to carry certain Royalist gentlemen over to France for the sum of £60. The start was arranged to take place on the night of September 22nd. The Colonel returned to Trent to prepare the King, and at the same time sent his man Peters to Charmouth to engage rooms at the inn, and to say that they

[1] See page 316.

were wanted for an eloping couple. Colonel Wyndham and Peters acted as guides, the King was disguised as a servant, and with him was Miss Juliana Coningsby, riding pillion. Lord Wilmot followed, he was the Romeo to Miss Juliana's Juliet.

Unfortunately, the tavern at Charmouth was very full, owing to the holding of a fair at Lyme. Rooms, however, were secured. While Wilmot and Juliana sat in the parlour acting the part of anxious lovers, Charles was busy with the horses in the stable yard, while Wyndham and Peters went to the beach to look out for Limbry's boat, which was to come from Lyme. They waited there all night and returned disconsolate to the inn at the dawn of day with the announcement that the tide had gone out, but that of a boat there was no sign. Limbry's failure to fulfil his engagement was due to the fact that his wife —a cautious woman—had read an unpleasant proclamation to the effect that it was death to aid or conceal Charles Stuart. Having a suspicion that that Prince might be one of the "Royalist gentlemen," she locked her husband in a room, and having as a further precaution concealed the mariner's trousers, waited smilingly for the day.

The distracted party at the inn now agreed that the King, Juliana, and Colonel Wyndham should return to Trent by way of Bridport, and at the latter town should await Lord Wilmot and Peters, who were to remain to seek out the cause of Limbry's distressing conduct. Now, it came to pass that, after the King had left, the ostler of the inn took Lord Wilmot's horse to the blacksmith to be shod. That observant crafts-man noticed that the three remaining shoes of his lordship's horse had been put on in counties about Worcester. This, with other suspicious happenings, was enough for the ostler. He at once hurried to the parson of the village as being the representative of the intellect of the district. The divine, in-flated by this precious gossip, put on his hat and bustled in turn to the inn. He addressed the astonished landlady in the following abrupt and facetious manner : " Why, how now,

Margaret, you are a maid of honour." To which cryptic re-mark the hostess replied, "What mean you by that, Mr. Parson?" "Charles Stuart lay last night at your house," said the minister, in the tone of a convicting judge, "and kissed you at his departure, so that now you cannot but be a maid of honour." After this delivery Mr. Parson expected to see the landlady fall into a swoon upon the sanded floor. He was taken aback when the gallant Margaret made answer, "If I believed it was the King, as you say it was, I would think the better of my lips all the days of my life."

The tavern that saw these scenes was the "Queen's Armes." It is no longer an inn, and indeed the front of the house is new, while the building itself has been converted into two small dwellings. The back of the premises is probably not much changed since the King stayed in the house. In the smaller of the two houses are a huge chimney, a stone-paved floor, an ancient doorway, and mullioned windows. In the larger house is a handsome room, with fine old beams in the ceiling, This relic of the "Queen's Armes" stands next above a chapel, opposite to a picturesque inn of some age called the "George," but which dates from long since Charles Stuart's time. As the tourist who visits Charmouth insists on beholding the actual inn where the King stopped, the "George" is pointed out to him, to the great comfort of the quiet folk who occupy the genuine hostelry.

The Charmouth of the present day is a place of little interest and small simplicity. The village is composed mainly of lodging-houses and red-brick villas, while the little street is busy all the summer with wagonettes and char-a-bancs. The church, rebuilt in 1836, is exceptionally ugly. In the church-yard is the tomb of James Warden, "who fell in a duel," April 28th, 1792. He had a dispute about some game with his neighbour and bosom companion, Mr. Bond. Incisive language followed, with the result that the two old friends met in a field near the Hunter's Lodge, on the way to Axminster.

They were not impetuous youngsters, for Warden was fifty-six and a retired naval officer. Pistols were chosen, and it was agreed that the angry men should fire in turn, the first shot being determined by the drawing of lots. Fortune in this particular favoured the naval officer, who fired at his boon companion, the ball passing through his hat. It was now

Lyme Regis from the Charmouth Road.

Mr. Bond's turn. He raised his pistol, took steady aim, and shot Warden through the heart. Bond fled away incontinently to "foreign parts." The body of Warden was carried back to Charmouth, and in due course buried, his wife Eliza inscribing four verses of poetry on his tombstone.

From the windy summit of Timber Hill, beyond Charmouth, the white high-road drops headlong into Lyme. From the height it is possible to look down upon the town as from the battlements of a tower. The place looks exceedingly small as it stands on the narrow ledge between the downs and the sea. So wide is the expanse of the Channel that the tiny settlement is dwarfed to a mere patch of colour on a beach. Lyme, from the heights, is nothing more than a jumble of red roofs, from which rises a grey church tower, and from which trail into the sea the curving tendrils of the cobb or pier round a clump of schooners and brigs.

According to Leland, " Lime is a praty market town set in the rootes of an high rokky hille down to the hard shore. There cummith a shalow broke from the hilles about a three

Lyme Regis. The Church and the Harbour.

miles by north, and cummith fleting on great stones through a stone bridge in the botom." This description befits the Lyme of the present day. The " shalow broke " is the River Lym or Buddle—a stream any one can step across—and it comes " fleting on great stones," and passes still under a stone bridge. The place no longer does a large trade with France, Spain, and the West Indies, but it has been dignified by the name of " Regis " since the time of Edward I., when that sovereign turned a poor fishing village into a borough and a haven. A part of the town once belonged to the Abbey of Sherborne, of which possession some testimony survives in a street called Sherborne Lane.

Lyme Regis is, on closer view, a sober, drab town, lodged in a gorge or cleft which opens upon the Channel. The houses, like the Gadarene swine, appear to be running down a steep place into the sea. At the end of the street they are only prevented from tumbling into the ocean by a sudden sea-wall, over which they hang unsteadily. Just a few escape and wander along the beach. Lyme-of-the-King is a very undecided town, a place of wandering and unrealised ideas. The main street on its way to the shore wavers to and fro like a drunken man. The lanes are in disorder, as if they could never determine which way to go. There is an esplanade or marine walk, but it has neither orthodox beginning nor end. It starts, in a way, with an assortment of houses, a new red-brick building, an ancient thatched cottage with a bow window, and a pompous villa. It then lapses into a green bank of bushes, fir-trees, and a wild undergrowth, a garden or two, and the blankest of blank walls. Finally it takes to houses again, but in the form now of a solid clump.

There is a piece of sea wall by the stream which seems to have been built at ten different periods from ten different points of view. Many of the houses of Lyme are ancient and very picturesque. They are all irregular, however, for the unmethodical seaport seems to have changed its mind many times as to its intentions. At present it is carrying out a rustic attempt to found a seaside resort.

The Town Hall, built in 1888, is pleasantly placed above the sea wall, near the mouth of the river. It has suffered in turn from the indecision which has been characteristic of the settlement. It is a nondescript building, which offers a sort of epitome, or olla podrida, of architectural styles. It is bright in colour, and is just such a *Stadthalle* as would be found in a German toy box of building bricks for boys.

The old fossil shop near by, "patronised by Prince Alfred," is as curious a house as any in the town. Here can be purchased, at the same counter, fresh prawns or fossil ammonites, filleted soles or pieces of a saurian's backbone.

Some few millions of years ago the vicinity of Lyme Regis was a favourite resort for saurians, fearful monsters, who have never been seen when living by the eye of man. One of these awful creatures, the Ichthyosaurus Platydon, twenty-five feet in length, lay down to die in the ooze near to the spot

Lyme Regis, looking Seawards.

where Lyme now stands. His sleep remained undisturbed for hundreds of thousands of years, and nothing that had life gazed upon him. At last, in 1811, his long rest was broken in upon, and the saurian and the human being met. The disturber of his sleep was a schoolgirl, aged ten, named Mary Anning, the daughter of a curiosity shop keeper in Lyme. Of all dramatic meetings—including the incident of Beauty and the Beast—this *rencontre* between the inquisitive Miss Anning and the twenty-five feet saurian (her senior by millions of years) is one of the most curious. The disturbèd saurian now lies in state in the Natural History Museum at South Kensington, while a stained glass window in Lyme Church keeps green the memory of Miss Mary Anning.

A Lane in Lyme Regis.

The parish church, like everything else in Lyme Regis, climbs uphill. It is a building whose little beauty is marred by a covering of stucco. Within are a fine Jacobean gallery and pulpit of carved wood, the gift of Richard Harvey, one of the merchant-adventurers of the town. In the gallery is some ancient and gracious tapestry, whose vivid reds and blues have faded into the gentlest tints of pink and lavender.

It may here be noted that this town on the Buddle has

been the birthplace of many remarkable men, among whom may be mentioned the following. The first is Arthur Gregory, whose fame is based upon his "admirable talent of forcing the seal of a letter in such a way that it appeared untouched." This gift commended him to Sir Francis Walsingham, then member for Lyme. With Gregory's aid that statesman was enabled to acquaint himself with the correspondence of the foreign Ambassadors to the Court of St. James, as well as with the private letters addressed to Mary Queen of Scots. In such fashion the labours of the Foreign Office of the time were greatly lightened.

From Lyme also came Dr. Case, a very famous quack and astrologer of the days of James II. Having realised a fortune by the most nefarious methods, he retired from practice, and to indicate his return to virtue had arms painted upon his carriage with this simple motto, "The Case is altered."

The Lyme notables, however, were not all Gregorys and Cases. From the town came Sir George Somers, the discoverer of Somers Island, better known as the Bermudas ; also that most honest and kindly shipwright, Thomas Coram, who, after infinite labour, established in 1741 the Foundling Hospital in London.

The cobb or stone pier is the chief glory and delight of Lyme. It is a sturdy work, laid down on mysterious lines and bearing a resemblance to no marine structure of like intent. It combines in one series of stone banks the functions of a breakwater, a quay, and a pier. It has somewhat the curve of a shepherd's crook, with an adventitious tentacle of masonry projecting from the summit of its bend. It wanders into the water in a hesitating manner which is quite in keeping with the uncertainty of the town. The cobb, or a cobb, dates from the time of Edward I., since when it has been many times destroyed by storms and as many times rebuilt. The present work belongs to 1825, when it rose afresh from the ruin wrought by the memorable gale of the previous year.

The most curious quarter of Lyme Regis is that which crowds about the banks of the Buddle River. So very narrow is the stream that the houses upon the two sides of it nearly touch one another, especially as they are brought nearer by overhanging stories propped up by ruffianly-looking timbers. Certain of the dwellings are built actually over the stream, so that the halting watercourse runs partly through a tunnel and partly by a dark gully between precipitous house backs. The dwellings, faded and sinister-looking, would appear to keep to such simple old customs as the emptying of slops and rubbish out of windows. This obsolete riverside place is particularly evil looking at night. There is a suggestion of trapdoors, of dark entries, and of dungeon-like, mouldy cellars. It has been—if the stories are true—a smugglers' alley of the fine old cutlass and pistol type. To the imaginative it is a water lane of muffled footsteps, of dark lanterns carried with suspicious slowness, of hoarse whispers and an occasional low whistle, of sudden lights at dirty windows and of ropes mysteriously lowered into the gloom.

From the sea wall near the mouth of this miniature Wapping is a glorious prospect of the coast towards the East, made especially beautiful when the sunlight is full upon it. Here on the way to the Chesil Beach are cliffs of many colours, slate-blue and ashen-grey, slashed with patches of green and yellow, while on the crowning headland is a cap of gold. The line, too, of the coast downs undulates like a wave. In one trough is Charmouth, in another Stanton St. Gabriel, in a third the sea town of Chideock.

Lyme Regis has a great and interesting past. It was from the hills above the town that was witnessed the beginnings of the engagement with the Spanish Armada in 1588. This battle was watched with breathless interest by the folk of Lyme, because they had contributed two ships of their own to the enterprise.

In the Great Civil War the town was held by the Parliament,

T

and held right well. The garrison of some 500 men was under
the command of Governor Ceely. Prince Maurice laid siege
to the place with no fewer, it is said, than 4,000 men. The siege
began on April 20th, 1644, and lasted until June 15th, when
the town was relieved by the Earl of Essex. Thus it came to
pass that Lyme was never taken. The garrison, we are told,
"defended it with amazing obstinacy and enthusiastic courage,

The Esplanade, Lyme Regis.

inflamed by the sermons of twenty-five seditious lecturers."
During the two months in which the twenty-five lecturers
laboured to so great purpose shots from demi-cannon and
whole culverins were poured into the town, together with
granadoes, fire-arrows, and " divers balls of wild fire." Houses
were burned down, breaches were blown through the walls, and
many assaults were made, but the gallant men of Lyme,
inspired by their lecturers, never budged an inch and never
suffered a reverse.

Another remarkable experience happened to the stalwart
town on June 11th, 1685. At daybreak on that morning the

early lounger on the cobb and the shepherd on the hill were alarmed to see three mysterious vessels approaching Lyme. No colours flew from their mastheads and no guns could be seen from their sides. The town was promptly roused, and its curiosity was in no way appeased when mariners of experience stated that the vessels were Dutch. As the uncanny craft drew nearer the surveyor of the port set out to inspect them. He failed to return. An awful suspense followed. In due course

The Town Hall and Sea-wall, Lyme Regis.

seven boats full of armed men put off for the shore. This was enough for Gregory Alford, the Mayor. He gave the order for the drums to beat the alarm, and, hastening to his stable, he mounted a horse and fled towards Honiton. He was well on the road before the boats reached the cobb. As the rowers drew near there could be seen seated in the stern of the leading galley a tall man in a curled wig, wearing a hat with a plume of black ostrich feathers. He was dressed, moreover, in purple, and wore a star on his breast. When he landed he and his followers knelt upon the beach and prayed, while at the same

time a deep green banner was unfurled bearing the words
"Fear nothing but God."

The River Buddle, Lyme Regis.

It became at once known that this pious man was no
other than the Duke of Monmouth, and that the object of his
landing was to claim the throne of England. The Duke,

with his followers, marched solemnly to the market-place, and here the dreamy, effeminate son of the late King proclaimed his purpose. The people were delighted with his discourse, so that the narrow lanes of Lyme Regis were soon crowded with men shouting ".A Monmouth! a Monmouth!" It must have been a fine picture, this scene at the market cross. The man in purple with a star upon his breast speaking graciously to the eager mob, his lieutenant standing by his side armed to the teeth—the reckless, swaggering Lord Grey—while at the foot of the cross was seated Fergusson the plotter, the lying poltroon, the false secretary, with his ink horn and pen, writing down the names of the stupid yokels who were eager to enlist. When Monmouth marched out of Lyme he had behind him no fewer than 3,000 horse and 2,000 foot. How it all ended is a tale that has been already told,[1] a tale of four weeks, in which befell the battle of Sedgemoor, Monmouth's capture in a ditch near Horton, and his execution on Tower Hill. The hat with the plume of ostrich feathers is not among the regalia of England, but lies in a museum in Bath.

[1] See pages 82 and 120.

CHAPTER XVII

MARSHWOOD VALE AND THE WEST BORDER

THE country about Lyme is beautiful and very varied. It is a land of hills and vales, of wooded hollows and heather-covered heights, of deep lanes buried in green and of luxuriant slopes of pasture. From any western height, such as that by Hunters' Lodge, is an incomparable view over the counties of Devon and Somerset on the one side and of the sea coast, as far as Hardy's tower and the Isle of Portland, on the other. Hunters' Lodge is a solitary thatched inn on the summit of the Roman road, from whence bustling highways lead to Honiton, to Beaminster, to Bridport, and to Lyme.

To the north of the coast road is the Marshwood Vale, a somewhat sullen hollow, shunned by man, for there is hardly a habitation in it. It is, as the name implies, marshy and full of trees. Crowe speaks of it as " cold, vapourish, and miry," while in Hutchins's time it " was hardly passable by travellers but in dry summers." The Vale is open and undulating. In the early summer it is a garden of wild flowers, and throughout the county it is famous for its oaks. One more boast it has, that there is not a stone within its confines. Hills encircle it on all sides. The view to the West is shut in by Lambert's Castle, and to the South by the coast hills. Northwards are the heights of Lewesdon and Pilsdon Penn, while to the East it opens reluctantly to the far-away sea. The roads through

the valley are narrow and grass-grown, for those who have
business in its highways are few. Tall hedges shut in
the roads, so that the place has ever the aspect of being un-
traversed by man.

The village of Marshwood is on a ridge on the northern wall
of the Vale. Its church, when seen from the valley, stands up

Whitchurch Canonicorum.

against the sky line. The place is scattered and poor, yet it
was "antientlie of much accompt," had two parks, a Norman
castle, and a vineyard. Indeed, so desirable a property was it
that Robert de Maud "owed £380, five marks, five palfreys,
and four Norway hawks to have the Barony of Mirswude."

The capital of the Vale of Marshwood is Whitchurch
Canonicorum, or Canon's Whitchurch, so named because the
great tithes were divided between the canons of Salisbury and
of Wells. The village consists of a few scattered thatched
houses. The church, however, is magnificent—a cruciform

building of singular beauty and of exceptional interest.   It is
dedicated to Saint Candida, or Saint Wita, as her name was in
Saxon.   Her shrine stands in the north transept, and there is
little doubt but that the church was originally called St. Wita's
Church.   The fifteenth century tower is a landmark for many
miles around.   High up on its walls is carved on stone an
archaic ship and an axe, which inscription has led to the belief
that some merchant whose ways were upon the sea built the
great tower.   On the south wall, too, is to be seen in stone a
quaint two-handled vessel, which is believed by many to
represent the Holy Grail.   In the south porch is a Norman
doorway with four consecration crosses.   " These crosses it is
supposed were first marked in holy oil by the Bishop or Bishops
who were present at the consecration of the church or some
part of it, and were immediately afterwards chiselled in their
present form to commemorate the event."[1]   Over the church
is an old sacring bell hut, in which hung the bell that was
rung at "the sacring of the Mass."   Within the church are
many curious and beautiful arches, some belonging to the Late
Norman period and some to the Early English.   There are
elaborately decorated tombs to Knights of Catherstone, but no
stone marks the resting place of Sir George Sommers, the
famous admiral, who died here.

The north transept, built about the year 1220, presents
wall arcades with clustered shaft piers and finely carved capitals.
In this transept stands the shrine or tomb of that Saint
Candida to whom the church was dedicated.   It takes the form
of an altar-like erection of stone in which are three oval
openings.   Into these handkerchiefs and other articles were
placed, in the hope that through their medium healing might
be conveyed to those who were too sick to be brought to the
church.   In 1900, owing to a settlement in the foundations
of the transept, the shrine became displaced, and in the
process of its repair the interior was exposed.   Within was

[1] From the excellent pamphlet furnished to visitors to the church.

found a leaden casket containing the remains of a small woman apparently about forty years of age. The lid was thus inscribed :—

"HIC-REQUESCT-RLIQE-SCE-WITE."

Of the pious little lady who came to be known as Saint Wita, and who was thus sumptuously buried in the Marshwood valley, nothing whatever is known.

Catherston Leweston, a place of no present interest, near to Whitchurch, was for long the seat of the Wadhams. Sir Nicholas Wadham was he who founded Wadham College. He lived at Merifield, and was, according to Fuller, so very hospitable that "his house was like an inn at all times and like a Court at Christmas." His widow built the college about 1612. Oxen were brought up from Merifield to Oxford for the building operations by one John Clay, whose account of expenses incurred on the road has been preserved. It reads as follows :—

	s.	d.
Imprimis laid out at Stoke for bread and drinke		10
Evill[1] for the oxen	5	10
Sope...		4
Our suppers...	4	0
Our breakfasts	2	0
Paid the chamberlayne		2
Charleton Horethorne. For beare ...		2
Meere. For aqua vitæ for Thomas Heed...		4
The oxen	6	8
Sope...		4
Our suppers...	3	4
Our breakfasts	2	6
Given the chamberlayne there		2

The "chamberlayne" is apparently the degenerate "boots" of the present day. No explanation is given of the circumstances

---

[1] A pitchfork or hay fork.

which led Thomas Heed to require aqua vitæ while at Meere. The "sope," so much in evidence on the journey, was used not for toilet purposes, but for "dressing the wheels."

On the border of the Marshwood Valley are the most notable hills in the West of the county. Here are Coney's Castle and Lambert's Castle, two heights capped by ancient earthworks. Lambert's Castle is a fine ridge, terminating in a truculent headland distinguished by a clump of fir trees. The view from the summit is maintained by many to be *the* view of the county. From hence can be seen Portland, the sea breaking on the Chesil Beach, the Fleet, a long stretch of the Devon coast, and, far inland, the uplands of Wiltshire and Somerset.

To the North of the Vale are the twin hills of Lewesdon and Pilsdon Pen, the latter reaching the elevation of 907 feet. In these eminences the Dorset Heights end. So like are the two hills when seen from about Beaminster that there is, or was, a local rhyme dealing with the peculiarity : —

> " As much akin
> As Lew'son Hill and Pilsdon Pen."

Crowe, who was the public orator at Oxford, wrote in 1788 a poem on Lewesdon Hill, which was much admired at the time. He sees many things from the summit, including—

> " the kine
> Returning with their milky treasure home."

He also rejoices that the minute stream at the foot of the hill, which would not float a schoolboy's canoe,

> " yet flows along
> Untainted with the commerce of the world."

Pilsdon Pen is a bluff promontory like Lambert's Castle, and like it is covered on the top by ancient earthworks. It lacks the woods which makes beautiful the slopes of Lewesdon.

XVII   KING CHARLES AND PILSDON   283

In the vale at the foot of the Pen is the very insignificant
village of Pilsdon.   It consists now of no more than the
church, the manor house, certain farm buildings, and a cottage
or two.   Yet the place is famous in a humble way in history.
The manor belonged for many years to the Hody family, and
after them to the Wyndhams.   Here at the time of King
Charles's flight from Worcester lived Sir Hugh Wyndham, an
uncle of Colonel Wyndham, of Trent.   When the King and his
party left Charmouth on September 23rd they made for Trent
by way of Bridport, as has already been detailed.[1]   Those who
pursued them rode through Bridport on to Dorchester.   Find-
ing to their disgust that Charles had not come that way, they
hurried back along the same road and made straight for Pilsdon,
where they believed the King to be secreted.   They burst in
upon the astonished family with some heat, and commenced
their blundering proceedings by declaring that one of the young
ladies of the house was Charles Stuart in disguise.   When this
error in diagnosis had been corrected they placed the old
baronet, his lady, his daughters, his man-servants, and his maid-
servants in the hall under guard, while they set to work to search
every cupboard and loft in the house.   With what result is
well known.

The old manor house is little changed externally since the
soldiers ransacked the bedrooms while Sir Hugh Wyndham
fumed and swore in the hall.   It is a fine house of yellow-grey
stone, with mullioned windows and with dormers in the rugged
roof.   From these very diamond-pane windows the indignant
maids watched the soldiers ride sulkily away, while the young
ladies mourned over the dainty gowns and laces which had
been tumbled out of any wardrobe that could shelter Charles
Stuart.

The church in this out-of-the-world retreat is very small.   It
possesses an ancient pulpit, as well as a holy water stoup by the
door.   From an old inventory it would appear that the folk of

---

[1] See page 256.

Pilsdon were not at one time as careful about their church as
they might have been, for there is an entry to this effect :
"At Pillesdon there lacketh two bells which were stolen."

Broad Windsor.

At the foot of Lewesdon Hill, in a deep hollow full of
gardens, is Stoke Abbott, as pretty a village as any in Dorset.
Its position is most fascinating.   The cottages have walls of
light yellow stone and roofs of thatch.   Many of them are old
and curious.   Two pleasant houses, for example, are dated 1613

and 1762 respectively. The church is a graceful type of the simple village church of long ago, and has preserved many of its Early English windows.

A road passing through the gap between Lewesdon and Waddon Hills leads to Broadwindsor. It was through this village that King Charles passed in his flight from Charmouth to Trent,[1] and it was here that he halted on the evening of September 23rd. The party put up at an inn called called the " Castle," Charles still acting the part of a groom. The name of this tavern was later on changed from the " Castle " to the "George." The George Inn is still the chief hostelry of the place, but it is not the inn that Charles Stuart and Juliana Coningsby rested at. That building was burnt down in 1856. The village is large, rambling, and untidy, and is surrounded by singularly featureless country. The chief interest of the place is due to the fact that Thomas Fuller, who died in 1661, was at one time rector here. He was, it is needless to say, that copious writer and exponent of witty conceits known as " quaint old Tom Fuller." The church in which the quaint man ministered is a fine building of its kind. It has been liberally restored, but the most interesting of its ancient features, its Early English and Norman aisles and its Norman font, have been preserved. With especial care has been kept the ancient pulpit from which Tom Fuller preached. It is elaborately carved with floral designs, and if not as quaint as the preacher, is at least as florid.

One of the most pleasant corners in the far West of the county will be found among the uplands about Corscombe and Chelborough. Here is an undulating district of valleys and downs, of many trees, of deep lanes shut in by hedges so high that the narrow way is always in shade. The road through the Chelboroughs—going south from Closeworth—is as beautiful as any in the South of England. It follows a ridge from which can be seen on either side a rich, comfortable country, with

[1] See pages 256 and 265.

smooth slopes dotted with sheep, and hamlets so hidden in green that they are only to be discovered by their rising smoke.

East Chelborough, it may be said, consists only of a house or two on the high ground near about the "Castle." West Chelborough is below the fort on the way to the valley. Chelborough Castle stands on a conical hill isolated from the rest. It is represented now by a mound, surrounded by a rampart. The bold outpost advances to the very edge of the range of hills, and in the days of the Britons must have been one of the watch-towers upon which hung the safety of the colony. West Chelborough is a village so far from the haunts of men that the visit of a stranger causes some unrest. It is a delectable little place, beautifully bestowed. The ancient church is very quaint; its walls are of yellow masonry, its roof of slabs of stone, while its font, shaped like a tub, belongs to Norman times. There are many old memorials on the wall, adorned for the most part with village poetry, of which the following is a specimen :—

> " Look here, my friends, behold and see
> This house of clay in which I be
> Pray do you not lament for me
> But scan your own Mortality."

The most curious thing in the church is an altar tomb, upon which are the recumbent figures of a lady and child. The lady is enveloped in a species of down quilt, and is asleep. Such costume as is apparent pertains to the time of Elizabeth. The monument is without date or name, is surmounted by the arms of the Kymers, and is on the whole exceptional and unpleasant.

Corscombe church is placed high up on the side of the hill at the foot of which lies the village. This handsome building is among the many locked churches of the county. Its situation is exceedingly fine. At Corscombe lived the eccentric patriot, Thomas Hollis, who called himself "a true Whig," while his friends dubbed him a republican. He lived at

Corscombe in absolute seclusion. He named his farms and
fields after men whom he considered had been defenders of
liberty. In the middle of one of these fields he was buried in
1774. According to his own directions, no mark of any kind
indicates the spot where he lies.

As is known to all men, the object of greatest interest on the
West frontier of Dorset is Forde Abbey. This exquisite
monastic building stands in a secluded valley by the River Axe.
The monastery was founded in 1148 for an abbot and twelve
monks of the Cistercian order. The last Abbot was Thomas
Chard, who restored and greatly beautified the place, recon-
structing the cloister and refectory, which remain as he left them
to this day. Thomas Chard died in 1544. Over the front
entrance tower remains still this inscription :

"AN'O D'NI MILLESIMO QUINQUESIMO VIC^{mo} OCTA^o
A D'NO FACTUM EST THOMA CHARD ABB."

The date, it will be noticed, is 1528. At the dissolution the
Abbey was granted to Richard Pollard, and from his family it
passed in succession to those of Poulett, Roswell, Prideaux,
and Gwyn. The arms of these great folk appear many times
and in many parts of the old house.

At the time of the Great Civil War it belonged fortunately to
a Prideaux who was Attorney-General to the Commonwealth,
and so its walls escaped the fate of being "slighted." This
same Prideaux employed Inigo Jones to make additions and
alterations to the edifice, all of which works still survive. " In
1680 the son of the Attorney-General received a visit from the
Duke of Monmouth, who was making a pleasure tour through
the western counties. He had afterwards, however, to regret
the honour, for he was arrested as accessory to Monmouth's
rebellion, and kept a prisoner in the Tower until he had paid
a ransom of £15,000 to Judge Jeffreys. . . . . In 1815 the
Abbey was let for a term of three years to Jeremy Bentham,
who here wrote some of his works ; and here his favourite

disciple, James Mill, the father of John Stuart Mill, with his whole family, used to spend nine or ten months at a stretch." [1] The great building, situated as it is in a glorious garden, is a wonder to see.   Grey with age, yellow with lichen, green with ivy, it presents a long stretch of ecclesiastical windows, of embattled walls, of decorated buttresses, of turrets and towers, of steep grey roofs, and of quaint fancies in carved stone.   Over the gateway is an oriel window of much dignity and beauty, although worn and rugged with age.   Within are a chapel, dating from the time of Stephen, windows of early Tudor days, the great hall built by Thomas Chard in the sixteenth century, his vaulted cloister, together with the grand staircase and state apartments erected by Inigo Jones.

[1] Murray's *Wilts and Dorset*.   London, 1899.   Page 693.

CHAPTER XVIII

TOLLER PORCORUM is a convenient centre from whence to
visit certain of the midlands of Dorset. There is a station
there, although it has dropped the cognomen of Porcorum.
The name is peculiar, but of remarkable names of places this
Toller is by no means the only example in the county. We
have, on this side of Dorset, Whitchurch Canonicorum and
Ryme Intrinseca. We have also in the county the Wriggle
River and the Devil's Brook, God's Blessing Green and
Giddy Green, Grammar's Hill and Mount Ararat, Hungry
Down and Dancing Hill. The names of certain farms and
holdings are possibly more curious still. There is something
of the forlorn hope about Ratcombe Barn, Wooden Cabbage
Farm, and Labour-in-Vain. Starvington Farm, Poor Lot, and
Charity Bottom are not attractive titles for those who have
property to sell. Botany Bay Barn and Menagerie have no
doubt a story, while there is the sarcasm of utter isolation
about Bedlam, Marshalsea, and Bridewell.

Toller Porcorum, Swines' Toller or Hog Toller, is supposed
to derive its title from the circumstance that it was a notable
place for the feeding of swine. The village lies in a shallow,
well-wooded valley, and is so singularly free from pigs that it
would appear to be living down its early reputation. It is, it
must be confessed, in itself a place of no interest, but it
stands in the midst of an attractive district.

U

The village of Toller Fratrum, Toller of the Brethren, is much more agreeable. It is prettily placed on a ledge delved from the slope of a hill, over against the River Hooke. It belonged at one time to the Brethren of the Order of St. John of Jerusalem, and at a later period to the Fulfords. The mansion, built by Sir Thomas Fulford, the distinguished Royalist, still stands, and is to this day an admirable specimen of the domestic architecture of the early part of the seventeenth century. It is a house of grey masonry, bronzed by age, with stone - mullioned windows, and pinnacles formed out of monstrous heraldic beasts, overshadowed by chimneys of twisted stone. A building with a thatched roof near the house is said to be the refectory. On its outer wall, cut in stone, is the appropriate figure of a man eating a loaf.

The small, much-restored church contains a tub-shaped font ornamented with archaic carvings of human heads in an incongruous jumble. Some, who speak with authority, say that the font is Saxon, others that its decoration belongs to a debased Roman period. It is further declared that the sculptor has striven to represent the man-faced Lion of Judah succouring the human race. In a wall of the church is a rustic tablet representing Mary wiping the Saviour's feet with her hair. It is almost as unconventional a piece of sculpture as the font.

A pleasant valley road leads from the Tollers to Wynford Eagle. The place was once held by the barony of Aquila, or the Eagle, in Sussex. The family was Norman, and took its name from Aquila in Normandy. He who was the first of the house to settle in England owned Pevensey Castle. The chief interest of Wynford Eagle rests in the fact that it was the birthplace of Thomas Sydenham, the father of British medicine. On this account Dr. Crane, a poet of Dorchester, protests that the village should be approached with proper humility. He writes severely in the following strain :—

> " With aweful footsteps, stranger, tread this earth,
> The place rever'd which gave to Sydenham birth."

The manor of Wynford Eagle came in 1551 to the Sydenhams, an ancient family from Sydenham, near Bridgwater. Thomas Sydenham, the great physician, was born here in 1624. He studied at Oxford, where he took his degree. On the outbreak of the war he served in the Parliamentary army as a captain of horse, and was engaged in repulsing a Royalist attack on Dorchester. He was present also at the eventful battle of Worcester. During one of the many engagements in which he took part he was severely wounded, and recurrent trouble from this injury followed him for many years. Sydenham in 1655 began to practise his profession at Westminster, and very soon became the leading physician in London. He threw aside the jargon and ridiculous traditions with which medicine was then hampered, and applied to the study of it sound common sense. He was guided by personal observation and experience, and not by the twaddle of theorists. His writings show him to be a man both truthful and fearless, whose insight was unusually acute. He was himself a subject of gout, and his description of that malady is still—of its kind —quite unsurpasssed. He made an epoch in the history of medical science, and is recognised as the founder of clinical medicine as it is now known. He died at his house in Pall Mall in December, 1689, and was buried at St. James's, Westminster.

The end of the Sydenham family is rather deplorable. William Sydenham, the last of the house, became involved in financial troubles. In the hope of clearing himself he put the ancestral estate of Wynford Eagle up to a private lottery. It is generally reported that there was more trickery than chance in this speculation, and that the harassed William had so arranged matters that the winning ticket should fall to "a confidant of the family," who should privately restore the estate to the Sydenhams for a small sum. When the lottery took place it was surely enough to the confidant of the family that the prize fell. This fortunate individual was a woman, who, when required by the *deus ex machinâ*, William Sydenham, to fulfil her part of the bargain, basely declined. Her heart, it appears, had long been set upon matrimony. As the owner of Wynford Eagle, she was quite aware that a substantial step had been made towards the possessing of a husband. In fact, she at once married Doily Michel, who in due course sold the manor to George Richards. When she who was destined to become Mrs. Doily Michel refused to complete the *rôle* she had essayed to play, Mr. Sydenham and his two daughters declined in turn to surrender Wynford Eagle. They clung to the ancestral walls, and no doubt called down fire from heaven to consume the treacherous Mrs. Doily. The law of the country, however, prevailed against the desperate squire, so that in the end William Sydenham was committed to Dorchester prison in 1709, and died there nine years later. Thus ended miserably a tenancy which had lasted just one hundred and fifty-eight years.

The house of the Sydenhams still stands in Wynford Eagle, a beautiful specimen of the seventeenth century manor. It is a house of gables, and on the summit of the central gable is perched a great stone eagle, alert and strong. Under it is writ the date 1630. The house has handsome old brick chimneys, a fine porch with two chambers over it, and the large, many-casemented windows of the time. The village itself consists mainly of orchards and gardens, with a few farm buildings and a cottage or two. The church that Sydenham knew has vanished, to be replaced by a modern building of daring ugliness. In the wall of the new edifice is a Norman or pre-Norman tympanum from the ancient church. It shows two fearsome beasts in stone, who are apparently about to fight. They have the aspect of lobsters, with the heads of cats and the front feet of cats. A long curved tail they have also, but no hinder extremities. Authorities state that these creatures are "wyverns in opposition." The wyvern is described in dictionaries as a winged dragon with a barbed tail.

North of Toller Porcorum, amidst very beautiful country, will be found the many-gabled Elizabethan manor house of Wraxall and the mansion of Chantmarle. This latter place belonged to the Chantmarles in the reign of King John. The present building, erected by Sir John Strode in 1619, was never completed. Although now but a farmhouse, it is still a building of great distinction. Over the picturesque porch are two chambers almost hidden by ivy. The lower of the two rooms has a beautiful bow window. In all the casements are the little diamond-shaped panes of the time. The whole house presents a fine effect in colour, in greys and yellows, soft browns and green. The very quaint chapel, detached from the house, was built by Sir John Strode in 1612 "in a garden of herbs." He laid the first stone, and his wife Anne the second. Over his stone he placed a sheet of lead engraved by himself with writings to record what he had done. Sir John speaks thus of his chapel: "This chapel hath his inside plastered white and fretted over with the sun, moone, stars, cherubims, doves, grapes, and pomegranates." For this work he paid one Eaton £6 16s. It may be said that the chapel no longer has "his inside" so decorated.

Rampisham, just beyond Wraxall, is one of the most beautiful villages in Dorset. It stands in a valley of trees through which runs a stream. It is a place of old thatched cottages, with a tiny, creeper-covered inn of great antiquity and singularly low stature, bearing the ferocious title of the " Tiger's Head." In the churchyard is the stump of a fifteenth or sixteenth century cross, close to which is an altar tomb inscribed with the date 1606. The cross is very elaborately carved with figures representing—as Hutchins supposed—the stoning of Stephen and the martyrdoms of St. Edmund and St. Thomas à Becket. It bears the date 1516 and the name of one Porter who died in that year.

Among the crowd of little stone men on the pillar are two crowned figures seated at a long table, a man kneeling, St.

Peter, sundry monks, sundry fools, and two men in armour. With the exception of the tableau, reputed to be the stoning of St. Stephen, the sculpture is as faint as an almost forgotten tale. The cross itself, its pedestal and its steps, have become tanned by many summers to a rich golden brown. The stones are nearly covered by moss, while in the wide cracks in the masonry ferns and a few ambitious wild flowers are growing. From the summit of the high-road which crosses Rampisham Hill is a view of the sea lying at the foot of the Golden Cap, very mystic and wonderful.

At Rampisham was born in 1597 that distinguished physician, Francis Glisson. He studied at Cambridge, where he became in due course Professor of Physic. He was one of the founders of the Royal Society, and practised his profession in New Street, Fleet Street. Among his many valuable contributions to science was an account of the anatomy of the liver so precise that at the present day no description of that fickle organ is complete without the details of " Glisson's capsule."

The nearest town to Rampisham is Evershot, a neat, wholesome, over-grown village, which remains still modest and unassuming, although dignified by a railway station. As in Leland's days, it is even yet " a right humble towne." In 1732 John Wilkins left money to Evershot for many things, including one pound a year to the curate for catechising the children of the place once a week. Through his goodness of heart poor children were to be bought blue gowns and bonnets as well as new Bibles. Indeed, the soul of Wilkins seemed to be overflowing with a tender love for children, had he not in the same will disinherited his only child. The trustees, displeased by the inconsistency of Wilkins, and believing that his yearning to provide poor children with blue gowns and bonnets was sheer hypocrisy, refused to act, with the result, says Hutchins, that "no new ones have as yet succeeded them."

To those in search of out-of-the-way places where may be found the quiet of the boundless prairie I would commend

Batcombe. Its situation at the foot of a curving line of steep chalk
downs is most romantic; its approach from the South by a
headlong road which drops over the green cliff is most fearsome.
The village has long vanished, having fled apparently to escape
the boredom of unutterable solitude, leaving behind a church,
a farmhouse, and a few cottages. The church stands quite
alone at the bottom of the silent downs, which surround it on
three sides. So steep are these grass-covered heights that
from their summit it is possible to look down upon the flat
roof of the tower. The church possesses a font of most
archaic design, and many monuments which are evidently
the work of village stonemasons who had vivid fancies in
their brains.

On the embattled tower are four pinnacles, one at each corner.
Until a few years ago there were only three. The fourth was
knocked off by the hoof of the squire's horse when that
gentleman jumped from the crest of the down into the village,
clearing the church and tower on his way. The squire, whose
name was John Minterne, was better known as " Conjuring
Minterne." He had dealings with the devil, so the story goes,
and the extraordinary feats he performed by the aid of this
being must have kept the villagers in a state of chronic
uneasiness. Possibly the uncanny habits of the squire led to
the depopulation of the settlement. It is to be regretted that
The Life and Times of Conjuring Minterne has not yet
been written. Certain it is that he ceased to associate with
the devil before he died, for he is buried in the churchyard, in
holy ground. His tomb is pointed out with pride to any who
turn aside to visit this quaint place. It is small and square and
singularly carved, but lacks both name and date, as well as any
record of the life work of this alarming man. In the church
are wall tablets to Minterns : to a John Minterne who died in
1716, as well as to a John Minterne who " decessed " in 1592.
I am unable to say if either of these " decessed " squires can
lay claim to the name of Conjuring Minterne, nor do I know

in what century the open-mouthed villagers gazed upon their
lord of the manor floating over the church on his Batcombe-
bred horse. I can only state that no conventicle in Dorset
is better adapted for the performance of this particular feat.

This Batcombe of the Legends is an altogether dramatic
place. On the summit of the hill, on a wild heath such as
the witches in *Macbeth* might have haunted, there stands a
mystic stone called the Cross-in-Hand. It is a sort of Pillar
of Salt in a place of hushed solitude, where are only gorse
and heather and a never-tiring wind. It may be that there is
little in this scapegoat pillar to distinguish it from the base of
a lamp post when such posts were fashioned in stone. There
are, however, some who can see that the summit of the
column is carved into the form of a hand holding a bowl.
Even those whose vision is thus gifted do not claim that anything like a cross is grasped by the semi-invisible fingers. The
morbid declare that this enigma in stone marks the scene of a
murder, the imaginative that it was a place where a miracle
was wrought, while those of simple faith state that in the bowl
alms were deposited for needy wayfarers. For my own part, I
do not fancy that the pillar rose from the heath as the sword
Excalibur rose from the lake, but believe that it was placed
where it is by unpicturesque overseers to mark the boundary
of a parish.

North-west of Toller of the Pigs is the town of Beaminster.
A certain byway leading thither passes another Toller called
Toller Whelme. This Toller Whelme is not a much-frequented
place, but the guide-book says that a grange there once
belonged to Forde Abbey. Let the traveller go to the spot
and see. He will in time come upon a narrow, silent road,
grown over with grass, which drops into a deep glen of trees.
Here, hidden away in a niche among the hills, will be found
Toller Whelme sleeping its last sleep. There is no village, no
hamlet—not even the sign of living men. Toller Whelme is
merely a deserted grange tumbling into ruin. A more pathetic,

piteous, haunting spot cannot be found in this bright part of
England. The house is of grey stone and very old. Its roof
is of comely thatch, its windows have stone mullions and
graceful dripstones. There is a little stone porch to the house
and an ancient door. The shutters are closed, but here and
there a hasp or a hinge has fallen away, so that the sun streams

Beaminster.

into an empty room and lights up pale patches on a wall where
pictures hung, and shows the bare, ghostly mantelpiece over
the rusting grate. The place is lonely, desolate, dead. The
Prince who woke the Sleeping Beauty might ride down into
the glen and blow the loudest blast upon his horn, but beyond
the flutter of startled birds in the creepers under the eaves
there would be never a sign of life. There are none to wake.

In a little garden within the wicket gate is a happy myrtle in
blossom, while the face of the dead grange is covered with
yellow roses, which spread tenderly over the walls, as if touch-

ing them with affectionate fingers. The garden behind the house is a mere wilderness of coarse grass and weeds, with here and there some loyal flower, once tended by the lady of the grange. By the side of the homestead is a pond, grown over with weeds, while around it are farm buildings, deserted, silent, and crumbling into ruin. The thatch-roofed barn is empty; there is only some mildewed harness in the cart-shed; in the manger is the unfinished hay the horses were munching when they were led out for the last time. All the chattering, restless bustle of the farmyard has long ended; the pig-styes are still, the hen-coops are grown over with weeds, and some green thing is creeping across the many thresholds of the dove-cot. Save for the myrtle-bush, the yellow roses, and the swallows, the grange has been abandoned utterly by all who once made the life of it.

From the high-road which leads from Toller Whelme to Beaminster can be seen the great hollow, in the green centre of which the town lies. Behind the amphitheatre rise the twin heights of Lewesdon and Pilsdon Pen. Beaminster is a clean, cheerful, self-respecting county town, without pretensions, without offensively modern houses, and without red-brick suburbs. There are a few thatched cottages in the streets, but Beaminster mostly affects a cosy, yellow-brown stone and ruddy tiles for its dwelling-places. No two houses in the town are alike. They belong mostly to the early part of the nineteenth century, and are much given to stone porticoes and ample bow windows, full of red geraniums. Beaminster is never puffed up, and never obtrusive, while it is still sufficiently old-fashioned to call a girls' school a " young ladies' seminary."

The pride of Beaminster is not its queer little square, nor that fine, farmer-haunted inn of stone, the White Hart, but all such conceit as it may harbour is centred upon the church, and especially upon its glorious tower, which is unrivalled in the county. This gracious, golden-brown tower is worth a pilgrimage to see. It was built as long ago as 1520. It is a tower of many pinnacles, gargoyles, and niches, which is endowed with as lavish a wealth of delicate carving as a gold casket. Here are sculptures of the Blessed Virgin, of the Crucifixion and the Ascension, all in the same warm, golden-brown stone ; yet from this happy tower were hung, like carrion, the quarters of some of Monmouth's followers. The church itself does not attain to either the magnificence or the elegance of its tower. Indeed, the two are a little ill-assorted. There are, however, many notable monuments in the aisles, of one of which mention has been already made.[1]

The comparatively modern appearance of Beaminster is the outcome of the many unfortunate fires to which, in times past, it fell the victim. For instance, in 1644 nearly the whole settlement was burnt down. Prince Maurice was quartered in Beaminster at the time. The conflagration began at John Sargent's house in North Street, and was due to a musket discharged in the gable of the thatch. This firing was incidental to a falling-out between the French and the Cornish in the town. The whole loss, "valued by men of judgement, was one and twenty thousand and four score pounds at least." Even a year later, when Fairfax's army passed through the town, Beaminster presented "the pitifullest spectacle that man could behold." There was another great fire in 1684, and still another in 1781. As in Leland's days, Beaminster still "usith much housbandry," and is the centre of the district in which is produced the famous Blue Vinny cheese, without which no Dorset man is really happy.

At the present day, when there is such clamorous demand for rifle clubs or rifle ranges in every village, and for compulsory training in the use of arms, it may be of interest to know that at Meerhay, by Beaminster, there are two butts, erected in the reign of Henry VIII. in pursuance of an Act of Parliament, whereby "all sorts of men, under the age of forty years, should have bows and arrows and use shooting, and that butts should

[1] Page 100.

be erected in every parish." Those, therefore, who are alarmed by proposals which they consider revolutionary may be reassured by knowing that the suggestion is ancient and the practice long established by law.

In the environs of Beaminster are three notable houses, Parnham, Mapperton, and Melplash. Parnham is a large Tudor mansion, characteristic of the period, which was for many generations possessed by the Strode family. It is scarcely visible from the road.

Mapperton House lies in a beautiful glen approached by an

Mapperton.

avenue of trees. It is one of the famous houses of Dorset, and one of the most charming and most picturesque. The building belongs to the time of Henry VIII. In the reign of that sovereign the manor was possessed by Robert Morgan, who had the following patent granted to him : " Forasmoche as wee bee credibly informed that our wel biloved Robert Morgan esquier, for diverse infirmities which he hathe in his hedde, cannot convenyently, without his grete daungier, be discovered of the same. Whereupon wee, in tendre consideration thereof, have by these presents licensed him to use and were his bonnet on his hed at al tymys, as wel in our presence as elsewher, at his libertie."

In spite of "the diverse infirmities in his hedde," Robert Morgan built the beautiful manor house. According to Hutchins, this inscription was formerly in the great hall to record the deed :—

"Robt. Morgan and Mary his wife built this house in their own life time, at their own charge and cost.

> "What they spent, that they lent :
> What they gave, that they have :
> What they left, that they lost."

Mapperton Manor House.

Any ambiguity in this passage may possibly be explained by the unfortunate condition of Robert Morgan's "hedde."

The house is a building of two stories, with dormer windows in the roof. It is of grey-yellow stone, and is so disposed as to form two sides of a prim square, a third side being supplied by a venerable church of the humblest proportions. Perched on the gate-posts before the house are stone eagles with outspread wings, gazing at one another as if awaiting a signal to rise.

Elsewhere are heraldic beasts on pinnacles. The roof is tiled with slabs of stone, the chimneys are of stone twisted into spirals. Over the door of the porch is carved a gallant coat-of-arms. There are gracious bay windows, with stone casements and small panes, and an open stone parapet to crown them all. It is a house of many gables, whose aspect of great age is tempered by a growth of much ivy upon the walls and of moss between the stones, while it is saved from utter silence by a colony of garrulous rooks.

The mansion at Melplash, although much modernised, is still worthy of the princely days of the squires. It is said that over the chimney-piece in the hall are the arms of the Paulets, with the motto of the family, "Aimez loyaulté," and the date 1604. The manner in which the manor came into the possession of the Paulet family is somewhat remarkable. An heiress of the Melplashes brought the estate, in the fulness of time, to Walter More of Marnhull. Among the descendants of this gentleman was Sir Thomas More, who in the reign of Henry VIII. was made Sheriff of Dorset. He was a jovial being, who had an unusual view of his responsibilities. One day, after no doubt a generous use of strong waters, the Sheriff was tickled by the idea that it would be an excellent jest to let all the prisoners loose out of Dorchester gaol. To the gaol then the ruddy-faced gentleman hurried and, to the dismay of confused warders, ordered all the prisoners to be set free. The command of a Sheriff in Tudor days no man could withstand, so locks were sulkily turned and doors thrown back with silent protest. The inhabitants of Dorchester there and then enjoyed the spectacle of a few score of prisoners running for their lives down the streets to the open country, while the hilarious Sheriff stood by the gaol gate and cheered them on as if they had been a pack of hounds let loose from a kennel. That the warders sat in the empty prison that night and talked the matter over with upturned eyes and uplifted hands may well be imagined.

It can hardly be supposed that the greater powers in the land considered the exploit of the Sheriff to be quite as divert-ing as he found it. Sir Thomas, indeed, had to seek a pardon from the King. This was obtained for him by the Lord Treasurer of the day, who happened to be Lord Paulet. As a suitable recognition of this convenience, the merry Sheriff was required to give his daughter in marriage to Lord Paulet's second son. Thus it was that the manor came for a while to the family whose motto was " Aimez loyaulté."

CHAPTER XIX

SHERBORNE—the town of the *scir burne* or clear brook—lies pleasantly at the foot of a green slope where it glides into the valley of the Yeo. The country around is so prettily wooded and so dainty that Sherborne seems to be sheltered in the glades of an ancient park. The town first emerges into the light of history as the capital of Newer Wessex, that new land beyond the grim forest of Selwood which had been won for England by the arms of Kings Kenwealh and Kentwine. This fair West Country included Dorset and Somerset, together with the land of Malmesbury. Of all of it the city of the clear brook was the capital.

It was in A.D. 705 that it became the seat of the bishopric and its church a cathedral. The first bishop was the learned and kindly St. Aldhelm—he of the little chapel on St. Aldhelm's Head. For 370 years the see of the diocese was at Sherborne, during which time twenty-seven bishops reigned in the castle by the town. In 1075 it was removed to Old Sarum. These ecclesiastics were no mere pastors or bookworm scholars, no mere saunterers in cloister walks. They were fighting men. It is well to remember that when the Danes swept over England, " only in one corner of the land did Englishmen hold their own throughout, namely, in this part of Wessex of which Sherborne

is the centre.   Between the years 871 and 933 three Bishops
of Sherborne fell in battle against the Danes." [1]

St. Aldhelm built a church at Sherborne, on the site of
which stands the present magnificent Abbey.   At Sherborne,

Sherborne.   The Monk's Conduit and Abbey Tower.

moreover, was founded in St. Aldhelm's time a place of learning, a
school which still at the end of 1,200 years flourishes exceedingly,
and has gathered about it miscellaneous ancient and stately
buildings.   Here too, in the guise of a picturesque almshouse,

[1] *History of Sherborne.*   By W. B. Wildman.   Sherborne, 1902.   Page 3.

X

is the Hospital of St. John the Baptist and St. John the Evangelist, which, from the time of Henry VI. until now, has sheltered a grateful company of poor men and women. Finally there is the Castle of Sherborne, which played a valiant part in the history of Wessex, until it was "slighted" at the end of the Civil War.

Things change but little at Sherborne. The world has passed by, with its unrestful projects and its irreverent breaking up of old landmarks, but the Wessex town has kept green the memory of its past, and has so clung to its old possessions that it is to the up-to-date town as the page of a missal is to a newspaper print. The city of faithful memories is to this day the most picturesque town in Dorset, while many will aver that it is the most pleasant to dwell in. The description of Sherborne given by Leland centuries ago will apply to the place still with but little amendment. That traveller writes of it in this wise : " The toune of Sherburne stondith partely on the brow of an hille partely in a botom.   I esteme it to lak litle of a two miles in cumpace.   For a dry town or other, saving Pole that is a little thing, I take it to be the best towne at this present tyme in Dorsetshire."

It is a bright town, prim and old-fashioned, and unsullied by the aggressive villas and red brick terraces of the modern suburb. Although a small place, it is yet of much dignity. Its Abbey, its rambling school buildings, its venerable almshouse, its many ancient dwellings, show that it still may claim some of the prestige of a capital in miniature. There is about it much of the quaint solemnity and monastic calm of the cathedral town, much of the gravity of an ancient seat of learning, much of the sober business ways of the mediæval market.

There are divers winding ways in the place, streets that become narrow or wide, according to their pleasure, and dark lanes that run between high walls or nodding houses. The names of the streets are all in keeping, being such as " Cheap Street," " Acreman Street," " Horsecastles," and " Coldharbour."   The houses are of all heights, sizes, and periods. Here are timber-faced dwellings, where the upper story overhangs the lower, and where the roof breaks out into irrelevant gables ; houses with the stone-mullioned casements of Tudor days or the round bow window of the Georgian period ; houses with gateways under them leading into courtyards ; humble buildings fashioned out of stone filched from a church ; cottages with the arched doorways of a convent, or with buttresses worthy of a chapel ; pieces of old wall and other miscellaneous fragments which the town with its love for the past has never had the heart to cast aside. Over the grey roofs can be seen the trees upon the hill top, while over many a crumbling wall comes the fragrance of garden or orchard.

Set down casually on the pavement of the main street, with for a background an old roof of dormer windows and the Abbey tower rising above a clump of trees, is the Monks' Conduit. It was built in the sixteenth century, and stood originally in the cloister court of the monastery. It was removed to its present site some centuries ago. The building is many-sided, has fine Gothic windows and a groined roof. To it in old days the water was conducted, and here the monks washed and shaved. At the present time it affords a picturesque support for the shoulders of the lounger.

In spite of its many and solemn responsibilities, Sherborne in the past appears to have had outbreaks of light-heartedness which almost amounted to riotous living. A deed drawn up "in the XXI yere of the Reigne of our Sov'aigne Lord Kynge Henry the VIIIth " and still extant contains this dolorous passage : " The towne has suffered from vyces, Idelnes, and unlawfull games by reson of so grete and inordynat nomber of Alehouses, in tyme of plentifulness, by Journeymen, day labourers and other poor Artyfycers there and thyder Resortyng and usyng there ryotous expenses and unlawfull games to the grete trouble and inquyetyng of the inhabitaunts next thereto adjoynyng and to the grete Impouerysshyng and decay of the

Towne." At the present day the number of alehouses is still
"grete" and "inordynat," but the sobriety of the town is
beyond question.

Sherborne too was famous for its fairs, especially for the
"Pack Monday Fair"; for its "Church Ales," and for the processions and plays on Corpus Christi Day. The character of
these plays can be gathered from the Parish Accounts of 1572,
when it would appear that sixpence was paid for "a peck
of weathen meal to make Lot's wife" (apparently in the character of the Pillar of Salt). A carrier was also paid 10d. "to
bring Master Poyntz, and he that did playe upon the trumpete
took 10d. for his payns." Furthermore, Henry Stephens was
paid 14s. "for canvass, gurswebbe,[1] tinsall and nails towards the
making of the giant."

The Abbey Church of St. Mary the Virgin is a singularly
beautiful building, although externally a little spoiled by its
stunted tower. "It is," Willis writes, "essentially a Norman
church entirely transformed, the nave and presbytery into the
Perpendicular style. The transepts, tower, and other append-
ages still retain Norman characteristics with Early English
insertions and additions, especially a portion of a fine Lady
Chapel at the east end. The Perpendicular work is of an
unusually grand and beautiful character." One small fragment
is left of the church of St. Aldhelm, in the form of a blocked-
up doorway and a wall on the north side of the present building. The Norman Abbey was erected by Roger of Caen about
1122. This Roger was the chief minister of Henry I., and was
as great an architect as he was a statesman. Of his work many
specimens remain in the Abbey, notably the Norman arches
which support the tower. Indeed, the tower itself is Norman
up to the floor of the bell-chamber. The beautiful Norman
south porch was reconstructed in 1850. The church was rebuilt in the Perpendicular style in the latter half of the fifteenth
century. It was finally restored, with great taste and skill,

---

[1] The webbing used for making girths.

by the ever generous Digby family in the ten years between 1848 and 1858.

The Abbey is constructed of rich Hamhill stone, whose warm yellow tints are made more beautiful by contrast with the deep green of the trees around the church. The immediate impression that will befall any who enter the Abbey for the first time is an outcome of the magic tint of the Hamhill stone. The interior of great ecclesiastical buildings is apt to be chilly and

Sherborne Abbey. The West Window and South Porch.

grey, and the atmosphere about the vaulted heights to be hazy, as if a wan mist filled the place. Here, however, is a nave warm and ruddy, and so flooded with yellow light that the pillars and high walls seem to have caught the rays of the setting sun. The choir of the Abbey is most magnificent, harmonious, and inspiring. In many places its panelled walls are stained an Indian red by the great fire which befell the church about the time of its reconstruction. Most glorious is the fan tracery in the roof, which is said to be unrivalled in England; most suggestive is the contrast between the sturdy, unpretending Norman arches and the dainty, effeminate Gothic work which they support.

At the west end of the Abbey will be noticed a doorway which has evidently been narrowed since its first construction, and is at the present time blocked up. The most stirring episodes in the history of the Abbey are, strangely enough, connected with this small doorway, which indeed played an almost tragic part in the annals of the church. The tale of the narrowed entry is as follows :—

In very early times the monks allowed the townspeople to use part of the nave of the Abbey as a parish church. As Sherborne grew in size and importance this arrangement ceased to content, so in the fourteenth century the church of Alhalowes was built on to the west end of the Abbey. The large west doorway of the Abbey led directly into the new building, and this the monks caused to be so built up that it was reduced to a very insignificant entry. Now the font, where all the children were baptised, was still in the Abbey and this narrow door which led from the parish church was very inconvenient and was much resented. The townsfolk, therefore, put up a font in Alhalowes ; but to this the monks objected, on the ground that such an act was a usurpation of their rectorial rights. The parishioners did more than this : they took to ringing the bells of their church at such an early hour that the morning slumbers of the monastery were indecently disturbed. This matter of the bells brought the great quarrel to a head, so that in 1436 the Bishop was compelled to hold an inquiry. This he did, and at the end decided that the Alhalowes font, " set up with daring rashness," was to be utterly destroyed, and that the ringing of the bells was to be postponed to a later hour in the morning. Moreover, it was his pleasure that the narrow door should be enlarged. This judgment, however, satisfied no section of this Christian people ; feeling ran high, and finally both the monks and the worshippers at Alhalowes took the matter into their own hands. Their methods of

procedure are thus described by Leland.   The monks induced
" one Walter Gallor, a stoute Bocher dwelling yn Sherborne, to
enter Alhalowes, where he defacid clene the Fontstone.   The
townsmen, aided by an Erle of Huntindune lying in those
quarters, rose in playne sedition. . . . A Preste of Alhalowes
shot a shaft with fier into the Toppe of that part of S. Marye
Chirch that divided the Est part that the monks usid from
(that) the Townes-men usid ; and this Partition chauncing at
that Tyme to be thakked yn the Rofe was sette a fier and con-
sequently al the hole chirch, the Lede and Belles meltid, was
defacid."   How the flames of this conflagration made red the
stones of the Abbey choir can be seen to this day.   Peace was
finally restored when Alhalowes was without restraint, " usid for
the Paroch Chirch."   The narrowed entry, however, remained,
and is still to be seen in the west wall of the Abbey.

Retribution long after fell upon the monks.   The Abbey
was dissolved in 1539, and was devised in 1540 to Sir John
Horsey, of Clifton Maybank, who promptly sold the whole
property—the great Abbey, the ground about it, the lead, the
bells, and other " fittings "—to the townsfolk of Sherborne for the
paltry sum of £300.   Thus were the tables turned upon the
narrow-minded and selfish people of the monastery.   As the
parishioners had no further use for the church of Alhalowes, it was
promptly pulled down.   The outline of the vexed building can still
be seen, although little more than the foundations of it remain.

Of the famous school of Sherborne it is needless to say more
than that it was founded about 705, was unaffected by the dissolution of the monastery, and was refounded by Edward VI.
in 1550.   A statue of this monarch was set up in the school in
1614, and still stands with much glory in the ancient dining
hall.   " It is of painted stone, is the work of a certain Godfrey
Arnold, and cost £9 5s. 4d.   From time to time henceforth
we get entries in the school accounts of this sort : " " For washing of ye King—6d." "[1]

[1] Wildman's *History of Sherborne.*   Page 62.

The school buildings are exceedingly picturesque, being made up of rambling halls and houses of all ages, scattered about the Abbey grounds, as well as of secluded courtyards and lawns, of unexpected entries and passages, and half-subterranean cloisters. Some are grey with the burden of long years, some are buried in creepers, while many are of glowing yellow stone, which contrasts so vividly with the green of the trees in

Sherborne. The School Dining Hall, with the Lady Chapel to the left.

the precincts. The old Guesten Hall of the monastery is now the library, the school chapel was the Abbot's Hall, a fifth-teenth century building on an undercroft of Late Norman work; the Abbot's Lodging—a most quaint and beautiful house of the fifteenth century, with a fine canopied doorway, many niches, and a queer outbuilding of two stories—is now converted into studies. Surely boys have never learnt Latin and Greek under the cover of such a roof or by the light of such windows. Where stood the Abbey fish-ponds is now the headmaster's garden, ablaze with flowers, while the Abbey mill has been replaced by the school workshops.

The most charming entry to the ancient college is by the south, through the Old Court. Here an arched doorway in a high wall opens from a lane into a little yard covered with grass. Across the lawn leads a flagged path. To step into the tiny square is to step back into the seventeenth century. In front is the dining hall, once the schoolhouse, which bears well its burden of 230 years. It is a building of one story, with tall, stone-mullioned windows whose small diamond panes glitter from under a canopy of ivy. At the breaking of the roof is a stone balustrade, while over the doorway are the royal arms of the Stuarts. To the left of the quiet square is the Lady Chapel, a thirteenth century building which has long been cut off from the Abbey, has been provided with Tudor windows, and converted into a master's house. A more picturesque dwelling could hardly be imagined. The windows look into a nook of ancient England, while the ceiling of the upper bed- rooms is a vaulted roof with as exquisite fan tracery as any chapel can display.

The school, although ancient in its foundation, holds an advanced position as a place of modern learning. Its statutes have of necessity been many times recast. The following clauses from the statutes of 1679 are curious [1] :—

"Every Schollar that shall bee admitted into the saide schoole shall pay unto the schoolmaster one shillinge and six- pence, whereof fourpence shall bee for the Master, fourpence for the Usher and fourpence for Registering and sixpence towards the Increase of Bookes in the Library." If this clause be of interest to parents, the following will be of greater concern to schoolboys. "Boys in the Upper School are to speak nothing but Latin in School and also out of School, wherever they shall meet, under pain of the severest correction." There is little doubt but that by this provision the Latin equivalents

[1] Derived from Wildman's *History of Sherborne.*

of the verb " to swap," and of the nouns " marbles," " apples," and "a black eye," came to be well understood.

Another very interesting feature of Sherborne is the alms-house, founded, or refounded, in 1437. The old part of the present building was completed in 1448. It is a low, many-gabled house of two stories, with a roof of stone tiles and a beautiful oriel window looking down the street. It possesses

The Alms House, Sherborne. The Cloister and Chapel.

a queer little chapel, where the poor men and the prior occupy the floor and the poor women and the housewife the gallery. In this quiet nook is a quadrangle, with on two sides a stone cloister where the old men sit and smoke, dream in the sun over the past, and wait for the end. Here can be heard, mumbled by toothless mouths and jerked out by the stems of cherished pipes, the rare, enchanting dialect of " Dosset."

Last of all must be seen the ruins of the famous Castle of Sherborne. This stronghold stands on a knoll of rock in a park surrounded on all sides by trees. It was built by Bishop Roger (1107–42) on the site of the palace of the Bishops of

Sherborne. It was a mighty place. The curtain, of which great fragments are still standing, was seven feet in thickness, while the walls of the keep measured no less than nine feet across.

The Castle, like all other castles in England, had little peace, and was the scene of fierce attacks, of violence and scheming, and of dark deeds done in dungeons. In 1597 the Castle and

Sherborne. The Castle Gate-house.

manor were granted to Sir Walter Raleigh "for ever," but as that gallant adventurer was indicted for treason in 1603, he was not long possessed of his property. There is, of course, a stone seat in the grounds where Raleigh sat deep in thought and smoked his strange weed. During the Great Civil War the Castle was twice besieged—once in 1642 and once in 1645—with the result that it was taken by Fairfax for the Parliament and was in due course "slighted"—that is to say that it was blown up by gunpowder after the manner of Corfe Castle.

After the turmoil of centuries an eternal peace has fallen upon this truculent and troubled place. Little remains of the

Castle but the fine Norman gate-house (to which Tudor
windows have been added), the walls of the chapel and of the
keep. Here are to be seen still immense masses of masonry
standing up like rugged crags on a lawn, a Norman doorway,
a Norman window, a great Norman pillar. There are dingy,
barrel-vaulted chambers, traces of sunken passages, a wall
marked by a beautiful intersecting arcade, and a turret stair
winding up a rock-like tower to end in nothingness.

Among the many interesting places in the country around
the old capital, the most important is Trent. The way to
Trent is through Nether Compton. There was once a vicar
of this place named Thomas Naish, who was at the same time
one of the Sub-Deans of Sarum. " Mr. Sub-Dean Naish " was
an incessant smoker. One day he was going on horseback to
Sherborne Castle to dine with Lord Digby. He was riding in
full canonical dress, as was the custom of the time, and was of
course smoking. In a fit of absence he put a still lighted pipe
into his pocket. A farmer overtook him and told him he
smoked. "I know it," replied the divine; "no man smokes
more." " But you are on fire, sir," said the farmer earnestly,
and so Mr. Sub-Dean proved to be.

Trent is a straggling, most picturesque village, lying in a
valley of orchards. A worn pathway of flagstones leads
through the rambling street. It is a village of old stone houses,
of thatched cottages, and of many gardens, with no hint of
modernness about it. Any inhabitant of a century ago
who could revisit the place would find it but little
changed.

It was at the manor house at Trent, then in the possession
of Colonel Wyndham, that Charles II. lay concealed for more
than a fortnight after the battle of Worcester. The battle was
fought on September 3rd, 1651. On September 17th the King
reached Trent, attended by Jane Lane—whose servant he pre-
tended to be—and Cornet Henry Lassels. His two companions left him the next day. At the manor Charles occupied

Lady Anne Wyndham's room, and had access, in case of alarm, to a hiding-place with a double floor under the roof. It was at Trent that the King was annoyed by the ringing of the church bells, and was told that the village folk were rejoicing at the news of his death. The monarch, accompanied by Juliana Coningsby, Colonel Wyndham, and Lord Wilmot, left Trent for Charmouth on September 22nd. Their adventures at that place and at Bridport have been already described.[1] They returned to Trent on the 24th, and left that place again on October 5th for Shoreham, near Brighton.[2] The King's stay at Trent, therefore, amounted in all to sixteen days.

Colonel Wyndham and his wife lie buried in Trent church. At the Restoration the Colonel received £1,000 " for the buying of a jewel for his great and eminent service," was made a baronet, and granted a pension of £600. Eleanor Withers and Joan Halsenoth—the maids who waited on the King—received each one hundred pounds. Juliana Coningsby, who rode pillion with the King, was Colonel Wyndham's cousin. It is sad to note that as late as September 11th, 1665, she was compelled to petition for a reward, " as often promised," and received then a grant of £200 a year. She married a Mr. Hext, and lies buried in the north aisle of Low Ham church, Somerset.

The manor house at Trent stands near the church, in a gracious garden. The building has been much modernised, but the King's hiding-place and the rooms he occupied have been carefully preserved. By the kindness of the lady of the house I was able to see them. Lady Anne Wyndham's room is beautifully panelled with black oak, has massive ceiling beams, quaint window recesses, and secret cupboards for hiding valuables. The King's hiding-place is in a small projecting wing, and is over an ancient brewhouse, which has been allowed to remain unchanged. The entrance to the very narrow cell is through a triangular opening, which is really at the base of

---

[1] See pages 264 and 256.   [2] See page 130.

a blocked-up stone doorway. The double floor appears to be due to the building of the wing at a different level from that of the house.

The church of Trent is a very gracious building, standing in one of the most beautiful churchyards in the county, where are the shaft and steps of an ancient cross, as well as a venerable chantry house, built in the reign of Henry VI. The curious and wonderfully carved bench-ends in the church are brown with age, the rood screen is older still ; on the walls over the manorial pew hang rusted helmets and gauntlets while altar tombs of knights carry back the history of Trent into far-away centuries. The stone that marks the resting-place of Colonel Wyndham, who aided the King in his flight, is very simple. It tells that he died on July 8th, 1676, just twenty-five years after Charles Stuart found refuge in his house. On the same plain stone is carved in rustic fashion these lines :—

D^m A. W.
OB^t JVL. 19.
AN^o D^m
1698

This serves to show that by his side lies his wife, Dame Anne Wyndham, who survived him over twenty years.

In the pretty village of Sandford Orcas, near to Trent, is a most excellent grey-stone manor house, very tenderly restored. It has a rare gatehouse with chambers over, a porch brave with heraldic carvings and heraldic beasts on gables, and, above all, an old-fashioned garden, with a bowling-green suggestive of leisured ease, cakes and ale. In the exquisite church by the manor house is a curious monument, which tells a family history with remarkable terseness. The work is in the form of a small marble tablet, elaborately carved and as elaborately coloured. A knight in white armour is kneeling, and in his hand is a skull. In front of him is a lady dressed in black, with a wimple, who in her hand holds a Bible. Behind the knight is a second lady, also in black, but wearing a ruffle, and grasping in her hand a skull. Behind her, in turn, are four little corpses. From the reading on the stone, which is dated 1607, it would appear that the white knight is William Knoyle, and that he first married "fillip, daughter of Robert Morgane, by whom hee had yssve 4 children and bee dead." The lady with the ruffle and the skull is evidently the deceased "fillip Morgane," and the four corpses behind her are those of her children. The knight married, in the second place, Grace Clavel, by whom he had three sons and four daughters. This wife, represented by the lady of the wimple, and the seven children evidently survived him, for she does not hold a skull in her hand ; and the three sons—very small—are to be seen kneeling behind the knight, while the four daughters are sheltered by the skirt of the lady of the wimple.

To the south-west of Sherborne is the famous church of Bradford Abbas, famous for its elaborate and graceful tower and its richly decorated west front. In this parish is the sole surviving wing of the great mansion of Clifton Maybank, which was the seat of the Horseys from the time of Richard II. It came to that family by the marriage of a Horsey with the heiress of the Maubanks, the earlier possessors of the manor. The present house was built about 1586. In an account of it, written in 1648, it is described as a "faire, yellowe freestone buildinge possessing a square green court and a curious gate-house with lodgings in it, also a faire chappel and a bowling greene with fower mounted walks about it, all walled about with a batteled wall and sett with all sorts of fruit." What remains of the mansion is a dignified house, with a rich, open parapet along the front, and high up under the side gable the quaintest little oriel window, ornamented with the Tudor rose and the arms of the Horseys—to wit, three horses' heads, couped, bitted and reined, or.

Among other places about Sherborne may be mentioned Lillington the Obscure, a village reduced now to a church, a rectory, a handsome old barn of stone nearly as large as the church, a farmhouse, and a cottage or two. Here was once the seat of the Cole family, whose fine mansion was surrounded by both terraces and fish-ponds. I searched in the church in vain for a memorial to a member of the Cole family who died in 1669, and who—according to Hutchins—is distinguished by the following epitaph :—

> " Reader you have within this grave
>   A Cole rak'd up in dust,
> His courteous fate saw it was late
>   And that to bed he must.
> Then do not doubt the Cole's not out
>   Tho' it in ashes lies,
> The little spark, now in the dark,
>   Will like the Phœnix rise."

At Purse Caundle lies buried that distinguished physician, Dr. Nathaniel Highmore. His father was the rector of the place. Highmore—who died in 1685—studied at Oxford, and was a friend of the great Harvey. He practised at Sherborne, and is rendered immortal by his anatomical work. A portion of the human skull will always bear the name of the "antrum of High-more." This antrum is a cavity in the face, and Nathaniel states that his attention was drawn to it by a lady who had an abscess in that situation. In the poor village of Purse Caundle most of the thatched roofs of the cottages have been replaced by corrugated iron, the churchyard is in a ruinous condition, while in the church the stone marking Highmore's grave is partly covered up. The beautiful Elizabethan manor house, with its many gables and its miniature oriel window, was the seat of the Hanhams, the Hoskins, and the Longes. One Hanham, buried in the church in 1576, is credited with being " a good housekeeper and comfortable to all poore."

Yetminster, the chief place near Sherborne, is a picturesque townlet, full of quaint old houses and venerable thatched cottages. The dates on the buildings belong mostly to the

early part of the seventeenth century. In the main street is an old
thatch-roofed inn, as well as many houses in ancient stone with
stone-mullioned windows and fine gables. Most of the dwellings are covered by creepers, and none seems to lack a garden
or an orchard. Yetminster is probably the most consistent
old-world village or townlet in the county, for of modern buildings it has but few examples. The church is one among the
many in Dorset which are kept locked, to enforce apparently
the doctrine that people should worship only on Sundays.

CHAPTER XX

THE COUNTRY BEYOND THE HILLS

CROSSING the county from East to West is a line of chalk downs called the Dorset heights. These grass hills—the hills of the sheep—are for the most part bare of trees, and are so steep and abrupt that they look like a great earthwork drawn across the land. Beyond the hills, on the side away from the sea, is the comely hinterland, the land of the Blue Mist, of which some account has been already given.[1] That part of the hinterland which lies between Sherborne and the hills is perhaps the most delectable of all. It is an undulating country, gentle, comfortable, and very green—a place of pasture land and many gardens, of tree-covered slopes and tree-secluded villages, of little streams and shady Devonshire lanes.

The most charming village in these Western backwoods is Melbury Osmond. This is one of the three Melburys in Dorset, its especial name depending upon the circumstance that its church is dedicated to Saint Osmund. The church, standing at the head of the village, was rebuilt in 1745, is of no great interest, and is slowly hiding all its shortcomings under a generous cloak of ivy. The people buried in the church appear to have been possessed of quite phenomenal virtues. Here lies, for example, the Rev. John Biddell (1732), who was "a person of such universal goodness that 'tis difficult to single

[1] Pages 23 and 101.

out any virtue in which he was more particularly eminent."
Here rests also Mrs. Mary Ainslie (1757)—

" A wife more than 21 years
To Mr. William Ainslie
Who never saw her once ruffled with anger
Or heard her utter a peevish word ;
Whether pained or injured, the same good woman
In whose mouth, as in whose character
Was no contradiction."

The village clings to a narrow waving lane on a steep slope,
at the top of which is the church and at the bottom a stream.
The little lane is deeply wooded all the way, so that its road is
always freckled with shade. On either side are ancient
thatched cottages, some with thatched porches and others with
relics of past pretensions in the matter of stonework. All are
covered with creepers. There are many gardens along the lane
side, surrounded by ivy-clad walls or by hedges of laurel. Near
the stream at the base of the hill is the most comely cottage of
all, together with a single-arch footbridge protected by a white
rail. The view down the village lane is very pleasant—a winding line of trees, with glimpses of roofs of russet thatch, of
patches of bright flowers in old-fashioned gardens, and of moss-
covered orchard walls. In the gap between the tree tops is a
view of the near hills and of white clouds.

There is one modern house in the settlement, which seems
as out of place as a circus cart in a convent close. It is
scarcely to be believed that this exquisite village in the lane
ever dabbled in commerce, much less that it ever drove,
as Hutchins declares, "an extensive trade" in horn buttons
and plated buckles, or that it engaged robustly in the
manufacture of dowlas.[1] At the present day it is the village of
the pastoral poem and of the rural lyric, dainty enough
for the feet of Amaryllis and attuned to the love songs of
Strephon.

[1] A strong unbleached linen cloth, much used in the sixteenth century.

At Melbury Sampford is the picturesque seat of the Fox-Strangways, Earls of Ilchester, who share with the Digbys, the Portmans, and the Bankeses the position of the great families of Dorset. The most ancient lords of this manor were the Sampfords, then the Earls of March, then the Brownings. Monuments to these ancient folk are to be found in the small fifteenth century church. In the reign of Henry VIII. William Browning sold the manor of Melbury Sampford to Henry Strangways for 600 marks. These same Strangways belonged to an old Lancashire family who were always loyal to the Crown. The present house was built by Sir Giles Strangways, who died in 1547. Additions were made at later dates, the east front, for example, pertaining to the time of Queen Anne.

Another Sir Giles Strangways, who died in 1675, rendered a substantial service to Charles II. when that monarch was hiding at Trent,[1] after the battle of Worcester. Colonel Wyndham, of Trent House, was anxious to find a shipmaster who would carry the King across the Channel. In his perplexity he appealed to Giles Strangways of Melbury. That worthy seems to have been impressed with the sound value of the family motto, " Faire sans Dire," for without further palaver he sent the King, by Colonel Wyndham, one hundred pounds in gold—the most seasonable present Charles Stuart ever received—and then directed him to a certain mariner at Lyme.

The village of Leigh, not far distant from the Melburys, is famous for its Miz Maze. This maze is one of those which were common in this part of England some centuries ago, and which are, or were, represented in Dorset by the mazes at Pimperne,[2] Leigh, and Troy Town. I believe that the British for maze is "caertroi," and that "troi" means a turning or winding. It is needless, therefore, to say that the name Troy Town has no reference to the Greek city. The maze appears to have consisted of low banks and trenches arranged in an

[1] Page 316.   [2] Page 73.

intricate figure, which the youths of the village, accompanied no doubt by the maidens, were wont to thread at certain seasons of the year. The amusement must have been of a primitive type, only to be appreciated by a people who could dance all day round a maypole. The maze at Leigh is on high ground in an open field. Of the winding passages no trace now survives. Nothing indeed is left but the low bank and the ditch with which the place of entertainment was surrounded. The enclosure is circular and very small. It would not content the present-day villager, who needs for his open-air pleasures a barrel-organ, a roundabout, plenty of swings, a row of cocoanuts to " shy " at, and, if possible, a fat woman in a tent.

In speaking of Iwerne Minster [1] I have alluded to one process under the influence of which the gracious old-world village is fast disappearing. Leigh provides an example of another method of disintegration—the corrugated iron process. In Leigh is a dignified house, dating probably from Tudor times, with stone-mullioned windows, dripstones, a gable with a little window in it, and over all that delicacy of colour which belongs to very old grey stone. The roof of thatch has been removed from this homestead, and has been replaced by a covering of corrugated iron, which for some reason has been painted a bright red. It may be that red was selected as being the tint best able to resist the heat rays of the sun. Whatever may have been the motive for the decoration, it has caused this picturesque relic of old days to be hopelessly degraded. For a parallel one must imagine the shapely head of the Venus of Milo crowned with a scarlet motor cap. In the village of South Perrott, away to the West, there is, however, provided a spectacle which puts even the glaring roof of Leigh into the shade. Here is a beautiful and ancient house of two stories, with the date 1672 carved over its doorway. The whole of the front of this building is covered.

[1] Page 53.

from roof to footpath, with corrugated iron, painted brown. Holes are cut for the stone-mullioned windows, which gleam like the eyes of a fair woman whose face is hidden by an iron mask. In the West of Dorset especially the use of corrugated iron is spreading like a pestilence, so that it would seem that the unique and unrivalled beauty of the English village will soon be only a memory of the past.

In the centre of the village of Leigh is an ancient stone cross, the shaft of which has been at one time elaborately carved. As the sculptured figures have long since faded, and as the pillar may appear to some to be untidy, the suggestion presses that the poor old cross should at least be granted a coating of red paint.

From Leigh, by way of Gudgin's Bank, Drummer's Castle, and Crocker's Knap, the traveller may come to Hermitage. The place is well named, since it is very far from the haunts of men. This tiny Rip Van Winkle village lies at the foot of High Stoy, the most engaging of all Dorset hills—a hill of 800 feet, made up of green slopes, a cliff, and a mantle of trees. There was once a hermitage here belonging to the order of St. Augustine. A more peaceful solitude can hardly be imagined, yet the monks seem to have left the retreat as long ago as 1460. What the traveller will find now is this—a small common with cows, surrounded by trees and by a few venerable thatched cottages. At one corner of the green are a farmhouse, an orchard, and a church. This is all. The church is, I should think, the smallest in Dorset. It is of drab stone, has a roof of rough slabs, a queer bell gable, and curious windows. On the church wall is a stone engraved

> "T. G. 1682
> R. F. 1799."

The churchyard is unkempt and wild, while wandering among the ancient tombs is a dissolute company of geese. To any who may wish to find themselves "right away from towns," or who may long to bury themselves in the "heart of the country," I would commend Hermitage.

Some 300 years ago this very sleepy spot was the scene of a curious disturbance in the form of a landslip. According to the historian, it was on Sunday, January 13th, 1583, that the villagers were aroused by the awful sight of their sober fields in movement. A close of three acres, it is said, "was carried clear over another close, the space of 40 goad,[1] and stopped up an highway that directed towards Cerne." Since this date nothing in Hermitage has moved, and it is a question now if even an earthquake would rouse it.

High up among the hills over Hermitage is Minterne Magna, the "Great Hintock" of Thomas Hardy's novels. The village itself is of little interest, being made up of a church and a few modern cottages, but its situation is most charming. It lies in a shady dip between the summits of Dogbury Hill and High Stoy, on the southern slope of the range. From the crest of High Stoy is a view to the North, the East, and the West which is not likely to be forgotten. It embraces the North of Dorset, the South of Wiltshire, and ranges over Somerset to Glastonbury and the Mendip Hills. Whether it is possible, as some declare, to see the two Holmes in the Bristol Channel I am unable to say.

Here is Minterne House, the seat of Lord Digby. The property belonged formerly to the Churchills, and the rebuilding of the house is ascribed to General Charles Churchill, who died in 1714. He began his career as a page of honour to the King of Denmark, became in due course a general of the army, Lieutenant of the Tower of London, and one of those who fought at Blenheim in 1704. Two years before this eventful engagement he married the sole heiress of James Gould, of Dorchester, to his great advancement.

The church, small and picturesque, stands close to the road

---

[1] A goad is about five yards.

side. It is full of monuments to Napiers, Churchills, and other great folk. Most of these memorials are florid, pompous, and over-elaborate. Some are quite oppressive by reason of their stilted grandeur and overbearing magnificence. Among them all, however, is one very small, very plain tablet of white marble, on which is engraved in the simplest manner the following :—

> " Here reposeth ye most virtuouse,
> Most obliging and charitably good
> Lady Blanch Napier."

She died in 1695, "languishing," it is sad to say, "under a tediouse sickness." Amidst all the monuments in this church of noble dames and famous men there is none so gracious as this token in white stone to the memory of the "most obliging and charitably good lady." A large brass on the south wall of the nave tells that there lies buried Sir Henry Digby, Admiral of the Blue, who commanded H.M.S. "Africa" in the great battle of Trafalgar, and who died at Minterne in 1842.

Due north of the hills of Minterne Magna and near to the handsome church of Wootton Glanville is the manor house of Round Chimnies. The mansion, built about 1590, was once the residence of John Churchill, the first Duke of Marlborough and the hero of Blenheim. It derives its name from the fact that its chimneys are round, although in no other way conspicuous. Hutchins considered it to be "one of the best planned and most comfortable houses of the age of Elizabeth." In his time the north side had been pulled down and the building was ruinous and uninhabited. Round Chimnies has been restored and modernised, and is now a farmhouse. It is a mansion of many gables and quaint windows, which has managed still to retain no little of its ancient dignity.

Near to Wootton Glanville, in an insignificant village, is the interesting church of Pulham, which, like so many others in the district, is kept piously locked. Over the porch is a small

room a little like the porch chamber at Loders.[1] Hutchins
states that it was provided with a chimney, and was used for
the dressing and undressing of infants "when immersion was
used in baptism." By the west door, as terminals to the drip-
stone, are two archaic figures, one squatting in prayer, the other
apparently in chains. Upon a flat stone in the churchyard
near to the tower was, Hutchins says, the following epitaph
without date. I searched for it in vain. There are ancient
flat stones in the burial ground with fragments of inscriptions
still legible, but none accord with these lines given by the
county historian :—

> " Under this monument enter'd doth lie
>   The mirror of admired husbandrie
>   Dic Carter's corps—whose soul with triumph sings
>   Sweet hallelujahs to the King of Kings."

In the parish of Pulham is King's Stag Bridge, which affords
a quite insignificant passage over the River Lydden. Somewhere in the levels of this bland valley King Henry III., when
hunting, came upon "a beautiful and goodly white hart." So
moved was he by the comeliness of the startled thing that he
spared its life and forebore to follow it, save with his eyes.
Some time afterwards it came to pass that Sir Thomas de la
Lynde, Bailiff of Blackmore Forest, encountered the same
white hart in the woods, and, being untouched by its loveliness,
turned upon it, and after a boisterous chase struck it dead at
the foot of this very bridge. When this exploit reached the
ears of the King he was deeply offended, and was so stirred to
wrath that he seized Sir Thomas and his companions, cast
them into prison, and loaded them with heavy fines. Such,
furthermore, was his sorrow at the loss of the comely stag that
he laid a tax upon the very land its gentle feet had traversed.
Thus it was that for many years to come "white hart silver"
was paid by surly squires and yeomen into the Exchequer, and

[1] Page 261.

the Vale of Blackmore grew to be known as the Vale of the
White Hart. Moreover, the descendants of that Sir Thomas
de la Lynde who brought this evil upon the glen bore as their
arms "three harts'·heads in a field gules."

Now, those who are learned in matters of this kind aver that
there is little truth in this story; that there was no Sir Thomas
de la Lynde, and that neither the Pipe Roll—whatever that
may be—nor any document of authority contains an account
of such a fine or amercement. They are, however, unable to
prove that there was never a breathless moment when the
King and the white hart gazed at one another across a clearing in the forest, nor can they say that the monarch was not
filled with sorrow when the pale stag died. They allow that
there were moneys called the white hart silver, and acknow-
ledge that the Reverend Thomas Fuller, the merry rector of
Broadwindsor, paid the same with the remonstrance, "Myself hath paid a share for the sauce who never tasted the
meat." Moreover, there is the King's Stag Bridge, to show
where the hart beloved of the King fell dead.

The bridge is very small, but is supported by two powerful
buttresses, and is approached by an avenue of white posts and
rails. The stream by whose banks the stag of the legend
died is a quiet, lazy, little rivulet, idling along in the sun. It
is shaded by weeping willows, and its channel is almost hidden
by rushes, water lilies, and forget-me-nots. There is an inscription on the bridge, but it is not in any way concerned
with the death of the white hart. It merely states, with ferocious bluntness, that anyone who damages the structure becomes
thereby "liable to be transported for life."

At Mappowder Church, south of Pulham, is a curious recumbent effigy about two feet long. The tiny manikin is clad
in complete armour, and is furnished with both helmet and
sword. He lies cross-legged, like the most valiant crusader,
while in his hands he holds a heart. There is neither date
nor inscription appended. The figure is supposed to be a

monument to a boy, erected by a fond mother who had dedicated him to the Crusades, or to a son who had died while his
father was fighting under the banner of the cross against the
Saracens. In other churches these little armed figures holding
hearts in their hands have been found.

Mappowder was for many years the seat of the Cokers,
whose mansion, built in 1654, has been long since pulled down.
On its site is now a farmhouse, while the sole relics of the
ancient manor consist of two curious stone gateposts surmounted by still more curious human heads. These are the
heads of "Blackamores," those indefinite natives of the
tropics having been used for the crest of the Coker family.

One place alone remains to be noticed in this district, and
that is Holnest. The village, with the exception of a
scattered house or so, has departed. The ancient church
remains, and in the ample churchyard around it is the
astounding object which has made Holnest a place of some
notoriety. This object, which has been described by one
critic as "of marvellous hideousness," is a colossal mausoleum
to a local squire. It is almost as large as the humble church,
which is overshadowed by its vulgarity. Its general appearance
at a distance is that of a pumping station. On nearer
inspection it proves to be a gaudy building, in the Byzantine
style, made up of grey and yellow stone, worried by much
carving and enlivened by highly polished granite pillars.
The rounded roof, which to be consistent should be of
corrugated iron, is of lead. The boastful memorial serves by
contrast to exalt the dignity of the little village church by
its side. This church is of the type common in Dorset—a
low, square tower, a motherly porch, a cove roof, and within
old high pews with doors and a pulpit with a sounding-board.

CHAPTER XXI

THE CERNE ROAD

THE high-road from Sherborne to Dorchester passes through both Holnest and Minterne Magna, and after climbing laboriously over the chalk hills drops down into Cerne Abbas.

There was a time when Cerne was a stately place. It is humble enough now, although it is still dignified on the maps with capital letters. Cerne owed its greatness to the Abbey which was founded here in A.D. 987 by Æthelmar, Earl of Devon and Cornwall. The sacred settlement passed through the varied experiences which were usual to abbeys in early days. It was attacked and plundered at one season, and endowed with rich lands and gold at another. There were many noble folk in England who were ready to do much "for the health of their souls," and in this part of Wessex that peace which the world cannot give could be secured by lavishing wealth upon the Abbey at Cerne. The holy house grew in power and magnificence, while about its walls sprang up a grateful town, only too eager to live upon the crumbs which fell from the rich monks' table. For many years the Abbey guarded and sheltered Cerne. Then came the Reformation, like a devastating cyclone, and now the town shields in its bosom the few poor relics of the long dead Abbey.

In the annals of the monastery there is at least one episode

of interest. Here, in the spring of 1471, came Margaret of
Anjou, wife of Henry VI., with her only son. Her husband

The Gate-house, Cerne Abbey.

was that poor feeble King of England who was destined to be
the last of the Lancastrians. and who, after he sank into a

state of idiocy, became a mere puppet to be thrown from hand to hand by a scrambling crowd. Queen Margaret was a woman of indomitable will, of keen intellect, and of ferocious courage. The whole of her life was spent in warfare, for it was this Margaret the Queen who brought about the War of the Roses, and who with her own persistence maintained that fight to the dismal end. She fought for her boy, to secure for him the Lancastrian succession to the English throne, and she fought like a tigress who is being robbed of her cub.

Henry VI. had been deposed, Margaret had been defeated at the battle of Towton, and, hugging her boy to her bosom, and dragging her idiot husband with her, she had fled to France. For never a moment did she rest. When the great Warwick sided with her, the drivelling King was dragged over to England again, and was restored for the moment to his throne. It was her pleasure to follow later with her son, and with substantial aid from France. She landed at Weymouth, only to learn that on that very day Warwick had been defeated at Barnet and killed, that the King was imprisoned in the Tower, and that the Lancastrian cause was lost for ever. It was then that she and her boy came across the hills from Weymouth and sought sanctuary within the quiet walls and comely gardens of Cerne Abbey. No defeat, however, could crush her spirit, and no long waiting could she brook. At the head of the Beauforts she marched towards Wales, and was met by the Yorkists at Tewkesbury. Here a battle was fought, the Lancastrians were cut to pieces, and Margaret and her son were taken prisoners. The boy—now about eighteen—was murdered in cold blood, and so the fierce mother's fighting was over. She was allowed once more to cross the Channel, and to end her days in France. That her husband was put to death in the Tower after Tewkesbury would have added little to her misery. It was for her boy that this Queen tigress defied the world, and, had he lived, she would have battled with the same savage determination until death came upon her. Such then were the French lady and the lad who passed through the gateway of Cerne Abbey in the spring of 1471.

Of the Abbey little now remains but the gate-house, a glorious building of golden-grey stone, covered with much ivy, and standing in a cluster of trees. It possesses a most exquisite, two-storied oriel window, the casements of which are separated by escutcheons and bands of panelling carved in stone. The beauty of this ghostly building, like a pale light among the trees, is a wonder to look upon.

In a part of the old Abbey buildings near by—now used as a stable—is a tiny oriel window of the quaintest kind, with little Gothic lights full of diamond panes, and a roof of stone slabs covered with moss and weeds. Its childlike simplicity is in strong contrast with the majestic window of the gate-house. Any who looked out of this casement on a day in April, 1471, would have seen Queen Margaret and her son go by, for this part of the house was built by Abbot John Vaune, who died in 1470.

The town of Cerne Abbas, when viewed from the Dorchester road, is a cosy settlement tucked away in an amphitheatre of sage-green hills. There are many trees in the town, so that, compared with the poor bare downs that close it in, it looks warm and comfortable, and curled up like a dormouse in a sunny corner.

On entering the main street of Cerne it is evident that some trouble has fallen upon the Abbey town. It is silent and well-nigh deserted. Sad to tell, Cerne Abbas is dying, and has already fallen into a state of hebetude. The joy went out of its life when the Abbey was taken away. The inhabitants in their affliction tried to make of the place a manufacturing town. They made boots, and no doubt made them well. They made beer, and became for a time famous. They developed a market They took to smuggling, and met for a time with most

encouraging success. Nothing, however, went well for long in
Cerne after the last monk slinked out of the Abbey. One
enterprise failed after another. There was still the great
high-road left with its coaches, for Cerne was a comfortable
stage from Dorchester. When railways made their brutal
advance into Dorset the heart of Cerne gave way utterly; the
coaches ceased one by one, and from that moment Cerne
Abbas has never smiled again.

It is a clean, trim, old-world town, which has remained
unchanged for Heaven knows how many years. Its streets are
quaint and picturesque, for they all belong to the England of
the coaching times. No two houses are alike; some are
tiled, some thatched, some roofed with stone. In not
a few of them the first floor overhangs the causeway, according to a forgotten fashion. The place, however, is
empty and decaying and strangely silent. Grass is growing
in the streets; many houses have been long deserted,
many have their windows boarded up, or are falling into listless ruin. Here are empty barns, gates falling off their hinges,
and doorways grown up with weeds. There are quaint old
shops with bow windows, but the windows are empty of everything but a faded red curtain, while over the door, in very dim
paint, are traces of a name. One feels compelled to walk
very quietly through the echoing streets, and to talk in whispers,
for fear that the sleep of Cerne should be broken. There are
many bright flower gardens in its midst, while through the
town runs a cheerful stream, whose banks are protected by
white posts and rails.

At the end of one street is the Abbey farmhouse, a handsome
old building of many gables, and in this same street is the church
of Cerne, with its commanding tower. In a canopied niche
above the door is a statue of the Virgin. Within, the church
is, like the town, unchanged. There are high pews with
doors, a fine oak pulpit dated 1640, with a sounding-board
above and a clerk's pew below. Before the present organ was

Cerne Abbas. The Parish Church with the Abbey Farmhouse at the end of the Street.

built the music for the service was provided by a barrel-organ.
There are some fifteenth century chairs in the chancel, while
the fine altar-table bears the year 1638.

z

One of the many memorial tablets within the church seems to have tuned itself to the spirit of the dejected town. It is to the memory of Joseph, son of George and Edith Sommers, who died in 1702, aged nine, and runs as follows :—

> " A little time did blast my prime
> And brought me hether :
> The fairest flowar within an hour
> May fade and wether."

Sydling St. Nicholas.

So sleepy and indifferent has Cerne become that it has even neglected its Giant. This colossal human form is carved on the slope of one of the barren hills which surround the town. The figure is of great antiquity, and dates—so the learned say—from pre-Roman times. Of its history and its purpose nothing is known. The Giant is a fine figure of a man, for he stands 180 feet in height; the length of each of his fingers is seven feet, and the length of the club he wields is 120 feet. Cerne Abbas the Depressed has so long ceased to care for its

Giant that the poor Goliath has become grown over with grass, and is nearly invisible to the eye.

A short way from Cerne, on the Dorchester road, is Nether Cerne, a village long since depopulated. The place consists now of a little old church of stone and flint with a square tower, placed among trees and gardens by the side of the Cerne River. The roof of this queer Early English building is gold-green with moss. Close to the church is a venerable thatched manor

Sydling St. Nicholas.

house with stone-mullioned windows. These ancient old cronies, still hobnobbing together, make up the whole of the settlement of Nether Cerne.

Farther along the road is the unsophisticated village of Godmanstone, where by the side of the stream is the smallest place of entertainment I have knowledge of. This is the Smith's Arms inn, a building of such humble stature that it is possible to touch the roof of thatch. By the side of the door is a window, about one foot high and a yard wide. This constitutes the façade or elevation of the tavern. On the side away from the road the little building is apparently saved from tumbling into the brook by a large willow tree. There is a post-office in Godmanstone, but as it projected too much into the road, a corner has been chipped off it, a procedure that seems to have been simpler than the widening of the highway.

To the right of Cerne road and across the hills is the hidden village of Sydling St. Nicholas. The village, which lies at the end of a valley, is the most charming in the

Cattistock.

district. It is largely made up of old thatched cottages and liberal flower gardens. Many of its roofs are covered by a solid green mantle of moss. At the entrance to the place are the shaft and pedestal of a cross of yellow stone, standing near to a Georgian house of no slight pretensions. The venerable church is worthy of the old-fashioned village, and is quite famous for its numerous and amazing gargoyles.

Sydling St. Nicholas was once owned by Sir Francis Walsingham, the minister of Queen Elizabeth. In the great tithe barn they say there is to be found carved on a beam the letters

"L. U. W. 1590," the initials of Lady Ursula Walsingham. The barn is magnificent; its buttresses are worthy of a church, and its timbers, even if much decayed, are still most illustrious. For the initials of the Lady Ursula I sought, however, in vain. The barn has, as is fitting, a heavy roof of thatch. Melancholy to tell, this is being gradually replaced by corrugated iron. It would seem that an Elizabethan tithe barn is not among the "ancient buildings" in the preservation of which any are concerned.

Away to the right again and over more hills are Cattistock and Maiden Newton. Cattistock is a cheery townlet, with a very noble church, recently rebuilt. The church is over-much decorated inside, but its glory in the minds of the villagers would seem to depend upon its carillon of thirty-five bells and the enormous size of its clock.

Much of the interest in Maiden Newton from the point of view of the tourist has vanished since the pulling down of its famous inn, the White Hart. This beautiful building has been replaced by an hotel of the most uninteresting type. The old White Hart was a charming specimen of the seventeenth century hostelry. It was a house of two stories, with dormers in the roof. The roof was of course of thatch, and the windows provided with stone mullions and dripstones. A gateway, with a chamber over, led under the house to the stable yard at the back. There are now few relics of the olden times left in this progressive settlement, if exception be made of the church and the mill on the River Frome.

The church, which contains much Norman work, is the most charming feature of Maiden Newton. Its surroundings are peculiarly fascinating. The churchyard is a garden of flowers, a vine climbs over the old church porch, lichen and moss have added rich tints of yellow, brown, and green to the drab walls, while between the windows and reaching up to the very roof are masses of roses.

Well to the left of the Cerne road, and approached from that

town by a byway along Kiddle's Bottom, is Piddletrenthide.
Here is a church which claims to be the finest village church
in Dorset.   It is an imposing building, situated by the side of
the stream.   Its lofty pinnacled tower of ashen stone has been
tanned to a gentle brown by the sun of centuries.   It is a
tower with immense buttresses about its sides, with a fine gold
weather-cock on its summit, and numerous gargoyles under its
battlements.   The sundial over the south door bears the date

The Mill, Maiden Newton.

1662, while an inscription in the Latin tongue on the west
side was carved there in 1487.   Both the south doorway and
the piers of the chancel arch belong to the time of the
Normans.   The colouring of the church is not among the
least of its charms, for the greys and yellows and browns of
its walls are contrasted with the deep green of ivy and the red
of many roses, while in the foreground are ancient yews, and
in the distance the jade green of the downs.

CHAPTER XXII

DORCHESTER

THERE is little doubt that the embryo of the town of Dorchester stood within the great ramparts of Maiden Castle, and was already a place of consequence when the Romans landed in Britain. As years advanced and as times grew more peaceful, the Celts who crowded the pit dwellings on the hill came down to the river-side and founded there a town upon the site of which the Dorecestre of the Domesday Book and the Dorchester of to-day arose in turn. The capital of the county lies on the great Roman road, the Via Iceniana, and there is evidence to show that the Romans made of Durno-varia—as they called the place —one of their chief cities of the South. They carried roads from out of it in many directions, and built a massive wall to shut it in, of which a fragment exists to this day.

Very numerous indeed are the Roman remains which have been found in and about Dorchester. The town, as Thomas Hardy says, "announced old Rome in every street, alley, and precinct. It looked Roman, bespoke the art of Rome, con-cealed dead men of Rome. It was impossible to dig more than a foot or two deep about the town, fields, and gardens without coming upon some tall soldier or other of the Empire, who had lain there in his silent, unobtrusive rest for a space of fifteen hundred years." In the museum are piles of Roman relics. The town itself still conforms to the lines laid down by the builders f om Rome—a town of four main streets, North, South, East, and West. On the outskirts are a famous Roman amphitheatre, as well as two British camps, Poundbury and Maiden Castle, which both show the signs of Roman occupation.

Dorchester has never been insignificant. In the days of Edward the Confessor it boasted of no fewer than 172 houses or huts, while by the time King Henry VIII. ruled in the land the number of dwellings had increased to 349.

The history of the town differs little from that of other English settlements endued with ambition. It was duly ravaged by the Danes, received unappreciated visits from King John, was the scene of many hangings, drawings, and quarterings, was laid low by the plague, and was more or less destroyed at sundry times by fire.

The most notable fire broke out at two on an August afternoon in 1613. It began at the house of a tallow chandler, and at a time when most of the townsfolk were unfortunately away, being busy in the harvest fields. It destroyed 300 houses and two out of the three churches of the place, St. Peter's alone being spared. Considerable use was made of this conflagration to collect money for the building of a hospital and a house of correction, it having been pointed out that the fire had arisen because " it had pleased God to awaken them [the inhabitants] by this fiery trial." The townsfolk, who had been thus rudely aroused, provided the money, but at the same time built a brew-house, intending that out of the profits derived from the sale of beer the hospital should be maintained. It is doubtful if at the present day the charitable public would be disposed to devote a portion of the Hospital Sunday Fund, for example, to the purchase of remunerative public-houses. The repentant folk of Dorchester, in their character of " brands snatched from the burning," had still unregenerate conceptions of business and of public morals. They failed to see the impropriety of tending the sick with the money derived from making them drunk.

There were minor fires in the town in 1622, 1725, and 1775. It is no matter of wonder, therefore, that the city fathers developed a dread of fire. On May 13th, 1640, for instance, the churchwardens of St. Peter's were ordered to provide "tankards [*i.e.*, leather buckets] to be hanged up in the church." In June, 1649, it was proposed to expend £30 to £40 "for buying of a brazen engine or spoute to quench fire in times of danger." This engine was a brass syringe, held up by two men and worked by a third. In December, 1653, we find that two officials were wisely told off for each parish, "to see and view iff there bee any badd or dangerous chymnyes or mantells and to see that all psons keepe their wells, buckets, ropes, tanckets, malkins, and ladders fit to make use of uppon occasion."

In the Great Rebellion Dorchester was so strong for the Parliament that it is described by Royalists as being "the seat of great malignity." In 1642 the town was fortified at great expense with walls, forts, and platforms. When, however, the Earl of Carnarvon, on behalf of the King, approached the stronghold, the courage of the defenders abruptly vanished, and, without firing a shot, they surrendered the town, with all its arms, ammunition, and ordnance. For many months this "seat of great malignity" suffered extremely, and was no doubt woefully uncomfortable. It was taken and retaken, so that the nerves of the inhabitants can only have been restored when Dorchester was finally seized by Lord Essex for the Parliament.

It was in this town, on September 3rd, 1685, that Judge Jeffreys opened in earnest his Bloody Assize. The purpose of his visit was to try all those who were suspected of being concerned in Monmouth's mad rising, and to pass sentence on such as were found guilty. The Duke of Monmouth, it may be remembered, was captured at Horton [1] on July 8th, and executed

[1] See page 121.

on Tower Hill on July 15th. Macaulay has thus described the
opening of the Assize :—" The Court was hung, by order of the
Chief Justice, with scarlet ; and this innovation seemed to the
multitude to indicate a bloody purpose. It was also rumoured
that, when the clergyman who preached the assize sermon enforced the duty of mercy, the ferocious mouth of the Judge
was distorted by an ominous grin. These things made men
augur ill of what was to follow. More than 300 prisoners were
to be tried. The work seemed heavy, but Jeffreys had a con-
trivance for making it light. He let it be understood that the
only chance of obtaining pardon or respite was to plead guilty.
Twenty-nine persons, who put themselves on their country and
were convicted, were ordered to be tied up without delay. The
remaining prisoners pleaded guilty by scores. Two hundred and
ninety-two received sentence of death. The whole number
hanged in Dorsetshire amounted to seventy-four." [1] In many
instances the only charge brought against these unfortunate
people was that they had been "absent from their habi-
tacons from and att the tyme of the Rebellion."

Jeffreys was thirty-seven years old at the time of the Great
Assize. He remains notorious in history as a corrupt judge, a
foul-mouthed, malevolent bully, and a fiend who delighted in
cruelty. He was a drunkard, a man of the coarsest mind, with
a ready command of blasphemous expressions. I am a little
disposed to think that the violence of this contemptible being

---

[1] From a paper by W. B. Barrett, in the *Proceedings of the Dorset Field
Club* (Vol. V. page 99), it would appear that the returns of Jeffreys's work
in the county are as follows :—

Presented at the Assizes	312
Executed	74
Transported	175
Fined or whipped ...	9
Discharged	54
	312

Dorchester. The High West Street, looking Eastwards.

was in some part due to disease, for he is said to have been
"tortured with the stone." His portrait, by Kneller, is singularly unlike any conception that may be formed of the judge of
the Bloody Assize. It shows a slight man, clean-shaved
according to the custom of the time, with a refined, gentle, and
intelligent face and dreamy eyes. For his hideous work in
Dorset and Devon Jeffreys was made Lord Chancellor of
England. His end was as horrible as his life had been. He
was committed to the Tower of London, where he died at the
age of forty-one—a diseased, hounded, and accursed wretch.
The last sound of the outer world that broke upon his ear, as
he crossed the drawbridge of the prison, was "the roar of a
great city disappointed of its revenge."

There are two relics of Jeffreys still in Dorchester. In the
West Street is a picturesque timber house with an overhanging
story. It is now a shop, but it was in this building that the in-
famous judge lodged when he visited the town for the purpose
of the Assize. In the Town Hall also is preserved his chair,
a bland and homely piece of furniture, with no suggestion of
villainy about it. To these relics may be added a third. In
the museum is a spike from the porch of St. Peter's Church,
upon which was set the head of one of Monmouth's rebels to
blister and to blacken in the sun.

Dorchester shows by its records [1] that it was always jealously
mindful of the personal morals of its inhabitants, as well as of its
own dignity. For example, in June, 1632, Robert Foot was
charged with being "severall tymes drunke and wishing that
fire and brimstone would fall on this town, it being sufficiently
proud." For this expression of his opinion as to the pride of
the town and the best means of curbing it Mr. Foot was
ordered to prison, "to be sett close to worke." Again, Mr. W.
Hardy, gentleman, who facetiously described himself to the
authorities as "dwelling evrywhere," was fined for calling the
constables "a company of dampnd creaturs." Scolding was

[1] To be found in the *Proceedings of the Dorset Field Club.*

severely punished. In January, 1632, four women are declared
to have "spent the most part of two daies in scolding."
For this long-sustained flow of unpleasant speech they were
ordered to be "plounced"—that is to say, to be ducked.

It is well to note that the magistrates of the town were
very indulgent towards women who had drawn upon themselves the terrors of the law.   Thus, on May 6th, 1631, "Mary
Tuxberry, for scoulding at the sergeants when they did goe
about for mersements,[1] was ordered to be plounced when the
wether is warmer."   As the "scoulding" took place early in
May, Mrs. Tuxberry must have felt that she was treated with
every consideration a lady could expect.   Alice Cox too, in
the same year, was ordered to be placed in the stocks for
drunkenness, but the sentence was "forborne for a week, she
being unfit then to be stocked, and since was stocked."   Here
it will be seen that time was thoughtfully granted to Alice Cox
to recover from the nervous depression consequent upon her
indulgence.

The rulers of Dorchester were very strict regarding the
proper observance of the Sabbath, as will be seen from the
following records :—On January 17th, 1629, Hugh Baker was
put in the stocks for two hours for leaving church before
prayers were over.   On October 12th, 1632, Ursula Bull was
fined one shilling for absence from church, although "she saith
she was amending her stockings."   A very unseemly outrage is
dealt with in the following entry of August 29th, 1631 : "Jo
Kay and Nicholas Sims did play at All Saints' in sermon time
and laughe, and Sims did stick Kay a box on the ear and carry
themselves very unreverently."   For this offence they were
both committed to prison.   Of the many culprits dealt with at
Dorchester for neglect of the Sabbath, I think that J. Hoskins
showed not only the most enterprise, but also the most versa-
tility of character.   On January 2nd, 1634, Mr. J. Hoskins
the Abandoned went out of church before the end of the

---

[1] Fines.

service. He went first to a neighbour's house to warm himself. Thus refreshed, he betook him to the "Broad Close" to serve cattle. Here the impious Hoskins found a bull, and promptly put him into a pound and baited him with a dog. Hoskins, when he had exhausted the pleasures of this sport, returned to the church and to his interrupted devotions. His absence, however, had been observed; possibly he chuckled audibly to himself over the bull-baiting during the final prayers. Anyhow, he was charged on the Monday and fined one shilling, the punishment evidently of a sympathetic judge.

The town authorities were very liberal also in the treatment of their sick. In the annals of 1640 is an order to pay Peter Sala Nova £5 for cutting off Giles Garrett's leg. About this period it is noted that Master Losse received £8 per annum "as fee as physician in taking care of the poore of the Towne." When occasions arose which were beyond the powers of Master Losse a specialist was called in. Thus in 1654 is an order "for the widow Devenish to be sent down to Master fforester for cure of her distemper." This cost no less than £15: "out of the town purse £5, out of her owne state £5, out of honest people's purses £5." On occasion a lady doctor was employed by the town. Her name was Canander Huggard. She does not appear to have been a lady of great professional initiative. It is noted, for instance, that on January 5th, 1654, she was paid £3 not for her own advice but "for finishing the great cure on John Drayton otherwise Kense."

Dorchester in olden times must have been, like many other country towns, a most picturesque place. The old Town Hall, for example, was a quaint and dignified building, with an ample balcony from which to address the crowd. There were, Hutchins says, some Flemish buildings of plaster and timber in the Corn Market and about St. Peter's Church. In the centre of the town stood the Cupola or market-house. "It was removed in 1782, its situation being found inconvenient on account of the great increase of travelling. It was built in the form of an octagon, supported by eight handsome pillars, and covered on the top with lead, on which formerly stood a little room capable of containing ten persons, and made use of for some of the corporation to meet on particular business. It was encompassed with balustrades, and was in the form of a cupola, whence it had its name." In the North Street was a footway made for passengers, paved with square stones and guarded by posts. Here also was "the Blind House for confining disorderly people for the night."

The houses crowded casually into the road, so that the streets were much narrowed. At the corner of South and East Streets—opposite to the present Corn Exchange—two dwellings stood so near together that their upper rooms joined over the highway, which was thus converted into a mere passage. The streets were not only narrow, but very untidy, and covered by uncouth cobble-stones. The kennel was full of garbage and miscellaneous litter. The houses were mostly of timber, with roofs of thatch. They were rich in gables and dormers, in windows with diamond panes, in outside galleries, and in overhanging stories. There were inns too whose stable yards were the centres of the bustle of the town as well as of the gossip of the county. Before the red-curtained bow windows stood a drinking trough for horses. The shops were low and dark, so that in fine weather the goods were set out by the road side, while in each of the little marts the tradesman could be seen busy at his trade.

To complete the conception of the bygone town the streets must be pictured as filled by people in the costumes of past days : by the yokel in his smock, by the soldier in the uniform that Hogarth drew, by the sailor with his pigtail. Here would come by a company of sheep guided by a shepherd, then three pigs driven by an old woman, a pedlar with a box of bright ribbons, a wandering knife-grinder, a donkey laden with baskets full of geese, and a man in black, who might be one of the ushers at the school. Now and then a sedan chair would swing across the road, especially when the days were wet; and on rarer occasions a carriage of some of "the quality" would lumber by, bumping over the ruts and splashing with mud the children who ran by the side of it.

The Dorchester of to-day is a bright, trim town, which, so far as its four principal streets are concerned, can claim to be still picturesque. The ancient houses are being gradually replaced by new, while all around the grey old town are arising those florid suburbs which in days to come will make the present era famous for architectural ugliness.

At one time the country came up to the very walls of the town. The North Street ended abruptly in a mill by the river, the South Street came to a sudden end in a cornfield. The East or Fordington side of the town remains unchanged in this particular, so that it is from this quarter that the approach to Dorchester is the most pleasing and the most reminiscent of past days. Here the water meadows reach to the very garden hedges and to the actual walls of houses. Indeed, cows pasturing by the river might shelter themselves from the sun under the overhanging story of one of these ancient dwellings on the fringe of the town.[1] In Hutchins's *History of Dorset* is a plate showing Dorchester as viewed from the East, from near a bridge over the Frome called Grey's Bridge. The date of the plate is 1803, and it is interesting to observe how very little the aspect of the place as seen from this point has altered in these one hundred and three years.

Dorchester was long prevented from extending its boundaries by being hemmed in on nearly all sides by Fordington Field, a wide stretch of land of over 3000 acres, "held under the

---

[1] This quarter of Dorchester is well displayed in a beautiful water-colour drawing by Walter Tyndale in Clive Holland's *Wessex*. London, 1906. Page 168.

Duchy of Cornwall in farthings or fourthings [the quarter of a hide[1] or caracute[2]], from which it derives its name in the original form of Fourthington."[3] The tenure of land in this field was hampered until recently by such restrictions as to make development of the town beyond its ancient limits difficult or impossible.

One of the most beautiful features of Dorchester is its *ceinture* of green, for on three sides it is surrounded by avenues of trees— of sycamores, limes, and chestnuts. On the fourth side runs the River Frome through reedy meadows. These avenues, called "The Walks," were planted between 1700 and 1712 on the lines of the ancient walls. Until quite recent years the Walks formed the outermost boundaries of the town, beyond which no house ventured to stray. The town indeed, as I recollect it, was still "huddled all together, and shut in by a square wall of trees, like a plot of garden ground by box-edging," as a character in one of Hardy's novels observes. These formal avenues or boulevards give to Dorchester an uncommon air and a little of the aspect of a foreign town. The principal roads, too, which approach the capital enter it with great solemnity through avenues of fine trees.

The best view of the town is from the top of the West Street. From this height the town slopes downhill to the river. There is a long, straight, yellow road, with a line of irregularly disposed houses on either side of it. No two are of quite the same height. They favour white walls, ample roofs, bow windows, and stone porticoes. Where there are shops there are patches of bright colour, striped sun-blinds, and a posse of carriers' carts. Over the house-tops rise the stolid tower of St. Peter's, the clock turret, and the pale spire of All Saints' Church. Then, at the far-away foot of the slope, the diminished road

---

[1] A measure of land enough to support a family.

[2] As much land as could be tilled with one plough (with a team of eight oxen) in one year.

[3] Murray's *Wilts and Dorset*. Page 518.

can be seen running out into the green water meads, to be
finally lost among the trees of Stinsford.

In the exact centre of the place, and forming, as it were, the
Arc de Triomphe of Dorchester, is the town pump—very large,
very parochial-looking, and very self-conscious.   Near it is the
handsome and venerable church of St. Peter's, which has witnessed and survived the great dramatic events in the town's
history—the fearful fire of 1613, the alarms of the Great Rebellion, and the horrors of the Bloody Assize.

The church is well preserved, even to its south door, which
dates from the late Norman period.   In the porch, in front of
this door, lies buried the Reverend John White, who is better
known as the "Patriarch of Dorchester."   Born in 1575, he
became the rector of Holy Trinity in 1606.   He was a masterful old Puritan, and an absolute autocrat in the town.   During
his rule there was never a beggar in his parish.   Fuller says of
him that "he had perfect control of two things—his own
passions and his parishioners' purses."   He was, curious to
relate, one of the founders of Massachusetts, for in 1624 he
despatched a company of Dorset men to that remote part.
He raised money for them, procured them a charter, and sent
them out their first Governor in the person of John Endicott,
of Dorchester.   That official sailed for New England in 1629
in the *George Bonaventura.*   In 1642 a party of Prince Rupert's
horse broke into John White's house, and stole his books.
He fled to London, where he became rector of Lambeth.
When peace was restored he returned to Dorchester, and died
there in 1648.

The church contains many ancient monuments, some of
which have been described as " noble " or " superb," and others
as merely " very lofty."   A memorial which can claim to be
ridiculous is one to Denzil Holles.   He it was who, entering
Parliament in 1624, was one of the "five Members" whom
Charles accused of high treason and attempted to arrest in
1642.   He was also one of the redoubtable gentlemen who

held the Speaker forcibly in his chair whilst certain resolu-
tions in which he was interested were passed. This active
person is represented as reclining, with a fine air of boredom,
on a cushion. He is dressed in the costume of an ancient
Roman. On his feet are the sandals of the days of the Caesars,
while on his head is the full-bottomed wig of the time of the
Stuarts. He is attended by unwholesomely fat cherubs, who
are weeping.

Outside the church is an excellent statue to William Barnes,
the Dorset poet. On the pedestal are engraved these lines
from one of his own poems :—

> " Zoo now I hope his kindly feäce
> Is gone to vind a better pleäce ;
> But still wi' v'ok a-left behind
> He'll always be a-kept in mind."

By the side of St. Peter's is the County Museum, where
is to be found one of the most interesting collections out
of London. Many of the objects in the museum have been
already referred to. Here are to be seen leg-stocks and hand-
stocks, a collection of most devilish man-traps, and certain of
the wooden reeve staffs of Portland, on which, by means of
notches, details as to the tenure of land were recorded. Here
too the curious will find the blade of a halberd which had been
converted into a sword by a smuggler, from whom it was taken
at Preston in 1835. Furthermore, amidst relics of Roman
days and of prehistoric man will be seen the humstrum, an
old Dorset viol, which has long since passed away, but
which at its best was hardly worthy of a tribe of Hottentots.
Of this quaint musical instrument Barnes has written in the
following strain :—

> " Why woonce, at Chris'mas-tide, avore
> The wold year wer a-reckon'd out,
> The humstrums here did come about,
> A-soundèd up at ev'ry door.

> But now a bow do never screäpe
> A humstrum any where all round,
> An' zome can't tell a humstrum's sheäpe,
> An' never heärd his jinglèn sound."

Very handsome is the ringers' flagon in the museum, from the belfry of St. Peter's Church, with the date 1676 ; very horrible are two leaden weights, marked " MERCY," which were made by a kind-hearted governor of the gaol to be tied to the feet of a man who was hanged for arson in 1836, and who was so slight that the governor thought he would be long in the strangling.

In the South Street is the grammar school, founded by Thomas Hardy, of Melcombe Regis, in 1569. This worthy, who lies buried in St. Peter's Church, was one of the family of the Le Hardis of Jersey, from whom Nelson's captain was descended. "After the lapse of three centuries his crest— a wyvern's head—is still worn on the cricket caps of the Dorchester *alumni*."[1] The original schoolhouse was newly built in 1618, after the fire of 1613. This building I had reason in my youth to know only too well. It was pulled down in 1879, when the present edifice appeared in its stead. Through all its vicissitudes the school has preserved a certain stone in the wall upon which are carved Queen Elizabeth's arms, supported by a lion and a wyvern, and the date 1569.

Next to the school is " Napper's Mite," a small almshouse, with a charming little cloister and enclosed garden, founded by Sir Gerard Napier in 1615.

In the same street, but on the other side of the way, was the school kept by William Barnes. He came to Dorchester from Mere,[2] and the dwelling in question was the third he had occupied since he tried his fortune in the larger town. It was here, at a tender age, that I had my first experience of school life. My recollection of the poet and philologist is that of the

[1] *Three Dorset Captains at Trafalgar.*   London, 1906.   Page 9.
[2] See page 19.

gentlest and most kindly of men. His appearance was peculiar. He had white hair and a long white beard, and always wore knee breeches and shoes with large buckles. Out of doors he donned a curious cap and a still more curious cape, while I never saw him without a bag over his shoulder and a stout staff. During school hours he was in the habit of pacing the room in a reverie, happily oblivious of his dull surroundings. I remember once that some forbidden fruit of which I was possessed rolled across the schoolroom floor, and that I crawled after it in the wake of the dreaming master. He turned suddenly in his walk and stumbled over me, to my intense alarm. When he had regained his balance he apologised very earnestly and resumed his walk, unconscious that the object he had fallen over was a scholar. I have often wondered to which of his charming poems I owed my escape from punishment.

Just to the South of the town, on the Weymouth road, stands Maumbury Rings, a Roman amphitheatre, which is by far the finest work of its kind in Great Britain. It is an oval earthwork covered by grass, the enclosing rampart of which rises to the height of 30 feet. On the inner slope of this embankment the spectators sat. The arena measured 218 feet in length by 163 feet in width, while the amphitheatre itself will accommodate from ten to twelve thousand spectators. "Some old people," writes Thomas Hardy of this place, "said that at certain moments in the summer time, in broad daylight, persons sitting with a book, or dozing in the arena, had, on lifting their eyes, beheld the slopes lined with a gazing legion of Hadrian's soldiery, as if watching the gladiatorial combat, and had heard the roar of their excited voices ; that the scene would remain but a moment, like a lightning flash, and then disappear. It was related that there still remained under the south entrance arched cells for the reception of the wild animals and athletes who took part in the games. The arena was still smooth and circular, as if used for its original purpose not so very long ago. The sloping pathways by which spectators had ascended to their seats were pathways yet. But the whole was grown over with grass, which at the end of the summer was bearded with withered bents that formed waves under the brush of the wind."

Until 1767 the public gallows stood within this tragic enclosure. It was here that, in 1705, Mary Channing met her fearful fate. When a mere girl she was forced by her parents to marry Richard Channing, a grocer of Dorchester. Her life with him was dull, for her heart was elsewhere, and she longed to be free. At last she poisoned him, they said, by giving him white mercury, first in rice milk and then in a glass of wine. She was found guilty and condemned to death, but pleaded pregnancy. She was removed to prison, where her child was born eighteen weeks before she died. On a spring morning in 1705 Mary Channing, still only nineteen years of age, was dragged to the arena of Maumbury Rings, clamouring forth her innocence all the way. From the centre of this arena the solitary girl faced a crowd of ten thousand men and women. Here she was strangled by the public hangman and then burned, whereupon the virtuous and Christian folk who had walked miles to see her die returned home satisfied.

There are two famous earthworks outside Dorchester with which the dawning history of the town is intimately concerned. These bluff strongholds of Poundbury and Maiden Castle appear to have been made by the Britons, and to have been occupied and modified later by the Romans. Poundbury stands on high ground above the river. In early days there was to the North of the encampment a great lake, a mile wide, fed by the Frome. Hence it is that to the North there is only one rampart to defend the enclosure. A well-marked trackway leads out of the north-west corner of the earthworks.

Maiden Castle—the Mai-Dun or Hill of Strength—stands some two miles South of Dorchester, in a solitude on the downs not far from the Roman road. Whether it was a fortified town, or a great camp, or a city of refuge matters little ; it remains to this day the most stupendous British earthwork in existence. It stands on the flat summit of a hill, where it covers an area of no less than 115 acres. The enclosure within the ramparts measures alone 45 acres. This gigantic structure was made by men who worked with horn picks and with hatchets of stone or bronze. When the inhabitants left the camp centuries ago they left it for ever. It remained as desolate as a haunted glen. It became a solitude; no man meddled with its walls, so that its great valla became merely shelters for sheep. Thus it is that Maiden Castle survives in perfect preservation, an astounding monument of the work of those busy Celts whom the Romans on their coming found in the occupation of England.

The defences follow the natural lines of the hill, and consist of three or more ramparts, 60 feet in height and of extreme steepness. It is not an easy matter even now to gain this Celtic fortress, unless an entry be made by one of the four gates, and these in turn are made hard of approach by overlapping ramparts and labyrinthine passages. The perimeter of this unique stronghold of the Round Barrow Men is no less than two and a quarter miles.

Maiden Castle, to the mind of the Celt, lacked nothing in perfection as a site for a founding of a town. It realised to the fullest his ideals of a home. Here is a hill on an open down, a height so commanding that none can approach it unseen, a place ready to defend, with all around it grazing land for sheep and no patch of cover for wild beasts or the creeping foe. At its foot are the lowlands of the Frome, where could be grown such crops as the man had knowledge of, and where he could find fish for his eating and the wherewithal to build his mud and wattle huts. In primitive grandeur—in the grandeur of the sheer cliff and the Titanic rock—there is nothing in Dorset to surpass this hill-town, this city of refuge, with its grass-covered ramparts rising, tier above tier, against the sky-line.

CHAPTER XXIII

THE ENVIRONS OF DORCHESTER

FORDINGTON is an appendage to Dorchester, not a suburb. It is an independent village, which many centuries ago attached itself parasitically to the town. The Church of St. George at Fordington is an interesting building, whose tall, battlemented tower is the first token of Dorchester that meets the eye when the town is approached from afar. Within the walls are Norman arches and pillars, a curious holy water basin, and a stone pulpit bearing the date " 1592, E.R."

Over the Norman door on the south wall is an archaic carving purporting to represent the performance of St. George at the battle of Antioch in 1098. The saint, seated upon a horse, is attacking certain knights in armour in a very casual and supercilious manner. These knights are really Saracens or Paynims, although they are clad in Norman armour of the kind shown in the Bayeux tapestry. St. George grasps a spear decorated by a flag. He has thrust the end of the spear into the mouth of a semi-prone idolater, who is trying to pull it out with his right hand with obvious anxiety. Other Paynims are lying about dead and much bent up. Their spears too are broken. Certain of the enemy are kneeling, and with canting looks are praying for mercy.

Away to the east of Fordington is the little village of Stinsford, the "Mellstock" of Hardy's story, *Under the Green-*

wood Tree. The church and the churchyard are both charming and very typical of the old-world Dorset village.

Near by are the two dainty Bockhampton hamlets, the one by the bank of the stream, the other on the fringe of the Great Heath. At Upper Bockhampton an ancient cottage is pointed out which is almost hidden from sight by the bushes of its old garden on the one hand and by the slope of the downs on the other. It is the birthplace of Thomas Hardy.

On this side of Dorchester too are the lovely village of West Stafford, with a church and rectory good to see, and the quaint little settlement of Whitcombe, which is content to remain as it was a century or so ago.

About a mile and a half to the north-west of Dorchester, in the Frome valley, is Wolfeton House, for long the seat of the Trenchards and a fine example of the domestic architecture of the reign of Henry VII. The house was built by Sir Thomas Trenchard in 1505, and was remodelled by another Trenchard in the time of James I. The gate-house is supported by circular towers with conical roofs. The part that this house played in the fortunes of the noble family of Bedford has been already referred to.[1] Thomas Hardy, in his *Group of Noble Dames*, describes Wolfeton as "an ivied manor house, flanked by battlemented towers, more than usually distinguished by the size of its mullioned windows."

In these northern environs of Dorchester are the two delightful villages of Charminster and Frampton. Charminster is a rambling place of gardens, with many old thatched cottages and an ever cheerful stream—the Cerne. Its church is full of memorials to Trenchards, and indeed the stately tower was reared some time in the early years of the sixteenth century by that Sir Thomas who built the mansion of Wolfeton.

Frampton is a village of trees. It is the Frome Town, just as Charminster is the Cerne Minster. In the eyes of Leland

[1] See page 250.

Frampton was "a praty husband towne," and the same it remains still. It once belonged to the Church of St. Stephen at Caen, and was then possessed for centuries by the family of the Brownes, who claim very many of the memorials in the church. I remember, as a boy, that on the Dorchester side of the church—in a shady corner by a wall—were the village stocks. Any who were "stocked" at Frampton had at least a beautiful prospect to gaze upon had they the ease of mind to enjoy it.

To the South of Dorchester are the Winterborne villages, all pleasant places enough, in the shallow valley of a stream which flows only in the winter. Of these venerable villages Winterborne St. Martin is probably the most picturesque and its church the most imposing.

The church of Winterborne Steepleton shares with those of Iwerne Minster and Trent the distinction of possessing the only ancient stone steeples in the county. On the outer wall of this church, close to the south door, is a curiously ridiculous figure of an angel carved in stone, which sculpture is supposed by some to date from before the Conquest. The angel is flying horizontally and apparently with great swiftness. The most indecorous feature about her is the unrestrained manner in which she is kicking up her heels in her flight. This embodied spirit would have afforded a suitable decoration for the tomb of Mrs. Bent, of whom it is written—

> " Here lies the body of Margaret Bent :
> She kicked up her heels and away she went."

In some respects the most interesting of the Winterbornes is Winterborne Came. The place derives its name from Caen, in France, for it once belonged to the Abbey of St. Stephen in that town. It cannot be said that there is any coherent village at Came. There is an unattractive mansion, in what is called the "classic taste," as well as a rectory and a church. The church is a thirteenth-century structure, placed in a well-

wooded park, where it is to be found among the outbuildings
and kitchen gardens of the classic house. It is a lovable little
church, with a minute, ivy-covered tower and architectural pro-
fessions of the very simplest.   Within is a finely-carved wood
screen before the chancel, and a much-decorated pulpit bearing
the date 1624.   It was from this pulpit that William Barnes,
the Dorset poet, preached for many years, for he happily

The Front, Athelhampton.

ended his days as the rector of Came. In the garden-like
churchyard he lies buried, beneath a simple cross and under
the shadow of the plain little tower.

The rectory—Barnes's rectory—is far away from the church,
a solitary house by the roadside, as homely as a cottage, but
with a garden which has all the pampered prettiness due to
centuries of care. In the account of his life the rectory is
described as " a thatched cottage with wide eaves and wider
verandah, on whose rustic pillars roses, clematis, and honey-

suckle entwine. It has a flowery lawn in front, and a sheltering
veil of trees at the side." [1]

In this pleasing spot the bard of Dorset died in 1886, at the
age of eighty-five. Mr. Gosse gives, in a letter, a very graphic
picture of the last days of this remarkable old man. " Hardy and
I went on Monday last," he writes, " to Came Rectory, where he
[the poet] lies bedridden. It is curious that he is dying as

The Garden, Athelhampton.

picturesquely as he lived. We found him in bed in his study,
his face turned to the window, where the light came streaming
in through flowering plants, his brown books on all sides of
him save one, the wall behind him being hung with old green
tapestry. He had a scarlet bedgown on, a kind of soft biretta
of dark red wool on his head, from which his long white hair
escaped on to the pillow; his grey beard, grown very long,
upon his breast; his complexion, which you recollect as richly
bronzed, has become blanched by keeping indoors, and is now
waxily white where it is not waxily pink; the blue eyes, half

[1] *The Life of William Barnes.* By Leader Scott. London, 1887.

shut, restless under languid lids. I wish I could paint for you the strange effect of this old, old man, lying in cardinal scarlet in his white bed, the only bright spot in the gloom of all these books." [1]

On the North-east side of Dorchester is the great Blandford road, which, after climbing the steep hill through Yellowham Wood and skirting Troy Town, comes to Puddletown. On the outskirts of this curiously named place is Athelhampton.

Athelhampton Hall—the ancient home of the Martins—is one of the most glorious relics of the Dorset of bygone years. The oldest lords of the manor were the Londons and the Pideles. Then came the FitzMartins, the first of the family being Martin of Tours, who was one of those who crossed to England with William the Norman. At Athelhampton the Martins lived for four hundred years—from the early part of the thirteenth century to the end of the sixteenth—a gallant company of Dorset squires.

The house is without question the most picturesque in the county. The greater part of the building belongs to the fifteenth century, while a wing described as "new" was added by the Martins in the reign of Henry VII. The exquisite gate-house of two floors, with its great oriel window and gabled roof, was pulled down in 1862, in which year also the chapel was sacrificed. The mansion contains a grand banqueting hall with an oak roof, a state bedroom with fine panelling of the time of the first Tudor King, much old window glass, and certain remarkable staircases.

Athelhampton Hall, standing by the water meadows of the river, is a low building of grey stone, covered with chocolate-coloured tiles. It is an irregular, rambling structure of many gables and many roofs, much given to dormers, to stone chimneys, and stone-mullioned windows with from three to sixteen lights. Over the front porch is a little chamber sur-

[1] *Ibid.*, page 325.

mounted by battlements. In the wall to the side of this are Gothic windows of strange proportions, and heavy buttresses whose stones are concealed by a mantle of ivy. Over this part of the house also a beautiful magnolia is growing. Where the stone is not covered by creepers it is bountifully cared for by moss and lichen.

Around the house are terraced gardens, trim lawns, formal flower-beds, and fountain pools; while in one corner is an

The Garden, Athelhampton.

ancient culverhouse, or dove-cot, in which no doubt many generations of ladies of the Martin household took kindly interest.

Puddletown, the Town on the River Puddle, and the "Weatherbury" of the Wessex novels, affords an agreeable *mélange* of the old and the new, of the semi-pretentious house and the humble thatched cottage. The ill-named river runs through the streets, the houses of which are much scattered and broken up by delightful orchards and gardens. There is one particularly quaint corner in the town where a thatch-roofed cottage has broken out into a Georgian bow window worthy of a town hall. This upper window is supported by pillars, and in the porch-like space beneath it is a parterre of flowers.

The feature of greatest interest in Puddletown is the church, one of the few in the county which has been happy in escaping the hand of the restorer. There is in the nave a beautiful

A Corner in Puddletown.

panelled ceiling of Spanish chestnut, the beams of which are bare alike of varnish and of paint. There are the old oak pews of past days still in use, a handsome singing gallery for the village choir, bearing the date 1635, an ancient wood pulpit with a clerk's stall beneath, and a Norman font shaped like a drinking tumbler. The general colouring of the nave is very pleasing, the pews and ancient woodwork being a rich autumn brown, the walls grey, the ceiling, with its myriad shadows, the tint of cinnamon.

But for the organ and the lamps, here unchanged is the village church of two centuries ago. On these very benches sat the farmer's men in drab smock frocks and their womenfolk in homespun. In this actual gallery the farmer's young wife led the singing—a prim woman in a poke bonnet and an ample flounced skirt, with a white tippet over her shoulders and mittens on her wrists. In this very porch the villagers bobbed and curtsied as the squire of Athelhampton and his lady swept by to the manorial pew.

No church in the county can compare with this in human interest, and nowhere can one come into closer communion with the homely spirit of the Dorset of the past.

The most picturesque corner of the church is the south chapel or Athelhampton aisle, so called because it is devoted to memorials to the Martins, the ancient possessors of Athelhampton. This little chapel is guarded or walled in by an altar tomb, on which lies an armed man carved in alabaster. It is entered through a quaint archway as if it would withdraw itself from the church. Buried in this chapel are the Martins of many generations—the first of the race in 1250, the last in 1595. Many of their effigies are grievously mutilated, but they make together the *dramatis personæ* of a pathetic old world story in stone.

A great company they are! Men of one family and from one house, who, succeeding each other as father and son, ruled for nearly four hundred years as squires of the little village kingdom. Those who rest together in this chapel lived through the reigns of sixteen English sovereigns, for the first Squire Martin came to Athelhampton in the time of Henry III. while the last lived far into the days of Elizabeth. It is little to be wondered that they clung with deepening affection to the manor-house—the home that had sheltered them all for so long a time. Everywhere is to be found valiantly carved on the tombs the family crest—the token of three monkeys, or "martins segeant." [1]

[1] Martin, an obsolete word for ape.

There is on the chapel wall this prayer from the lips of certain of the Martin brotherhood :—

> " Here lyeth the body of Xpofer Martyn Esquyer,
> Sone and heyre unto Sir Willym Martyn, Knyght.
> Pray for there soules with harty desyre
> That bothe may be sure of eternall lyght."

The last of the Martins was the Knight Nicholas—he who died in 1595—and it is fitting that the closing epitaph of the devoted family should end as it does with the words "Good night, Nicholas." It is as if all the old squires of Athelhampton rose in their little chapel, and, lifting the visors of their helmets, joined together in wishing a dreamless sleep to the new comer, to the youngest of their clan, to the very last of their ancient race. "Good night, Nicholas."

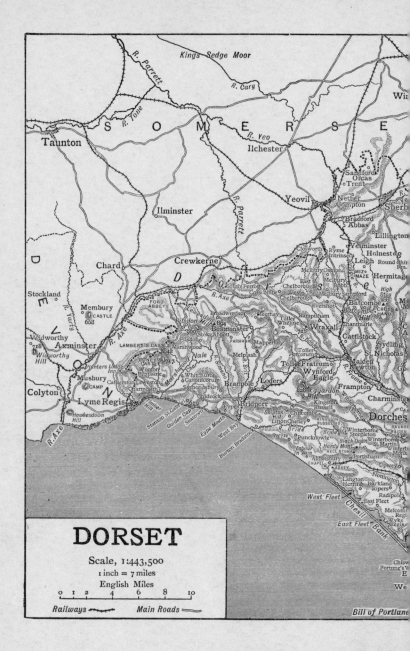

Kings Sedge Moor

R. Parrett

R. Cary

R. Tone

S O M E R S E

R. Yeo

Taunton

Ilchester

Yeovil

Sandford
Orcas
Trent

Nether
Compton

Wir

Bradford
Abbas

Sherb

Lillington

Ilminster

R. Parrett

Closworth

Ryme
Intrinseca

Yetminster

Holneste

Leigh

Round
Chu

Pn.

Chard

D

O

South Perrott

Crewkerne

Melbury Osmond

East
Melbury

Babb

MAZE
MIZ.

Hermitage

High
Sta.

Stockland

R. Yarty

Membury
CASTLE
658

FORD
ABBEYS

R. Axe

Pilsdon H.

Chelborough
East
Chelborough

Wraxall

Closworth

Chilfrome
Wraxall

Melbury
Bubb

Wynford
Eagle

Melbury
Sampford

Evershot

Batcombe

Batcombe
Hill

CROSS

LAND

Chantmarle

Cattistock

Sydling

St. Nicholas

D
E
V
O
N

Widworthy

Axminster
CAMP

Widworthy
Hill

Hunters Lodge
Inn

Musbury

Colyton

Lyme Regis

Hawkesdown
Hill

R. Axe

Broadwindsor

Bettiscombe

LAMBERT'S CASTLE

Marshwood
Vale

Beaminster

Stoke Abbott

Wootton
Fitzpaine

Whitchurch
Canonicorum

Charmouth

Catherston
Leweston

Symondsbury

Sidlock

R. Synford

Mapperton

Melplash

PARNHAM

Powerstock

Toller
Porcorum

Toller
Fratrum

Maiden
Newton

Frampton

Bradpole

Brampole

Loders

Eggardon
Hill
826

Kingston
Russell

RUSSELL

Charminster

Dorches

R. Frome

R. Bride

R. Char

Stanton St. Gabriel

Golden Cap

Seatown

Lyme Mouth

West Bay

Bridport

Shipton
Gorge

Chilcombe

Litton
Cheney

Shyre

Burton Bradstock

Hive

Long
Bredy

Litton
Cheney

Punknowle

Hardy Mont.
HELL STONE

Embury
in Vain

Abbotsbury

CHAPEL

ABBEY

Bride
Steepleton

Black Down

Portisham

Langton
Herring

Nottington

Buckland
Ripers

West Fleet

East Fleet

Chesil Bank

East Fleet

Winterborne
Steepleton

Winterborne
St. Martin

Upwey

Radipole

Melcombe
Regi

Wyke
Regis

Chisw

Fortune's Well

E

We

Bill of Portland

DORSET

Scale, 1:443,500

1 inch = 7 miles

English Miles

0 1 2   4   6   8   10

Railways   Main Roads

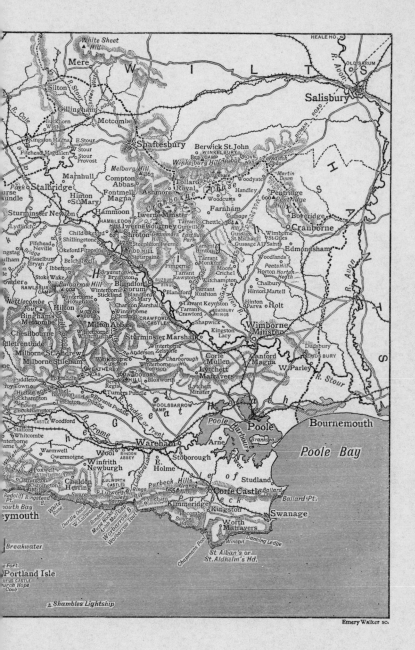

HEALE HO.

R. Avon

OLD SARUM

White Sheet
Hill

Mere

W I L T S

Salisbury

Silton

Gillingham

Motcombe

Buckhorn
Weston

R. Cole

Kingston Magna

E. Stour

Fifehead Magdalen

E. Stour

Shaftesbury

Berwick St.John

WINKELBURY

CAMP

Winklebury Hill

ROMAN ROAD

Tollard
Royal

GROVE

Fonditch
Chase

Stour
Provost

Marnhull

Compton
Abbas

Melbury Hill
A 363

Ashmore

C r a n b o r n e

Martin
Down

Stalbridge

Hinton
St. Mary

Fontmell
Magna

Handley

Woodyates

Pentridge

Peatridge
600

Boveridge

Sturminster Newton

Hammoon

Iwerne Minster

Woodcuts

Farnham

Gussage
St. Michael

Cranborne

HAMBLEDON
HILL

Iwerne Courtney

Gunville

Chettle

Tarrant
Gunville

Pimperne East Bury
Park

Tarrant
Hinton

Gussage All Saints

Wimborne
St. Giles

Edmondsham

Lydlinch

Childe Okeford

Shroton

Steepleton Iwerne

Fifehead
Neville

Shillingstone

Okeford Fitzpaine

NOD HILL

Stourpaine

Belchalwell

Tarrant
Monkton

Moore
Crichel

Woodlands

Peats Hill

Horton Horton
Heath

Ibberton

Bryanston

Bryanston

Stoke Wake

Turnworth

BUZBURY
RINGS

Tarrant
Rawston

Watchampton

Chalbury

RAWLSBURY
CAMP

Burbarrow Hill
902

Blandford
Forum

Winterborne
Stickland

Blandford
St. Mary

Blandford

Tarrant
Rushton

Hinton Martell

Nettlecombe
Tout

Hilton

Winterborne
Houghton

MILTON
ABBEY

Charlton Marshall

Tarrant
Keynston

Tarrant
Crawford

BADBURY
RINGS

Hinton
Parva

Holt

Bingham's
Melcombe

Milton Abbas

Winterborne
Clenston

Shapwick

Kingston
Lacy

Wimborne
Minster

Chesilbourne

Winterborne
Whitchurch

Sturminster Marshall

Didsbury

CLOUDS BURY

Milborne St. Andrew

Winterborne
Zelstone

Anderson

Charborough
Park

Corfe
Mullen

Canford
Magna

W. Parley

Milborne Stileham

WEATHERBY
CAS.

Winterborne
Kingston

WOODBURY
HILL

Winterborne
Thomson

Lytchett
Matravers

R. Stour

Puddletown

Tolpuddle

Bere
Regis

Bloxworth

Lytchett
Minster

Troy Town

Affpuddle

Turners Puddle

WOOLSBARROW
CAMP

Athel-
hampton

Bryants Puddle

Tincleton

G r e a t

Puddle

o r

T r e n t

Bournemouth

Woodford

Frome

G

Wareham

Poole Harbour

Brownsea

Poole

CASTLE

Stafford

Warmwell

Wool

BINDON
ABBEY

Arne

Poole Bay

White Horse

Whitcombe

Owermoigne

Winfrith
Newburgh

E.
Holme

Stoborough

Studland

Foxwell

Chaldon
Herring

LULWORTH
CASTLE

Grange

P u r b e c k

Corfe Castle

Ballard

Ringstead

Redcliff

ARISH MELL

E. Lulworth
Lulworth
Cove

Tyneham

Purbeck Hills

Kimmeridge

Kingston

Ballard Pt.

Swanage

mouth Bay

White Nore

Purdie Door
W. Lulworth

Mupe Rocks
Worbarrow B.
Worbarrow Tout

Kimmeridge
Bay

Worth
Matravers

ymouth

Dancing Ledge

Breakwater

Winspit

Chapmans Pool

St. Alban's or
St. Aldhelm's Hd.

Fort

Portland Isle

RUFUS CASTLE
urch Hope
Cove

Shambles Lightship

Emery Walker sc.

INDEX

INDEX

THE END

R. CLAY AND SONS, LTD., BRUNSWICK ST., STAMFORD ST., S.E.

THE
HIGHWAYS & BYWAYS SERIES.

Extra crown 8vo, gilt tops, **6s.** net each.

London. By Mrs. E. T. Cook. With Illustrations by Hugh Thomson and Frederick L. Griggs.

GRAPHIC.—"Mrs. Cook is an admirable guide; she knows her London in and out; she is equally at home in writing of Mayfair and of City courts, and she has a wealth of knowledge relating to literary and historical associations. This, taken together with the fact that she is a writer who could not be dull if she tried, makes her book very delightful reading."

Middlesex. By Walter Jerrold. With Illustrations by Hugh Thomson.

EVENING STANDARD.—"Every Londoner who wishes to multiply fourfold the interest of his roamings and excursions should beg, borrow, or buy it without a day's delay."

DAILY TELEGRAPH.—"A model of its class, for it is difficult to see how descriptive work of the kind could be performed with a more sympathetic and humane touch."

Hertfordshire. By Herbert W. Tompkins, F.R.Hist.S. With Illustrations by Frederick L. Griggs.

WESTMINSTER GAZETTE.—"A very charming book. . . . Will delight equally the artistic and the poetic, the historical and the antiquarian, the picturesque and the sentimental kinds of tourist."

ST. JAMES'S GAZETTE.—"Cram full of interest and entertainment. The county is singularly rich in material for gossip and comment, and Mr. Tompkins has made a very charming book from it. Nothing more can well remain to be said, yet all that is said in these pages is to the point."

Buckinghamshire. By Clement Shorter. With Illustrations by Frederick L. Griggs.

WORLD.—"A thoroughly delightful little volume. Mr. Frederick L. Griggs contributes a copious series of delicately graceful illustrations."

OBSERVER.—"A very full, pleasant, and informing book. . . . Mr. Griggs again gives us of his best."

Surrey. By Eric Parker. With Illustrations by Hugh Thomson.

DAILY TELEGRAPH.—"Author and artist have combined to give us one of the very best books on the most variedly beautiful of the home counties."

SPECTATOR.—"A very charming book, both to dip into and to read. . . . Every page is sown with something rare and curious."

Kent. By WALTER JERROLD. With Illustrations by HUGH THOMSON.

PALL MALL GAZETTE.—"A book over which it is a pleasure to pore, and which every man of Kent or Kentish man, or 'foreigner,' should promptly steal, purchase, or borrow. . . . The illustrations alone are worth twice the money charged for the book."

Sussex. By E. V. LUCAS. With Illustrations by FREDERICK L. GRIGGS.

WESTMINSTER GAZETTE.—"A delightful addition to an excellent series. . . . Mr. Lucas's knowledge of Sussex is shown in so many fields, with so abundant and yet so natural a flow, that one is kept entertained and charmed through every passage of his devious progress. . . . The drawings with which Mr. Frederick Griggs illustrates this charming book are equal in distinction to any work this admirable artist has given us."

Berkshire. By JAMES EDMUND VINCENT. With Illustrations by FREDERICK L. GRIGGS.

DAILY CHRONICLE.—"We consider this book one of the best in an admirable series, and one which should appeal to all who love this kind of literature."

Oxford and the Cotswolds. By H. A. EVANS. With Illustrations by FREDERICK L. GRIGGS.

DAILY TELEGRAPH.—"The author is everywhere entertaining and fresh, never allowing his own interest to flag, and thereby retaining the close attention of the reader."

Shakespeare's Country. By The Ven. W. H. HUTTON. With Illustrations by EDMUND H. NEW.

PALL MALL GAZETTE.—"Mr. Edmund H. New has made a fine book a thing of beauty and a joy for ever by a series of lovely drawings."

Hampshire. By D. H. MOUTRAY READ. With Illustrations by ARTHUR B. CONNOR.

WORLD.—"Mr. Moutray Read has written a well-nigh perfect guide-book, and he has been thrice blessed in his illustrator, Mr. Arthur B. Connor."

STANDARD.—"In our judgment, as excellent and as lively a book as has yet appeared in the Highways and Byways Series."

Dorset. By Sir FREDERICK TREVES. With Illustrations by JOSEPH PENNELL.

STANDARD.—" A breezy, delightful book, full of sidelights on men and manners, and quick in the interpretation of all the half-inarticulate lore of the countryside."

Somerset. By EDWARD HUTTON. With Illustrations by NELLY ERICHSEN.

DAILY TELEGRAPH.—" A book which will set the heart of every West-country-man beating with enthusiasm, and with pride for the goodly heritage into which he has been born as a son of Somerset."

Devon and Cornwall. By ARTHUR H. NORWAY. With Illustrations by JOSEPH PENNELL and HUGH THOMSON.

DAILY CHRONICLE.—" So delightful that we would gladly fill columns with extracts were space as elastic as imagination. . . . The text is excellent ; the illustrations of it are even better."

South Wales. By A. G. BRADLEY. With Illustrations by FREDERICK L. GRIGGS.

SPECTATOR.—" Mr. Bradley has certainly exalted the writing of a combined archæological and descriptive guide-book into a species of literary art. The result is fascinating."

North Wales. By A. G. BRADLEY. With Illustrations by HUGH THOMSON and JOSEPH PENNELL.

PALL MALL GAZETTE.—" To read this fine book makes us eager to visit every hill and every valley that Mr. Bradley describes with such tantalising enthusiasm. It is a work of inspiration, vivid, sparkling, and eloquent—a deep well of pleasure to every lover of Wales."

Cambridge and Ely. By Rev. EDWARD CONYBEARE. With Illustrations by FREDERICK L. GRIGGS.

Also an **Edition de Luxe.** Limited to 250 copies. Royal 8vo, 21s. net.

ATHENÆUM.—" A volume which, light and easily read as it is, deserves to rank with the best literature about the county."

GUARDIAN.—" Artist and writer have combined to give us a book of singular charm."

East Anglia. By WILLIAM A. DUTT. With Illustrations by JOSEPH PENNELL.

WORLD.—" Of all the fascinating volumes in the ' Highways and By-ways ' series, none is more pleasant to read. . . . Mr. Dutt, himself an East Anglian, writes most sympathetically and in picturesque style of the district."

Lincolnshire. By W. F. RAWNSLEY. With Illustrations by FREDERICK L. GRIGGS.

PALL MALL GAZETTE.—"A splendid record of a storied shire."

Nottinghamshire. By J. B. FIRTH. With Illustrations by FREDERICK L. GRIGGS. [*In the Press.*

Derbyshire. By J. B. FIRTH. With Illustrations by NELLY ERICHSEN.

DAILY TELEGRAPH.—"The result is altogether delightful, for 'Derbyshire' is as attractive to the reader in his arm-chair as to the tourist wandering amid the scenes Mr. Firth describes so well."

Yorkshire. By ARTHUR H. NORWAY. With Illustrations by JOSEPH PENNELL and HUGH THOMSON.

PALL MALL GAZETTE.—"The wonderful story of Yorkshire's past provides Mr. Norway with a wealth of interesting material, which he has used judiciously and well; each grey ruin of castle and abbey he has re-erected and re-peopled in the most delightful way. A better guide and story-teller it would be hard to find."

Lake District. By A. G. BRADLEY. With Illustrations by JOSEPH PENNELL.

ST. JAMES'S GAZETTE.—"A notable edition—an engaging volume, packed with the best of all possible guidance for tourists. For the most part the artist's work is as exquisite as anything of the kind he has done."

The Border. By ANDREW LANG and JOHN LANG. With Illustrations by Hugh Thomson.

STANDARD.—"The reader on his travels, real or imaginary, could not have pleasanter or more profitable companionship. There are charming sketches by Mr. Hugh Thomson to illustrate the letterpress."

Galloway and Carrick. By the Rev. C. H. DICK. With Illustrations by HUGH THOMSON.

Donegal and Antrim. By STEPHEN GWYNN. With Illustrations by HUGH THOMSON.

DAILY TELEGRAPH.—"A perfect book of its kind, on which author, artist, and publisher have lavished of their best."

Normandy. By PERCY DEARMER, M.A. With Illustrations by JOSEPH PENNELL.

ST. JAMES'S GAZETTE.—"A charming book. . . . Mr. Dearmer is as arrestive in his way as Mr. Pennell. He has the true topographic eye. He handles legend and history in entertaining fashion."

MACMILLAN AND CO., LTD., LONDON.

4

C.5.4.16.

Redwood Library

...IONS FROM THE RULES

...hree volumes may be taken at a time ...y three on one share. Two unbound ...of a monthly and three numbers of a ...ublication are counted as a volume.

...Books other than 7-day and 14-day ones ...kept out 28 days. **Books cannot be ...d or transferred.**

...oks overdue are subject to a fine of one ...for fourteen days, **and five cents a ...each day thereafter.**

...eglect to pay the fine will debar from ...the Library.

...book is to be lent out of the house of ...to whom it is charged.

...ny person who shall soil (deface) or ...lose a book belonging to the Library ...ble to such fine as the Directors may ...shall pay the value of the book or of ...e a part of a set, as the Directors ...All scribbling or any marking or ...ver, folding or turning down the ...ll as cutting or tearing any matter ...ook belonging to the Library, will be con-...sidered defacement and damage.